The Charter School Experiment

The Charter School Experiment

Expectations, Evidence, and Implications

Edited by
Christopher A. Lubienski
Peter C. Weitzel

HARVARD EDUCATION PRESS
CAMBRIDGE, MASSACHUSETTS

CAL: *for my daughters*

PCW: *for Laura*

Library of Congress Control Number: 2010931318

Paperback ISBN 978-1-934742-66-2
Library Edition ISBN 978-1-934742-67-9

Published by Harvard Education Press,
an imprint of the Harvard Education Publishing Group

Harvard Education Press
8 Story Street
Cambridge, MA 02138

Cover Design: Schwa Design, Inc.

The typefaces used in this book are ITC Stone Serif for text and ITC Stone Sans for display.

Contents

Acknowledgments

This volume represents one of the first efforts of the Forum for the Future of Public Education, an initiative based at the University of Illinois to bring empirical evidence to bear in critical policy areas, particularly those areas often characterized by more heat than light. The founding director of the forum, Stanley Ikenberry, provided the initial push for this volume. The current director, Debra Bragg, took up the cause and has actively encouraged us in this project. Additional resources for this endeavor were provided by the Bureau of Educational Research, the College of Education, and the Provost at the University of Illinois.

In addition to this institutional support, a number of individuals played crucial roles in bringing this project to fruition. First and foremost, the authors contributing chapters to this volume deserve our profound thanks for providing excellent insights into the important aspects of charter schools. We are very grateful that this group of elite researchers accepted our invitation to participate. Then, Jeff Henig and Kevin Welner offered valuable comments on the ideas in these papers. Finally, Jin Lee provided invaluable assistance in preparing and formatting the manuscript. All of these individuals and groups have our sincere gratitude.

The Charter School Idea

Jeffrey R. Henig

Policies evolve. They evolve as they are debated within legislatures, through negotiation and compromise needed to obtain winning majorities. They evolve during implementation, as bureaucratic agencies flesh out rules and regulations and develop (or fail to develop) modes of delivery, oversight, and enforcement. Policies also evolve as they are disseminated, as when one state borrows an idea from another but adapts it to better fit local needs, culture, tradition, demographics, capacity, and politics.

Policies like those that call for charter schools constitute broad changes in governance and institutional systems and evolve in more complicated and unpredictable ways than do policies like personnel strategy or restructuring of the school day, school week, or school year. There are at least two big reasons why this is the case. First, the presumed causal link between the policy intervention and the desired societal outcomes is much longer and more indirect for institutional changes. Systemic policy changes, such as charter schools, do not directly change the core of instruction and learning, and the multiple steps that may lead from the one to the other each represents possible stumbling points and unexpected detours.[1] Second, systemic and institutional changes can have important second-order, or policy feedback, effects.[2] These changes alter the landscape of markets, civil society, and political interests in ways that subsequently can alter the prospects for revising the original laws or for altering implementation regimes that determine how they unfold.

These things make a volume like this one important. As new policy regimes mutate and mature, it is critically important to step back, take a broad scan, and reconsider early premises and framings. Our contemporary understanding of charter school policies should be informed—but not determined—by the history of theories, expectations, and concerns that characterized their emergence on the scene nearly two decades ago.

As the charter school movement took shape in the 1990s, positions were staked out according to abstractions: idealized conceptions and formalized causal models. Small glimmers of evidence, filtered through these lenses of abstraction, reverberated in ways that exaggerated both expectations and fears.[3] Charter proponents offered pumped-up predictions of the ways that choice and competition would blast through the calcification of the existing educational system, allowing a flood of energy, innovation, and commitment that would simultaneously and rapidly raise overall levels of achievement and substantially narrow educational gaps. Charter school skeptics, skipping right past the possibility that charters would have only incremental impacts, proffered dire scenarios in which choice translated directly into stratification and competition into a downward spiral of disinvestment in the public education enterprise.

Niels Bohr, the Danish physicist, reportedly said, "Prediction is very difficult, especially if it's about the future." We can forgive early prognosticators if some of their projections were off the mark. The authors in this volume have the advantage not only of hindsight, but of the grist of an empirical record on which to chew. To those who like simple narratives, the result may be disappointing. The story of charter schools, as it unfolds here, is one of nuance and contingency. If the question is "Are charter schools good or bad?" the answer for now is a resounding "It depends." It depends of the type of charter school, on the ways the laws are formulated and implemented, on financing and other support mechanisms, on the local context as it affects children's needs and family demands, and on collective and individual decisions yet to be made.

I entered the charter debate as a skeptic. The evidence to date convinces me that blanket judgments are risky and the rush to issue summative judgments premature and ill advised. I continue to harbor some genuine concerns about how the charter school phenomenon may play out over time, and the weight of the evidence and interpretations in this volume does more to stoke those than to snuff them out. But American education has needed some shaking and prodding, and charter schools have delivered on that part of their promise. There are vitality and talent and resources in public education today that were flagging prior to the 1983 federal report *A Nation at Risk,* and while I do not believe that these are attributable to the market-based dynamics that some charter proponents continue to celebrate, I am reasonably convinced that charter schools have helped to bring this about.

In Kurt Vonnegut's *Cat's Cradle*, "ice-nine" is a substance that, once injected into water, acts as a seed crystal that freezes all liquid molecules in an unstoppable contamination.[4] Unlike ice-nine, the charter school phenomenon does not carry within it a preordained future. Charter schools operated within a framework structured by government, and public policy will have much to do with how they continue to develop and the consequences that will ensue. Many things will play a role in whether those policies steer us in the right or wrong direction. Some have to do with ideology, power, and interest-group politics, played out in various venues from Washington, D.C., through the states, to local districts, charter networks, and individual schools.

Good research and considered interpretation of evidence cannot determine how the charter school experiment will play out in the end, but they can help open-minded and pragmatic citizens and policy makers make better choices and strengthen their hand in contentious battles to shape future policies and practice. They cannot serve up a single, assured answer to the educational challenges that face us, but they can help us avoid foolish errors and increase the probability that we will get things more right than wrong.

This volume gives us good research and considered interpretation. The chapters circle in from various sides on the multifaceted and dynamic phenomenon that is the charter school experiment. The authors are clearheaded in their analysis, clear in their exposition, and appropriately modest in their claims. While not a recipe book for those looking for quick and tasty one-size-fits-all solutions, it is a model of what the slow, careful probing enterprise of good social science has to contribute. The book is not a final tally sheet on the charter school experiment, but an extremely helpful starting-off point for those who continue to believe that better understanding can lead to better policy and better social outcomes.

Two Decades of Charter Schools
Shifting Expectations, Partners, and Policies

Christopher A. Lubienski and Peter C. Weitzel

When charter schools first arrived on the American educational land-scape, few people suspected that within two decades, thousands of these schools would be established across most of the United States, serving almost a million and a half children. In 1991, a coalition of Minnesota progressives and conservatives drew on an obscure idea at the periphery of social policy to propose and pass the first state charter legislation. Now some forty states have embraced this reform, which has enjoyed the support of groups as varied as market enthusiasts, teachers unions, alternative educators, and religious conservatives. As schools that are publicly funded but free of much of the traditional education bureaucracy that characterizes district-run public schools, charter schools are part of a larger deregulation reform agenda in public policy that has seen broad political support—not just in education and not just in the United States, but also in many other sectors around the globe. A generation and a half of children has now passed through charter schools, and the movement continues to grow. We now have a sufficient track record available to make some overall judgments on the potential of these decentralized and deregulated schools to improve educational opportunities for all children.

Inasmuch as there is a single charter school "model" in this diffuse reform, the widespread popularity of these schools—with parents, community organizers, school management companies, mayors, reform advocates, and many other disparate parties—speaks to the unique and chronic desire for substantive change in American education. Policy makers, parents, and others have become increasingly frustrated with the cycle of "change" in American schools, where widely heralded reforms follow the previous generations of attempted improvements. For many, this seemingly endless tinkering at the edges of American education seems to have created little substantive change. Despite billions of dollars and decades of change, achievement appears stagnant, large gaps remain between groups, American schools slip in international rankings, and bureaucracies endure. Unlike many policy interventions, charter schools are designed to be game changers—uniquely positioned to break the cycle of ineffective reform. As an idea, charter schools are not about curriculum or pedagogy. Instead, they are focused on changing the fundamental governance and management structure of schooling: unleashing the creative potential of educators and communities, nurturing diverse options for families, encouraging parents to choose what is best for their children, and making schools directly accountable to the people who use them.

As an innovation in governance, charter schools aim to bypass the educational establishment; empower new institutions, organizations, and communities; and bring the competition that characterizes the consumer-driven economy of the United States to bear in education as well. Charter schools are essentially structural reforms, largely at the state level, where the alternative governance schemes are implemented. These reforms are intended to create incentives and opportunities for educators to develop new, different, and better approaches to meeting the needs of students. Greater flexibility for teachers and more entrepreneurial management strategies are among the intermediary objectives of these reforms, and these outcomes could serve as evidence that charter leaders are taking advantage of their greater institutional freedom. However, the ultimate goal for charter schools is improved learning opportunities for students—not only those who attend charter schools but also students at other schools that are affected by competition from charters.

Charter schools are indeed quite popular, reflecting the widespread desire for substantial change. But how well are they fulfilling the goals laid out for them? What do we know about actual outcomes and consequences? Much has been written over the past decade about charter schools, but researchers, policy makers, and reformers have tended to focus on charter schools as an idea (good or bad, depending on one's perspective), rather than as policy experiment in American education. Much of the available research is too often characterized by smaller-scale case studies or is overly ideological in selecting evidence in support or critique of these schools. After more than a decade and a half, it is time to take a measure of what we know about the accomplishments, shortfalls, and continued potential of this experiment.

This book represents an effort to take a step back and survey the past, present, and future of charter schools as an increasingly established fixture on the American educational landscape. We solicited chapters from some of the leading thinkers on charter schools, asking them to examine the record, role, and impact of these schools in view of the initial expectations set out for this reform. What you will see in these pages is a mixed assortment of authors, with varying perspectives on charter schools, examining the empirical record on this evolving educational reform. Contributors to this book include leading researchers on key charter school topics like student achievement, social segregation, competition with public schools, regulatory frameworks, and organizational structures and responses. As the charter school movement approaches the start of its third decade, these authors examine how the expectations for charter schools have changed in the first twenty years and how the research community's knowledge of charter schools' performance and impact has improved over time. In essence, this volume aims to review and evaluate both the policy rhetoric and the empirical record on charter schools in the United States.

In this introduction, we start by offering an overview of charter schools as a reform mechanism in American public education. We briefly look back at the origins of the movement and highlight the early promises of this form of decentralized educational governance. In fact, although charters vary from state to state, there has been a notable consensus on the goals for charter schools as a reform movement: introducing competition to the school sector, promoting more equitable access to quality school options through greater choice, encouraging innovation, and thereby creating more effective and efficient educational processes and outcomes. We also provide a short summary of the various chapters in the volume and conclude with some of the critical themes as charter schools enter a third decade. We conclude that charter schools are now beginning a new phase in their development, serving significantly different purposes from those originally set out for them by reformers.

OBSCURE BEGINNINGS AND STRANGE BEDFELLOWS

In the last twenty years, perhaps no issue in education has generated more optimism and bipartisan support than school choice and, in particular, charter schools. In an arena often characterized by severe ideological wrangling over the approaches and objectives of education reform, charter schools have certainly accomplished a remarkable feat. They have singularly brought together distinct and often conflicting elements from the fractured educational policy landscape around the idea of offering—within the publicly funded sector—alternatives to neighborhood-based public schools. This is actually an extraordinary achievement. Other efforts to introduce choice and competition, prod the public sector into improvement, or blur the boundaries of public and private institutions (such as, say, vouchers) have been much more divisive.

Though public education has always had a diverse set of stakeholders, charter reforms are one of the few policy changes that have enticed a wide range of actors—from small, local nonprofits to large corporations and foundations—that previously functioned at the margins of public education to participate directly in service provision. The politics of school choice has been noteworthy in its own right, as both charter school advocates and opponents have used research in new ways and sought strange bedfellows in their pursuit of policy change. Charter schools represent the confluence of otherwise disparate agendas for organizing education, including professional and for-profit models, community and commercial impulses, and curricular-instructional as well as social-entrepreneurial objectives. In fact, this is largely because charter schools, as a concept, are essentially an empty vessel. They have come to represent not a specific educational design, but a vehicle that can be variously used to advance both the small-schools movement and the franchising of corporate school providers; both back-to-basics and progressive pedagogical approaches; both traditional family values and progressive (or radical) political models for educating at-risk kids; and even efforts both to shore up and to undercut teachers unions.

In fact, this last contrast is itself quite telling. Charter schools have often been cast as union-busting devices, yet the initial idea found quite a bit of favor in union circles. Ray Budde, a former principal before moving to the University of Massachusetts at Amherst, presented preliminary ideas for school chartering as early as 1974.[1] He conceptualized charters as a way of encouraging small groups of teachers to explore alternative educational models. But it was not until Albert Shanker, president of the American Federation of Teachers, embraced and championed the idea in 1988 that the charter school movement really began to gather steam. In these early iterations, teachers were expected to be one of the primary drivers of charter school growth as they sought independence to implement instructional innovations. This concept found particularly fertile ground in Minnesota, where progressive educators emerging from the alternative schools movement and frustrated with district-run bureaucracies, succeeded—through the liberal Democratic-Farm-Labor Party—in securing the nation's first law authorizing charter schools. Charter advocates at the time envisioned small-scale, autonomous schools run by independent mom-and-pop operators who would be best positioned to respond to local community needs.

As the charter school movement developed, however, many of these expectations for grassroots growth seemed a bit idealistic. Rather than the laboratory unit where teacher professionals could try out new ideas, charter schools came to be seen as challengers or threats to the public school establishment, including teachers unions. School choice advocates, including some traditionally liberal constituencies, gained influence in statehouses and on Capitol Hill, areas where unions had long held sway. Whereas Budde and Shanker's concept of charters was expected to empower existing teachers, the notion of charter schools as competitors to public schools or antecedents to vouchers introduced the possibility that funds might eventually be drawn away from public schools and current teacher protections could be eroded. Indeed, the charter idea was rapidly gaining acceptance in more market-oriented education circles, including charters' promotion as a "second-best" alternative when voucher proposals failed in some states.[2] Consequently, unions and school boards began to actively oppose the expansion of charter schools, claiming that charters were part of a right-wing effort to subvert democratic control of schools.[3] These shifts in union stance from charter school promoter to opponent to collaborator are in many ways a microcosm of the charter school movement over its first twenty years. They are but one indication of how the fears, expectations, and political support of charter schools have shifted substantially over time.

GLOBAL CONTEXT

Like many educational reforms over the past quarter century, the charter movement can be seen as an outgrowth of the economic fears exemplified in *A Nation at Risk*—the landmark 1983 federal report warning of the "rising tide of mediocrity" in America's public schools.[4] In the years following the report, states and districts pursued a range of reforms to establish higher standards for schools, teachers, and students. A growing body of researchers attempted to identify common characteristics of successful schools. In the view of market theorists such as John Chubb and Terry Moe, however, these conventional reforms and recommendations amounted to little more than tinkering within a fundamentally flawed system.[5] As long as primary control of schools was left with an entrenched bureaucracy, conventional remedies were bound to fail. The educational crisis facing the United States required more than the usual incremental approach to change.

This rhetoric of deep, fundamental reform found voice not just among choice advocates but also among many leading politicians in the 1990s. In fact, educational policy makers around the globe were pursuing similar strategies, encouraging consumer choice and competition between schools as a way to leverage structural incentives for self-improvement within the education system. For instance, policy makers in England and Wales allowed schools to opt out of control and funding from local educational authorities and operate more autonomously as "grant-maintained schools" that had to attract students. Similarly, neoliberal reformers in New Zealand created a choice system within the state sector by freeing up family choice of schools. An even more dramatic experiment was in evidence in Chile, where the "Chicago boys," inspired by Milton Friedman's gospel of market-based social policy, implemented a nationwide voucher program that encouraged the creation of a new sector of for-profit schools.

Indeed, market-oriented reforms have increasingly been utilized in other dimensions of public policy as well. Financial support and so-called structural adjustment policies for the developing world through the International Monetary Fund and the World Bank often required that governments reduce regulation and direct provision of social services. While there has been a notable movement worldwide to privatize government enterprises such as telecom and other utilities, the move toward "contracting out" government services—rather than the institutions themselves—to private providers has also been popular in areas such as social services because of its potential to contain costs and improve consumer satisfaction.

The rhetoric for school choice reform has presented a compelling combination of both technical and ideological arguments. Not only are markets considered necessary to spur school improvement, but school choice itself has been cast as a civil right, one that is currently only available to middle- and upper-class families. Concerned parents, particularly those with children trapped in decaying urban schools, must be empowered to seek high-quality schooling alternatives. Disadvantaged urban populations and right-leaning, even libertarian, groups thus found themselves on the same side of the issue, and school choice came to be seen as a potential solution to racial and socioeconomic achievement gaps.

FROM THEORY TO RESEARCH

In the absence of data on charter school performance, the early discussions over charter schools necessarily focused on their theorized outcomes and impacts. These debates, often focused on the validity of market models for the public education sector, were valuable in their own right. Charter schools served as a mirror on public education in a market society, encouraging scholars and policy makers to revisit the balance of public and private interests in education. Although these theoretical debates certainly continue, this book is motivated by the presence of a sufficient and growing body of research to inform policy and practice on charter school issues.

Much of this evidence has challenged the early expectations and assumptions regarding the operation and performance of charter schools. Ideals of local responsiveness and heroic reformers have confronted the notion that schools are big businesses where economies of scale, political access, and branding can go a long way toward sustainability. Likewise, market-based perspectives that see competition as a rising tide that can lift all boats have collided with the realities of metropolitan segregation, parent preferences, and perverse incentives for schools to attract higher-achieving students rather than focusing solely on instructional improvements.

The introduction of new actors and market mechanisms in public education presented substantial methodological challenges for educational researchers, but the conversation around charter schools among the research community has gradually become more complex. For starters, many researchers and commentators have recognized that charter schools themselves can no longer be discussed as a monolithic entity. The label *charter school* can mean different things in different states, as these policies and reforms have been implemented within a range of different contexts and regulations.[6] Likewise, charter schools are now often parsed into categories like for-profit and nonprofit, local and educational management organization (EMO) affiliated, comprehensive and specialized, and high performing and low performing. As charter schools have proliferated and scholars have examined different markets, concepts like competition and innovation have also been refined. Competition for students is now often differentiated by levels of market penetration, types of choices available, and the prevalence of choice across a particular market.[7] Rather than simply noting if parents have publicly funded choices, researchers are now able to map the geographic distribution of schools across metropolitan areas to determine what realistic options are available to different demographics in a city.[8] Researchers have also examined education consumers and the selection process itself, often demonstrating that school choice may not be as rationale as early theorists predicted. The school information available to parents as consumers is now often categorized by its source, content, quality, and accessibility.[9]

Indeed, scholars from the fields of education, political science, sociology, and economics have substantially enhanced our understanding of the outcomes, policy issues, and market dynamics that have emerged in the first two decades of the charter school movement. This book, featuring chapters from accomplished scholars of school choice, attempts to compile and summarize this body of research. Within their respective areas of expertise, contributors examine both initial and later expectations for charter school reforms, review the evidence in light of these expectations, and identify areas for future research and debate. Although this volume is by no means an exhaustive examination of charter school issues and research, it does attempt to cover the most prominent questions and policy issues in this area of reform.

To that end, we have included chapters from leading experts in the field to consider the impact of charter schools in critical areas such as student achievement, social segregation, competition with public schools, parental choice, and education policy. Despite diverse interests, backgrounds, and topics, all of the contributors were asked to consider early intentions and expectations for charter schools, the current state of knowledge in their area, and emerging trends in policy and practice. Specifically, this volume is intended to provide insights on the following issues:

- The evolution of thinking on the various ways in which charter schools specialize, particularly the early expectations for charter schools and how the goals have been sustained or may have changed

- The current state of knowledge in these areas, especially the empirical record, including the strength of the evidence and analytical approaches
- Likely future directions of the charter school movement, as well as research and policy making around charter schools

In essence, this book aims to take a measure of the prospects and pitfalls of charter schools as the movement enters its third decade in American public education. In the remainder of this introduction, we provide an overview of the chapters included in this volume.

OVERVIEW OF THE VOLUME

In chapter 1, Peter Weitzel and Chris Lubienski review the performance of the charter school movement on three of the overarching goals laid out by supporters: more equitable access for students, competitive effects, and innovation. Though some advocates emphasize one or two of these goals more than others, most of the expected benefits of charter school growth fall under one of these categories. Thus far, many of the sky-high expectations for charter schools have not been met. Although charter school operators have been very innovative in some areas of management and marketing, they have not produced the substantial innovations in curriculum and instruction that many advocates anticipated. On the issue of more equitable access to schooling options, the growth of charter schools has certainly expanded the range of options for many traditionally disadvantaged groups. However, charter schools, particularly for-profit schools, often avoid poor neighborhoods, and there is growing concern that school choice may be exacerbating already high levels of racial segregation. Many advocates anticipated that higher student achievement in charter schools would attract students and drive public schools to improve performance in order to compete. At this point, charter schools, on average, are performing no better than traditional public schools on student achievement, and cities with high levels of competition for students are not experiencing greater improvements in student achievement. Chapter 1 reviews these three primary expectations for charter schools and examines the evidence of progress toward these goals.

The remaining chapters focus on specific issues in charter school policy and performance in greater detail. In chapter 2, David Garcia examines the hopes and fears of commentators regarding charters schools' potential to either reduce or increase existing levels of racial and socioeconomic segregation. Because school choice eliminates school assignment based on residential neighborhoods, which tend to be segregated, school choice has the potential to reduce segregation in the schools. On the other hand, if parents act on preferences for more homogenous schooling environments or use racial composition as an indicator of academic quality, school choice could actually increase already high levels of segregation. Garcia notes that initial concerns focused on white flight, but socioeconomic sorting and the self-segregating actions of all groups have become more prominent concerns in recent years. Research on these sorting issues has improved substantially, moving from nationwide comparisons to more useful, local comparisons. Student-level longitudinal enrollment data now enable researchers both to track students as they change schools and to compare the composition of the school the students left with those they selected. Most of these studies indicate that both white and black students, on average, are self-segregating through charters by leaving schools that are more diverse in favor of schools more segregated. Moreover, many parents are selecting lower-performing schools for their children than the schools the students departed.

Concerns about the diversity of charter school enrollments are not just present in the research community. In chapter 3, Suzanne Eckes examines states' charter school legislation and compares their approaches to regulating (or not regulating) enrollment composition in charter schools. Though many of the debates over charter schools often capture national attention, charter school policy is still very much a state issue, with substantial variation in these regulations between states. Not only do the regulations themselves vary, but states also demonstrate substantially different capacities and willingness to enforce the rules they have on the books. Eckes compares charter school enrollment diversity in states with different types of regulations. In effect, she asks, "Do the rules actually matter for shaping enrollment patterns?" Eckes concludes that the rules do appear to matter, but additional research is needed. Numerous lawsuits indicate a lack of clarity in many regulations, and Eckes offers recommendations for producing more carefully designed and better articulated rules.

Superior student achievement is undoubtedly one of the most prominent expectations for charter schools, and it is the most contentious issue in charter school research by far. In chapter 4, Gary Miron examines the evidence on student achievement in charter schools. Charter schools are expected to perform better than public schools because they are freed from many regulations that limit their ability to remove poor teachers or implement better practices. The combination of state and market accountability is also expected to push charter schools to greater performance. Miron outlines the improvements to charter school achievement research over time but notes that low-quality studies are still common. He takes a systematic approach to his synthesis of the research literature, categorizing studies by their findings and weighting them according to the quality of their data and methodology. On the whole, charter schools perform about the same as traditional public schools, but there are large differences in performance both within and between states. Larger-scale studies tend to produce results that are more negative for charter school performance, while small-scale studies tend to indicate results more positive. Rather than looking for a single, definitive answer on charter school achievement, Miron suggests that policy makers should consider how charter schools can be made more accountable and if other uses of public funds (such as reducing class size) might have greater effects on student achievement.

Charters, however, are not expected only to have an impact for the students they enroll. In chapter 5, Yongmei Ni and David Arsen examine the evidence on the competitive effects of charter schools in education markets. Charter schools, by breaking the district monopoly on publicly funded education, are expected to produce superior outcomes not only for charter school students (direct effects), but also for students remaining in other schools (indirect effects). Charter schools could attract so many students that the traditional public schools would be forced to improve to avoid going out of business. The result would be benefits for choosers and nonchoosers alike. On the other hand, critics contend that competition will leave the most disadvantaged students behind, creating "winners" and "losers" rather than collective improvements. Ni and Arsen summarize these theories of competitive effects, outline the potential competitive responses that schools might pursue, and review the methodological challenges and findings of quantitative research on competitive effects. The results of this relatively small body of research are mixed, even when studies in the same state are compared. When the positive effects of competition are found, they tend to be very small. Ni and Arsen note that several aspects of local context, including financial arrangements, regulations, and policy implementation, can substantially alter competitive dynamics. The researchers conclude that the expectation that widespread student improvement will emerge through competition is a compelling idea but not likely to be a reality in practice.

In current charter school policy, competition for students means competition for funds because the per-pupil state funding essentially travels
with departing students to their new school. In chapter 6, Those competitive dynamics were expected to create efficiencies, providing charter
schools with an incentive to do more with less. Luis Huerta and Chad
d'Entremont examine charter school finance policy and discuss how these
financial pressures can influence management decisions for charter school
operators. School finance is actually much more complex than a simple
per-pupil allotment, and research indicates that most charter schools end
up receiving significantly less in state funds per pupil than do traditional
public schools, though this difference varies substantially between states.
However, many charter schools also seek and secure substantial amounts
of private funding to support their work, though this pursuit of private
funds often entails trade-offs for school operators. School leaders must balance financial concerns with their need to pursue their specific mission and
seek institutional legitimacy in their local market. Huerta and d'Entremont
outline a neo-institutionalist framework for understanding the financial
decisions of school leaders and apply this framework to different types of
charter schools in New York.

Expectations for input from parents and other local stakeholders are
not just expressed by advocates for democratic governance but also often
included in charter school legislation. In chapter 7, Priscilla Wohlstetter
and Joanna Smith describe the variations in state regulations for parent
and community involvement and survey the research in this area. In many
states, charter school operators are required to work with local stakeholders in the charter application process. These types of partnerships highlight one of the ancillary outcomes of the charter school movement, the
increased involvement of new players—including community, faith-based,
and business organizations—in public education. Wohlstetter and Smith
draw on interviews with charter school operators, authorizers, and state
leaders to examine the extent of involvement by these organizations and
their impact on school operations. The researchers find that innovation
in this area has been rather incremental and that state policy could do
more to encourage substantial involvement from nontraditional education
stakeholders. In many cases, state policy outlines a goal for greater involvement from new partners but does not create any useful incentives or support to promote local activities toward these goals.

Many charter schools end up spending greater proportions of their budgets on administrative costs than do traditional public schools, in part

because charters have to recruit students and cannot rely on large district offices to handle many administrative functions. One approach to reducing these administrative costs is to work with educational management organizations (EMOs) that can provide substantial efficiencies of scale. In chapter 8, Janelle Scott and Catherine DiMartino examine the emergence of EMOs as major players in the charter school movement and in many other areas of education reform. EMOs include both nonprofit and for-profit enterprises, some of which operate schools directly while others provide a range of curricular support, technical assistance, and other materials and services. Scott and DiMartino describe the evolution of these organizations, including related precursors that appeared in the decades preceding the charter school era. Although EMOs control a relatively low percentage of charter schools overall, they dominate several urban areas through high market share. EMOs certainly offer advantages in dealing with administrative burdens and replicating successful school models, but they also fly in the face of expectations that charter schools will be more locally responsive and will develop targeted interventions to deal with unique educational challenges in particular contexts. Scott and DiMartino examine this tension and connect it to broader debates over educational governance and local input, particularly in urban school systems.

Many of the systemic changes expected to emerge from the charter school movement depend on the effective use of information by key stakeholders. In chapter 9, Chris Lubienski and Peter Weitzel outline these expectations for information usage and examine how particular types of information are used by two types of actors, state policy makers who develop charter school regulations and parents who select particular schools for their children. Charter schools are often presented as a policy experiment, implying that policy makers will consider evidence on their performance when enacting or revising policy. An examination of the spread of charter school laws in light of the available evidence on performance at the time suggests that policy makers acted on other interests or information in their pursuit of new charter school policy. The Obama administration's recent focus on charter school quantity rather than quality in the Race to the Top grant program serves as another example along these lines. This rational-choice perspective that many assume guides policy selection is also very much at play in understanding policymakers' assumptions about how parents will gather and use information on school academic quality when selecting schools for their children. Such "hard" evidence is in fact available and used by many parents, but "softer" information, often from "word-of-mouth," is quite influential for people choosing schools. Much of this information has to do with the racial composition of schools—a factor valued by parents, even when they claim otherwise in surveys and interviews.

In the book's conclusion, Weitzel and Lubienski provide recommendations for future charter school research. Researchers still need to better understand the differences between charter school students and traditional public school students. Also, little research has been conducted on the entities that authorize charter schools or the shifts in political power arising from the introduction of charter schools". Another key question concerns types of charter school accountability. Charter schools operate under a two-part model of accountability in which they are expected to answer to both consumers (parents) and public regulators. Given the emerging evidence that the market-based form of accountability is not working as expected, the implications of this development for the future of charter school regulation needs to be studied. Furthermore, the research community has only begun to examine the extent to which charter school regulations themselves actually influence outcomes on the ground. Finally, variations in state policy and local context have created a situation in which the words *charter school* can have substantially different meanings in practice. Researchers and policy makers should attempt to minimize discussions of charter schools as a singular model. Rather than focusing largely on school-level effects, researchers also need to crack open the black box of charter schools and determine what school-level practices are associated with better outcomes for particular student populations.

CHAPTER 1

Grading Charter Schools
Access, Innovation, and Competition

Peter C. Weitzel and Christopher A. Lubienski

In this chapter, we highlight the overarching goals of the charter school movement and review the existing evidence on the effects of charter schools in these areas. Since the inception of the charter school movement, three major goals have been set out for charter school reforms (as well as for other instances of expanded school choice): equity, innovation, and competition. These goals are by no means mutually exclusive; nor are they usually presented in isolation. Most advocates will include aspects of all three goals in their arguments, though many advocates will emphasize one or two of these goals over others, depending on their interests and political philosophies. For example, the Obama administration has largely emphasized equity and innovation, while many conservatives and neoclassical economists tend to emphasize competitive effects. These three goals are not necessarily independent, either. Expectations for competitive benefits in particular depend in part on innovations in curriculum and instruction leading to improved achievement. Thus far, contrary to the hopes and fears of supporters and skeptics, neither the most pessimistic nor the most optimistic expectations on these three issues have been realized. But that is, in itself, quite important.

EQUITY: ACCESS TO QUALITY EDUCATION OPTIONS

Of these three goals, the equity goal is perhaps the most foundational argument, and it underlines one of the most appealing promises for charters. Briefly stated, expanded school choice through charter schools will improve equity by extending to disadvantaged families the same types of options already available to middle- and upper-class families through residential selection or private school choice. (In this conceptualization, *equity* is more about equity of access or opportunity rather than equity of outcomes; some predictions for competitive benefits, however, indicate that improved equity of outcomes is a long-term possibility.) Families with sufficient financial means have been practicing school choice through residential location or private school attendance for decades, which enables them to select high-quality schooling options for their children. Indeed, in 2003 a quarter of surveyed families in the United States reported moving to their current location for the school, and middle- and upper-class parents were more likely to practice this type of choice.[1] Poorer families often do not have the same range of options, due to financial limitations, and the government has thus far failed to provide high-quality neighborhood schools to this population in any consistent manner. Since education is widely regarded as the primary avenue for economic mobility in the United States, disadvantaged students who are trapped in failing schools are also less likely to escape the cycle of poverty. School choice can thus be framed as a civil rights and liberty issue.

Expectations of improved equity of access predict that the proliferation of charter schools will provide parents with a menu of high-quality schooling options. Parents not only will be able to find a high-quality school but will also be able to match their academic, behavioral, cultural, or philosophical preferences with school communities sharing the same views. (School choice, in this sense, is a form of values expression. Frumkin suggests that facilitating values expression is one of the key functions of the nonprofit sector.[2] This view is reflected in more communitarian arguments for charter schools as vehicles for preference clustering.[3] Such preference clustering, when extended to the values and preferences of school personnel, is also predicted to enhance teacher effort and school productivity.[4]) More skeptical observers predict that school choice will lead to greater student sorting along racial and socioeconomic lines, exacerbating current problems of segregation and stratification in the public school system. Initially, white flight was the primary concern, but more recent research has increasingly focused on socioeconomic sorting and self-segregating behaviors across several demographics.

Assessments of how well charter school reforms have expanded options for poor families depend in part on how one defines opportunity and liberty. Modern conservatives tend to define liberty as the absence of government regulations or constraints. Liberals, on the other hand, tend to see liberty in terms of individuals having sufficient means and opportunity to make real choices in a market society. These different concepts of liberty inform two perspectives on the equity of access achieved thus far through charter school reforms. When viewing liberty as the absence of government regulation, there is little doubt that charter school reforms have freed many families from their residentially assigned public schools. Parents in dozens of states and cities can apply to enroll their children at any age-appropriate charter school in the district, city, or other administrative area. The parents of nearly 1.5 million children have chosen to do so. In some cases, their options are not just limited to an assigned public school and bricks-and-mortar charter school, but also include other traditional public schools, online charter schools, financial vouchers for private schools, and homeschooling. Although disadvantaged families in areas of expanded school choice still lack the full range of options available to affluent families, reduced government regulation has considerably expanded their range of schooling options, albeit with government funding.

However, adherents to the current liberal definition of liberty would argue that the mere existence of charter schools in an educational market does not guarantee that these schools will be realistic options for many disadvantaged families. Residential proximity is a major factor in many parents' school selections.[5] What's more, disadvantaged families often have limited transportation options.[6] If charter school operators do not locate near low-income or high-minority neighborhoods, many of the families in those communities will be considerably less likely to pursue or maintain enrollment in a charter school. Also, the ability to actively select schools requires knowledge of the available options. Social networks, much like residential neighborhoods, tend to be segregated by race and class.[7] This perspective on school access suggests that educational markets and enrollment data need to be viewed in relation to their specific demographic contexts, particularly in cities with high levels of socioeconomic and racial segregation.

Early nationwide comparisons indicated that charter schools were serving higher proportions of minority students, but some observers noted that such comparisons were of limited use because of the higher concentration of both charter schools and minority populations in urban areas. Comparing the composition of charter school enrollments with their nearby public schools indeed provides more meaningful indicators of sorting effects. Studies in several states and metropolitan education markets have taken this approach, and others have used longitudinal student-level data to directly compare students' initial public schools with the charters they selected. Charter schools exist in a segregated social landscape in the United States, so the real question is whether they are ameliorating or contributing to wider patterns of segregation. Although findings vary somewhat by the studies' methods and locations, most data indicate that charter schools are at least as segregated as, if not more segregated than, public schools in their area. Evidence from multiple states indicates that charters are now "the most segregated sector of public schools."[8] Such trends are disturbing, particularly in light of increasing racial segregation in much of the country and recent court decisions curtailing the ability of districts' to use race in school placement.[9]

Expanded school choice may also influence socioeconomic segregation in the public school system. Early concerns about the impact of parental choice on socioeconomic segregation in schools focused on the potential of charter schools to "cream" the more advantaged and higher-performing students from the traditional public schools, leaving the most disadvantaged students behind. Participating in school choice is, of course, not mandatory, and parents who are able to devote greater energy toward their children's education or who have greater knowledge of their local school market may be more likely to exercise choice. If active choosers tended to be more affluent than nonchoosers, and all charter school attendees are necessarily choosers, socioeconomic sorting through choice could occur. Indeed, the families of charter school students appear to be somewhat more advantaged than nearby public school students on traditional socioeconomic status measures, but the most pessimistic expectations of creaming have not been supported in the research thus far. However, a handful of studies have indicated that school choice may have a cropping effect, where the lowest-performing or most-difficult-to-educate students are less prevalent in charter schools. Both local and national data have demonstrated that charter schools tend to enroll lower proportions of special education and free- or reduced-lunch students.

Many of the studies on socioeconomic sorting thus far are limited by their reliance on school enrollment data. Choosers could be advantaged in ways that are not readily apparent in the limited demographics collected by schools. Many charter school achievement studies implicitly acknowledge this possibility, using random assignment to compare charter school students only against other choosers rather than traditional public school students in general. Preliminary work using more detailed datasets indicates that choosers may have advantages that are not easily observable in regular enrollment data, including smaller families, richer home learning environments, and higher rates of participation in organized preschool.[10] As the number of charter schools expands, it will be important to see how the differences between choosers and nonchoosers are affected by the market penetration of charter schools or the prevalence of choice among consumers in a particular market.

COMPETITION: COMPELLING IMPROVEMENT IN EDUCATION

From their origin in Minnesota, charter schools have been seen as a way to inject a degree of competition between schools into the publicly funded system, which has traditionally been shielded from competitive pressures.[11] The idea that schools would have to compete for students (and thus their per-pupil funding) sets out a mechanism for the system to be self-improving. According to early enthusiasts, expanded school choice could lead to a cascade of events eventually leading to improved outcomes across the board. This chain of events begins with dissatisfied parents pulling their children out of underperforming public schools and enrolling them in charter schools. These charter schools will produce higher student achievement, attracting ever more public school students and their per-capita public funding. Eventually, public schools will face financial pressure from losing students and will respond to competition by improving their services and raising achievement. Expectations for these broad competitive benefits for all students depend in part on the higher performance of charter schools in comparison with public schools in the same local market.

The cornerstone of many arguments for expanded school choice, particularly in the No Child Left Behind era, is that charter schools will produce higher academic achievement than public schools. The main question for researchers, policy makers, and parents is whether charters *cause* higher academic performance for students. This question becomes problematic when researchers are forced to compare outcomes for students in charter schools with outcomes for students in the public schools the charter students might have otherwise attended. Many charter schools students, in fact, transfer from private schools, and the demographic profiles of student populations in public and charter schools are demonstrably different on factors that are known to influence school success. The challenge, then, is to isolate the impact of charter schools on students' academic performance.

There have been a number of attempts to assess charter school performance relative to public schools using a variety of methodological approaches. Despite the wide range of approaches, we see a general pattern emerging around this issue. A few of the smaller-scale studies of specific localities show advantages for charter schools, but most of the large-scale studies indicate that charter schools are performing at a level about equal to, or somewhat lower than, public school comparison groups (see Miron, chapter 4 in this volume).

However, many advocacy groups have painted a remarkably different picture of charter school performance. Although the research on charter school performance is mixed, some groups have claimed that evidence of superior achievement in charter schools is overwhelming. Much of this debate has taken place in the mainstream media, leading scholars to re-examine the role of the media and standards of evidence in research dissemination and policy making. During a time when No Child Left Behind and achievement results dominated educational news, demonstrating superior achievement in charter schools may have been seen as a make-or-break issue for charter advocates. As Henig notes, the debate over charter school achievement became high stakes, carrying overtones of larger political differences about the role of the private sector in public services.[12]

The growing body of evidence that charters are performing no better than public schools appears to have dampened some of the expectations of market-oriented reforms. Recently, some influential choice advocates like Sol Stern have publicly stated that expanded choice alone may not lead to the sweeping changes initially predicted.[13] In a very public debate, other advocates have shot back, claiming that choice is working and needs to be further unleashed.[14] This raises intriguing questions about whether choice, as manifested in charter schools, is inherently limited in its potential to reform education, or if the limited choice experiments we now have, as with charter schools, need to be scaled up dramatically before the real benefits of competition can be realized.

Of course, while the obvious question is how students in charter schools are performing, perhaps an equally pertinent question is how competition from charter schools affects achievement in other schools. Charter schools still occupy only a small proportion of the total organizational landscape in American education, but they were advanced as a way to leverage improvements in the wider system. As noted above, schools faced with the loss of students would have to improve their effectiveness or lose per-pupil funding. Instead of creaming the best students from failing schools, as some critics feared, the competition generated by charters could lead to overall improvements—a "rising tide that lifts all boats."[15] A number of studies have attempted to examine competition directly, comparing school outcomes in areas with high and low levels of competition.[16] Earlier work by Caroline Hoxby found that higher levels of Tiebout choice (residential choice) were associated were more productive public schools.[17] However, this work was challenged for some of her methodological decisions.[18] A later study focused on the impact of charter school competition on public schools, finding that when competition reached a certain threshold, district schools responded by increasing their productivity.[19]

Recent studies by Yongmei Ni, David Arsen, and others, however, have not found such positive outcomes for increased competition, and in many cases, more competition appears to be detrimental to public schools (see Ni and Arsen chapter 5 in this volume). In order for competition to "work," leaders and teachers in schools with declining enrollments must not only perceive the loss of students to competitors but also be able to make improvements in response. Given the high mobility rates of poor urban students, there is a good possibility that students departing for charter schools would not attract special notice.[20]

INNOVATION: ENCOURAGING NEW AND DIFFERENT APPROACHES

Probably no other goal was more closely identified with charter schools than the hope for innovation. This expectation was prevalent in the early years of the movement, and the Obama administration's recent emphasis on the innovative aspects of charter schools underlines the point. Charter schools are predicted to produce superior achievement, in large part because they have been freed from the bureaucratic restraints facing public schools. In line with Ronald Reagan's memorable statement that "government is the problem," many supporters of market-oriented reform have pointed to the government's monopoly on public education and its bureaucratic bloat as the primary roadblock to substantial improvements across the system. Since public schools typically have limited choice in their management of teachers, use of resources, and selection of curricula and instructional techniques, they arguably do not have enough latitude to develop innovative approaches to common educational challenges.

Consequently, according to this line of thinking, the public education system will continue to "muddle through," making only incremental improvements at a very slow pace.

Since charter schools are not immersed in this bureaucracy, they are thought to have a much greater range of options for responding to local needs.[21] The need for greater innovation was particularly prominent in early calls for charter schools. In their call for charter-like schools, John Chubb and Terry Moe noted the failures of the "one best system," and Ray Budde foresaw teachers freeing themselves from constraining administrations in order to improve their professional practice. In many cases, innovation and improvement were expected to emerge from increased interaction between schools and their constituent parents and communities.[22] In these predictions, current teachers and local leaders, including those outside the education system, would start charter schools in order to develop solutions to unique local needs. Charter school innovations would include changes to both internal practices and external relations.

Charter schools are undeniably "innovative" in the sense that they are the result of a significant innovation in educational governance—usually through changes in policy at the state level. However, outside of their being a result of innovation, the bigger question is whether they would be innovative in the sense of cultivating new and different educational models, especially in the classroom. In fact, no goal was cited more frequently than the idea of creating new, alternative approaches to teaching and learning.[23] While policy makers continue to promote the "innovative" aspects on charter schools, researchers appear more convinced that charter schools are generally not much different than other public schools in the classroom.[24] While there are certainly notable examples of innovative charter school classrooms (as there are in other public schools), charter schools generally do not appear to be developing new and different instructional practices to the degree that advocates had anticipated. Indeed, many charter schools have adopted classroom practices developed in the wider public or private school sector, and even more appear to have embraced "basics" curricular and pedagogical practices.

To understand this apparent shortcoming, it is useful to look into the design of charter schools. Advocates argued that these schools would have both the opportunity to innovate because they were freed from regulation and the incentive to innovate because parents demanded better alternatives. As it turns out, though, faced with a sink-or-swim situation from being thrown into the competitive marketplace, many charter school operators preferred to adopt tried-and-true approaches that would appeal to educationally conservative parents and would be more likely to pay off in academic performance. Although charter schools have not produced many fundamentally new approaches to instruction, they still play an important role in expanding the implementation of educational innovations. It is important to distinguish between true innovation and the replication of existing models or differentiation in particular education markets. In other words, charter schools may not create entirely new practices, but they may help introduce practices and curricula that were previously unavailable in a particular market. In this role, charter schools are more like showcases than research-and-development units for classroom practices. Simply put, true innovation is risky and expensive, and charter schools, particularly new ones, may not be well positioned to pursue innovation. The common expectation for innovation in charter school classrooms has been covered extensively before, and researchers are coming to a consensus on the limited performance of charters on this issue.[25] Accordingly, we do not devote space in this book to that aspect of innovation.

But that is not to say that charter schools are not innovative. While they have generally not been as successful as some had hoped in inventing new educational practices, charter schools are a wonderful site where one can witness extracurricular innovations in other areas of the educational organization. For instance, charter schools pioneered the idea of school marketing in many areas, as they were forced to attract students accustomed to attending their assigned school. Furthermore, new organizational models such as teacher-owned cooperatives, management organizations, and contracting out for essential services have appeared in the charter sector. Online education, services to homeschoolers, and new governance and employment arrangements are also prominent on the charter school landscape.

Expectations, if not requirements, for parental involvement and other sorts of community collaboration are often enshrined in charter school law. The application process for new charter schools frequently requires the identification of local stakeholders and partners, though these guidelines can vary significantly from state to state. This is one of the areas where charter schooling is particularly innovative, in bringing new players and resources into the public education sector. Although many charters must pursue outside input at their inception, it is largely unclear how prevalent these influences remain as charter schools mature and how they affect performance and operations in comparison with traditional public schools. This is but one of several areas of research in which the research community is only beginning to crack open the "black box" of high- and low-performing charter schools.

In contrast to grassroots collaboration, educational management organizations (EMOs)—which include both nonprofit and for-profit companies—have become powerful forces both in the charter school movement specifically and in education reform in general. These regional, national, and even international corporations directly create and manage charter schools or indirectly influence charter school operations by providing materials, curricula, technical assistance, and other services for a portion of schools' funds. They emerged from earlier practices in contracting and decentralization of both instructional and noninstructional school services. Many of these EMOs have combined financial backing, packaged and branded curricula, and economies of scale with considerable political access to develop charter schools and secure government contacts to take over troubled schools. For example, the considerable political influence of these organizations was readily apparent in Philadelphia's experiments with school privatization and urban reform. At one point, state policy makers went as far as to threaten that all additional education funds for Philadelphia would have to be directed to Edison Schools and other private providers.[26]

Educational management organizations, which often use identical basics-heavy curricula regardless of school location, are in many ways the antithesis to visions of locally responsive, innovative charter schools. On the other hand, many of the charter schools that have emerged locally or have stronger grassroots orientations have also struggled to produce solid outcomes or even stay afloat. This is a particularly intriguing issue, because charter schools were essentially asked to "do more with less." That is, innovation as a goal does not mean only that charter schools were supposed to create a new product, but also that they would develop processes that would be more efficient in terms of organizational inputs and outcomes. While—as we note above—the question of outcomes has been studied extensively, even if charter schools are performing at a level roughly equal to that of other public schools, if they are doing so with fewer costs, then this would indicate that they have found efficiencies in a notably expensive public endeavor.

Researchers have demonstrated that many charters are actually short-changed in comparison with public schools, although the degree of this inequity can vary substantially with state policy (see Huerta and d'Entremont, chapter 6 in this volume). These financial challenges for charter schools are compounded because many of the schools are new organizations that must secure and develop new facilities, hire large numbers of new staff and faculty, and recruit and admit large numbers of students. Consequently, many charter schools spend much larger proportions of their overall revenue on noninstructional services than do public schools. Though charter schools have been tasked with innovating in the classroom, they also act entrepreneurially in securing resources to support their mission.

The challenges of small, independent operators and the explosive growth of EMOs serve as a valuable reminder that schools are big business, with considerable administrative burdens. Although depictions of charter schools as grassroots operations are appealing ideals, they are perhaps not realistic expectations for the development of new schools under current state policies. Charter schools face considerable start-up costs and many constraints that make it difficult to function, let alone innovate. If policy makers expect the charter school sector to drive innovation in public education, they may need to determine what organizational contexts are most conducive to experimentation and compare those contexts with the current incentive structure for charter schools. Indeed, research thus far indicates that most charter school innovations are in marketing and management rather than in the classroom.One of the greatest barriers to instructional innovation in charter schools may be the perverse incentives created by achievement-based accountability systems under No Child Left Behind.

POLICY-MAKING ISSUES

In view of how charter schools have (or have not) advanced toward the goals set out for them by proponents, it is important to consider how policy levers may have contributed to the patterns we are seeing, and how those levers might address any deficiencies appearing in the charter school track record. Charter schools themselves are a policy creation, and just as importantly, the context in which they operate—the environment that informs their strengths and failures—may be shaped largely by policy factors. Although charter schools are a policy innovation, they are also the result of a relatively laissez-faire approach to education reform. In contrast to other efforts where policy makers directly intervene in educational processes by dictating curricular standards, assessment regimes, or teacher training, charter policy essentially establishes an environment and incentives in order to encourage new ideas that might not otherwise emerge from centralized decision-making. Charter schools are generally deregulated schools, with policy makers looking to contracting and market-like forms of accountability to address issues such as qualifications and quality that policy makers decided not to directly regulate. Policy makers still shape that environment by implementing or abolishing caps on the number of charter schools, specifying the agencies that may grant charters, establishing funding plans for charter schools, or setting parameters on how charters may enroll students. However, although more market-oriented proponents of charters may see further deregulation as the key to creating a self-correcting system, others will argue that some adjustments are necessary in charter policy, and policy makers must take a more direct hand in improving charter schools. But questions remain as to whether policy makers have the will and the information to lead such improvements.

As concerns over student sorting in educational markets continue, changes in state policy are likely to be one of the most influential tools for public intervention (see Eckes, chapter 3 in this volume). Although national politics and presidential administrations have certainly played substantial roles in shaping both perceptions and policy on charter schools, the debates over state laws—such as those governing racial sorting in charter schools, types of financial support, and caps on the number of charters—are in many ways the key battlegrounds for advocates and opponents of expanded school choice. The likelihood of revisions to state policy depends heavily not only on federal pressure and political climate but also on awareness of these equity issues among legislators. Understanding the impacts of charter school policy requires policy makers to think about schools, achievement, and parent behavior in new and perhaps more complex ways. The complexity of these issues allows advocates on both sides of the issue to play substantial roles in trying to shape how policy makers frame and evaluate charter school policy and performance. Thus, the question of how policy makers access information on this reform becomes crucial.

In an age where policy makers require "data-driven decision-making," a focus on "what works," and the use of "scientifically based research" in advancing school reform, one would expect that policy makers drew on evidence of charter school effects in advancing the movement. However, a retrospective analysis of the evidence available at the time indicates that information on program effectiveness did not seem to be the primary driver of charter school expansion. Instead, policy makers appear to have drawn on other justifications regarding the theoretical potential of charter schools in embracing this model—and still do today.

Parents are also expected to make informed decisions based on school performance indicators. Two of the highly anticipated outcomes for charter schools, improved equity of access and improved achievement, depend on the actions of parents as consumers of education. In rational choice models that undergird much of the thinking on charter schools, dissatisfied parents will pick higher-performing schools for their children, creating competitive pressure on low-performing schools to improve to attract and retain students and funding. Schools that fail to improve will eventually "go out of business," according to charter enthusiasts, leading to academic improvement across the school system.[27] Several assumptions need to hold for these competitive benefits to be realized, and parent decisions are the crucial first step in the process. If parents lack sufficient knowledge about schooling options or about the academic performance of these schools, the dynamic predicted by rational-choice models may be less likely to occur. Likewise, parents might also select schools on the basis of preferences or information other than academic performance.

While the rational-choice model that undergirds much of the thinking on parental behavior on charter schools would predict that parents will collect and use information on the academic quality of various school options to best advance their child's future economic earnings, the evidence to date presents a rather different, and more complex, picture. Most surveys indicate that school data are reviewed by parents, but other sources of information, particularly social networks, tend to be more trusted.[28] Though parents consistently report that race is not a major factor in school selection, behavioral indicators and revealed preferences suggest otherwise.[29] In fact, longitudinal, student-level studies of student movements indicate that many parents are pulling their children out of higher-performing public schools in order to send them to academically inferior schools that are more segregated.[30] However, such patterns often simply reflect the types of information that are available to parents. Thus far, most data do not support the rational-choice model, but a recent experiment has indicated that parents are more likely to pick higher-performing schools if these parents are directly provided with simplified school performance information.[31]

POWER RELATIONSHIPS AND CHARTER SCHOOLS

As independent education agencies usually operating free of what Chubb and Moe famously lambasted as "direct democratic control" of local school boards, the idea of a charter school has the potential to substantially shift the power dynamics around American education.[32] The intermediate players that have traditionally been associated with maintaining the status quo—school boards, teachers unions, administrators, etc.—are essentially demoted from their primary positions of influence and thereby prevented from obstructing the immediate relationship between educators and students. This perspective is quite explicit in the advocacy work of some of the early champions of charter schools such as Ted Kolderie and Joe Nathan. A journalist and policy entrepreneur, Kolderie helped accelerate the charter school movement in Minnesota and across the nation, finding allies in centrist Democratic organizations such as the Progressive Policy Institute. He made the case that chartering was a way of removing the "exclusive franchise" that districts enjoyed over education funding.[33] "The groups that represent the people who work in K–12 education deeply do not want to lose the district's exclusive. They do not want the state making it possible for public schools to appear, which students may attend, that are out of the district's control. That exclusive is what protects them from the dynamics—the pressure to be responsive, innovative and economical—felt by most every institution today."[34] Thus, by ending the government monopoly on administering public education, new players and their ideas could be brought into the educational arena, and unions, while hesitant to cede power, would have to assume new roles to be relevant. Nathan, coming from the alternative- progressive educator tradition, lambasted unions for their opposition to substantive innovations and, therefore, charter schools.[35] He saw an irony in how unions were opposing or weakening charter legislation, since he argued that charters would in fact empower individual teachers, even if the teachers would lose collective bargaining protections such as seniority.

Charters thus represented a device that many education reformers, as well as some anti-union activists, found useful in undercutting the entrenched position of teachers unions, even though the late president of the American Federation of Teachers (AFT) was one of the prime movers for promoting the idea of charter schools. Many if not most reformers in the charter school movement saw unions as an obstacle to innovation and other efforts to focus on the interests of the child. Thus, for example, in the wake of Hurricane Katrina, Louisiana policy makers and national charter advocates arranged to fire the unionized workforce of New Orleans public schools (including the teachers) and reconstituted the schools using a charter school model as a primary template—reflecting efforts to portray charters and unions as being in opposition.[36] While there has been much attention recently to organizing efforts by unions at charter schools in major cities, and unions tend to publicize the few charter schools they run, a recent report from a federally sponsored study reports that "to date, relatively few charter schools have been unionized . . . it is hard to call charter unionization a trend."[37] These developments raise questions as to whether charter schools are changing the power relations in public education by empowering parents at the expense of unions, or whether these schools simply represent the institutionalization of anti-union interests.

Although unions are often portrayed as one of the key obstacles for reform efforts, focusing solely on their position in relation to charter schools or empowered consumers would fail to capture some of the other important changes in power dynamics that have occurred through the growth of the charter school movement. In cities like Chicago and Philadelphia, charter schools, contract schools, and other forms of privatization have enabled central district leaders to institute new modes of governance. In these "contract regimes," district leaders build governing coalitions that depend more heavily on formal links to private actors and may reduce the influence of unions and the traditional bureaucracy.[38] In these circumstances, district CEOs, often with the firm backing of mayor-appointed school boards, can use charter schools and contract schools to implement central plans relatively quickly, without working through a large public school bureaucracy.

While such approaches certainly can reduce the power of unions, this power shift is not inherent to the governance arrangement itself. For example, in Philadelphia, one of the key complaints of the teachers union was that teachers did not get enough support from administrators and the district on student discipline issues. District CEO Paul Vallas engineered the creation of four new charter schools that would handle severe disciplinary cases, enabling other schools to institute "zero tolerance" discipline systems and satisfy union leaders. In this case, charter schools were essentially used to make a side payment to the union, helping to secure the union's support in the overall governance regime.

The Renaissance 2010 initiative in Chicago demonstrates how charter schools have altered the power dynamic in the city, but not necessarily in a direct or even market-like way. Rather, charter schools in this sense can serve as a path of least resistance for elite actors to pursue their agendas. The Renaissance 2010 plan, a version of a proposal initially presented by a group of business elites in 2003, aims to close some traditional public schools and create one hundred new schools, two-thirds of which would be charter and contract schools. All of the new schools would initially function under governance arrangements that eliminate local school councils (LSCs), boards composed primarily of parents that have power over principals and discretionary budgets at the school level. City leadership had criticized LSCs heavily in the past for political amateurism, and one side effect of Renaissance 2010 was a net loss of influence for these boards in district operations. P. Lipman and N. Haines note that the decisions on new charter schools in Chicago appear to be made in closed-door sessions between the school CEO and business elites and that many of those actors also control the distribution of private funds to aid in charter school start-up.[39] Compared with philanthropic efforts that aim to reform traditional public schools, this arrangement seems to provide a more direct path for funders to pursue their goals. In order to implement the Renaissance 2010 plan, the Chicago CEO does not necessarily need a particularly broad coalition with many public voices.

As noted in our introduction, the charter school concept is more like an empty vessel or a new educational space than it is a targeted reform. In some visions of change for the charter school movement, these spaces will be filled by myriad private actors, each implementing a unique approach to schooling. Advocates who hope to empower parents and "let a thousand flowers bloom" might see the emergence of contract regimes as a setback because charter schools in these regimes can become tools for the implementation of centrally defined plans. Charter schools may even increase the power of central leaders, allowing them to circumvent much of the bureaucracy below them. On the other hand, the embracing of charter schools by leaders of public school systems could be seen as strong evidence that charters are indeed "public" schools serving collective interests.

CONCLUSION

Thus far, most research indicates that charter schools have not produced many of the substantial benefits in innovation and competitive effects predicted by advocates. The evidence on competitive effects is mixed, and when positive effects are found, they tend to be quite small. In student achievement, charter schools on average are performing no better than traditional public schools. Innovation research has found that many charter schools are implementing new ideas in management and marketing, but the schools tend to be very traditional and conservative in curriculum and instruction. Nonetheless, much of the political rhetoric around charter schools continues to emphasize their role as innovators, competitive catalysts, and exemplars of high performance.

It is somewhat more difficult to draw conclusions on the third goal for charter schools: equity of access. Equal opportunity to attend high-quality schools is hard enough even to define, let alone measure. What would equal opportunity look like? If one looks for the absence of regulations on school assignment and the pure range of options available in particular education markets, charter schools are undoubtedly a success on the equity question. However, many charter schools are not realistically accessible to the most disadvantaged student groups, and there is evidence that special needs students are substantially underrepresented in charter schools. If expanded school choice is primarily utilized by more motivated or affluent subsets of urban populations, this suggests inequitable access.

Many readers will undoubtedly find shortcomings in our typology of the three main goals for the charter school movement. We believe that most of the arguments in support of charter school expansion can be categorized under these three goals, but we acknowledge that this list is far from exhaustive. Moreover, these issues and their corresponding research are considerably more nuanced and complex than we are able to discuss in the space of this chapter. The following chapters examine particular goals for charter schools and the research on those predicted effects in much greater detail.

CHAPTER 2

Charter Schools Challenging Traditional Notions of Segregation

David R. Garcia

Where one stands on charter schools is a matter of perspective. They have demonstrated the paradoxical capacity of being nearly all things to all people. Charter schools have managed to garner bipartisan support while becoming the contemporary battle line in school choice debates.[1] Likewise, charter schools have been described as hope for disenfranchised communities and a sorting machine that perpetuates existing social inequalities.[2]

In the spirit of the retrospective nature of this book, I dedicate this chapter to a review of the research on the segregation of students by race or ethnicity and academic ability in charter schools. The chapter is framed in light of the prognostications that both opponents and proponents put forth on the emergence of charter schools in the United States. The prognostications are used as a backdrop to explore three transformations in the perspective of charter schools within the academic literature.

First, critics feared that charter schools would segregate students by race or ethnicity through white flight, that is, through the convergence of white students into charter schools. To the contrary, there is considerable evidence that charter schools may overrepresent minority students compared with district schools. White flight is not the primary driver in the creation of segregated charter schools. The prevailing trend is for minority students to self-segregate into charter schools. As a result, academics are becoming increasingly concerned with the quality of education that minority students receive in racially isolated charter schools.

Second, critics charged that charter schools would stratify students by academic ability because these schools were expected to become elite institutions via cream-skimming. Charter schools would enroll academically talented students, to the detriment of academically disadvantaged students left behind in district schools. But research has now shown that, with some exceptions, charter schools serve academically disadvantaged students in proportions comparable to district schools. The stratification critique, however, has not been laid to rest. Academics are considering more subtle ways that charter schools may stratify students.

Third, charter schools were framed as market-oriented schools governed largely by economic forces. Many state laws, however, either include racial balance provisions to avoid the transformation of charter schools into white enclaves or provide incentives for charter schools to serve at-risk students. There is emerging evidence that these state-level policies influence the student body composition of charter schools. As a result, the perspectives of charter schools within the academic literature are expanding to consider charter schools a public school choice and amenable to public policies that promote racial integration, similar to magnet schools.

In the remainder of the chapter, I discuss each of the three transformations in detail. In each section, I chronicle the relevant research and comment on how the perspectives of charter schools have changed over time. To begin, I review the prognostications of both charter school opponents and proponents at the beginning of the charter school movement.

THE CASE FOR AND AGAINST CHARTER SCHOOLS

When charter schools emerged in the 1990s, neither policy makers nor academics had experience with a large-scale, decentralized public school choice policy. Charter schools, a new hybrid option for public school choice, fused elements from both the public and the private schools that preceded them. On one hand, charter schools received public funds, were held accountable to public authorizing bodies, and remained public schools. On the other hand, charter school laws allowed those outside the traditional public school system to operate schools. The extension of school operations to entities outside the traditional public school system became a defining feature that aligned charter schools with privatization policies in the eyes of many.

Charter schools were associated with market motives, and opponents warned of the encroachment of privatization into public education. Certainly, a few academics linked the roots of the charter school movement to other public school choice initiatives such as magnet and community schools.[3] But most critics considered charter schools a precursor to vouchers.[4] These fears were rational, given that some pro-charter school policy makers did indeed view charters as a segue to vouchers, and states with Republican-controlled legislatures were more likely to adopt "strong" charter school laws that resulted in more market-like operating environments.[5]

To charter school opponents, "school choice arguments, including those that support charter schools, were ever about anything but increasing the role of publicly funded, privately delivered instruction."[6] Moreover, Elaine L. Halchin feared that charter schools could fundamentally alter the perception of public education:

> As a market-based education system, charter schools present education as a common good, with parents as consumers. The fragmentation of the school system, the weakening of the common school ethos, and explicit messages encouraging parents to shop around, all challenge views of education as a public good. In sum, the existence of charter schools could institutionalize education as a private good.[7]

Researchers applied the results from previous research on market-oriented school choice policies to charter schools to forecast how events might unfold in the new public school choice sector.[8] Opponents feared that charter schools would become a mechanism for white students to separate themselves from their minority peers. For example, Frederick Hess and David Leal grouped charter schools and vouchers together as "market-based reforms."[9] Using data on private schools, they found evidence of white flight and generalized the results to portend what policy makers might expect under charter schools. Casey Cobb and Gene Glass, in their charge against Arizona's "laissez-faire" charter school laws, asserted that "unregulated choice can intensify ethnic stratification by allowing parents to remove their children from integrated schools (e.g., White flight)."[10] In effect, charter schools were expected to increase segregation by discriminating against disadvantaged and minority students. When charter schools emerged, the concerns over racial segregation were not based on the idea that minority students would be overrepresented in charter schools.

On the sorting of students by academic ability, opponents argued that "charter schools were likely to 'skim-off' the most talented public school students and their highly involved families, thus leaving public schools to serve at-risk children and other students with special needs who may be difficult and expensive to educate."[11] In this view, district schools would become "dumping grounds" for students shut out of school choice options, as historically had been the case in many school choice policies.

In defense, charter school proponents went on the offensive. First, charter school supporters pointed out that American public education was already segregated before charter schools.[12] Independent of formal school choice policies, many parents "choose" schools according to housing preferences. Low-income families, many of which are minority, cluster in neighborhoods with affordable housing. In addition, American public schools have experienced dramatic demographic shifts due to the growth in the number of minority students.[13] Opponents made clear that "the existing system does not live up to its rhetorical commitment to complete racial mixing. Choice programs should surely be compared against the system's real performance, not its aspirations."[14]

Second, proponents portrayed charter schools as havens for struggling students, whom district schools have not served well and whom districts are willing to let leave.[15] They argued that charter schools with homogenous populations and a clear sense of mission are more beneficial to students than the status quo, where integration may be encouraged but academic focus is lacking.[16]

Third, school choice proponents advanced what I term the "charter school specialization theory" as a viable defense of racial segregation in charter schools. The charter school specialization theory is based on the premise that parents from similar social, economic, and cultural backgrounds hold consistent school preferences and may choose to enroll their students in schools with other students from similar backgrounds in light of these shared preferences.[17] Because parents with similar backgrounds make similar decisions, specialized charter schools may enroll a disproportionate percentage of students with similar demographic characteristics. Segregated charter schools, then, can be understood as the logical consequence of like-minded parents making decisions based upon a shared set of academic criteria, rather than divisions along racial or ethnic lines.

Bruno Manno, Gregg Vanourek, and Chester Finn Jr. used the charter school specialization theory to question the use of student racial characteristics as an appropriate standard to judge charter schools.[18] "The 'balkanization' charge must also contend with the fact that some charter schools are designed for specific sorts of children."[19] Indeed, one-fourth of charter school directors cited "serving special populations" as a major reason for starting their school.[20]

FROM WHITE FLIGHT TO RACIAL ISOLATION

Students attend charter schools with more students of the same racial or ethnic group than do district school students. There is evidence of white flight to charter schools. But the more prominent trend is for minority students to leave segregated district schools to self-segregate into more racially isolated charter schools. The revelation that minority students self-segregate has expanded the traditional frameworks about segregation to consider the implications of racial isolation as minority students congregate in charter schools.

The four-year study commissioned by the U.S. Department of Education (USDOE) was one of the earliest and most influential studies on charter schools and racial segregation. The results refuted claims by choice opponents that charter schools enroll disproportionate percentages of white students compared with district schools. In 1998–1999, 48 percent of students in the charter school sector were white, compared with 59 percent in the district school sector. Also, black and Hispanic students were overrepresented in the charter school sector by 7 percent and 3 percent, respectively.[21]

The USDOE results were challenged in later research on the grounds that national aggregate data masked considerable variability across states. Charter schools in racially diverse states tended to enroll more white students than district schools did. In states with predominantly white populations, charter schools enrolled higher percentages of minority and low-income students than district schools did.[22]

In 2003, another national report sparked additional controversy on the issue of racial segregation. The study found that the charter school sector enrolled 13 percent fewer white students, 14 percent more black students, and nearly identical percentages of limited English proficiency (LEP) students and special education (SPED) students than did the district school sector.[23] In response, Martin Carnoy and his colleagues used the same National Assessment of Education Progress (NAEP) data to complete a more detailed comparison of students attending the charter and district school sectors.[24] After disaggregating the data further by location (central city, urban fringe, and rural), the researchers found that the charter school sector enrolled a lower percentage of black, Hispanic, and white students who were free- or reduced-lunch eligible than did the district school sector, particularly for schools located in the urban fringe and rural areas.

The aforementioned national studies, however, did not address the important question of how students are distributed among charter and district schools. Another vein of research compared individual charter schools and district schools within smaller geographic boundaries, such as within a state or school district, in order to narrow the comparisons to the localized contexts in which charter schools exist.

Erica Frankenberg and Chungmei Lee compared the racial composition of all charter schools and all district schools within a state and conducted the analyses across several states.[25] They found that 70 percent of all black charter school students attended charter schools defined as "intensely segregated" with a high concentration of black students. In district schools, 34 percent of black students attended intensely segregated schools. In both district and charter schools, white students attended schools with a higher proportion of white students than the aggregate state percentage of white students, a sign of white flight. On average, however, white charter school students were more exposed to black students than white students attending district schools. Yet, few white students attended heavily minority charter schools. A follow-up study released in 2010 found little change in the aforementioned patterns of racial segregation.[26]

In Michigan, minority students were overrepresented, rather than underrepresented, in charter schools. In 2004–2005, more than 40 percent of Michigan charter schools were racially segregated with higher percentages of black students. The high number of segregated charter schools was credited with increasing the overall percentage of segregated schools in Michigan.[27]

The strategy to compare charter and district schools that share the same boundary is predicated on the assumption that charter schools attract students either exclusively or predominantly from within the host district boundaries. Students in school choice programs entered from more than just nearby district schools, and there is evidence that charter school students traveled farther in a choice environment than they would have to attend the neighborhood district school.[28] Thus, even among schools within the same boundary, there is considerable potential to mismatch charter and district schools in the comparison groups.[29]

In a study of Arizona charter schools, Cobb and Glass used geographic mapping to compare charter and district schools located close to another, rather than comparing schools within the same district boundary.[30] They grouped "nearby" charter schools and district schools using coverage areas ranging from five to twenty-eight miles and found that Arizona charter schools were typically 20 percent higher in white enrollment than nearby district schools.[31]

As charter school research evolved, dynamic models were introduced to compare the exact district schools that students exited with the exact charter schools that students entered the following year.[32] These models maintained accurate geographic and temporal school attendance sequences to track and evaluate the outcomes of school choice decisions.

The two most salient findings from research conducted with dynamic models include these observations: (1) segregated conditions in charter schools are more attributable to minority self-segregation than to white flight, and (2) the charter specialization theory is tenuous as an explanation of the differences in school compositions between charter and district schools.

In Texas, Gregory Weiher and Kent Tedin compared the exact district schools that students left with the charter schools they entered. White parents rated test scores as the most important factor in choosing a school, and black parents rated test scores as the second-highest priority.[33] Parents across all racial and ethnic groups rated school racial or ethnic characteristics as the lowest priority among all available choices.

After exercising choice, however, students from all racial and ethnic groups entered charter schools with higher concentrations of students from their same racial or ethnic background. The average black student entered a charter school comprising 15 percent more black students than the district school they exited. White and Hispanic students entered charter schools comprising 8 percent and 4 percent more students from the same racial or ethnic group than the district school they exited. Simultaneously, parents chose to send their students to charter schools where a lower percentage of students passed the state assessments than the district schools they exited. The Texas results are consistent with other school choice research that indicates a difference between parents' stated and demonstrated school choice behaviors. The outcomes of parental charter school decisions appear to divide along racial and ethnic lines rather than to improve student academic conditions.

In Arizona, choosers attended largely segregated district schools before leaving to attend charter schools. After students have exercised choice, there is evidence of white flight into charter schools but a stronger tendency for minority students from all racial and ethnic groups, except Hispanics, to self-segregate in Arizona charter schools with higher concentrations of students from their same racial or ethnic group.[34] From 1997 to 2000, the average white elementary student attended charter elementary schools that consist of 10 percent more white students on average than the district schools they exited. The extent to which white students were exposed to black and Native American students remained unchanged after they entered a charter school, but whites were less exposed to Hispanics.

For minority students, the average black elementary student entered charter elementary schools that enrolled 29 percent more black students than the district schools they exited. Native American students across all grade levels chose to attend charter schools concentrated with other Native American students, despite attending the most segregated district schools. Native American charter school students attended district schools composed of 82 percent other Native American students, on average. The typical Native American student then entered a charter school composed of 16 percent more Native American students. Hispanic elementary students, on the other hand, entered charter schools with 4 percent less Hispanic students than the district schools they exited.[35]

In North Carolina, policy makers included racial-balance provisions in their charter school law to prevent white flight. A dynamic comparison of the district schools that North Carolina students left to the charter schools they subsequently entered revealed both white flight and racial self-segregation. White students entered charter schools with 11 percent fewer black students than the district schools they exited. Also, black students entered charter schools with 19 percent more black students than the district schools they exited.[36]

In Texas, there was evidence of white flight as white students entered charter schools with 6 percent more white students than the district schools they exited. The self-segregation of black students, however, was more pronounced. Black students entered charter schools with 16 percent more black students. Of note, Hispanic students were the only group not to attend charter schools with high concentrations of students from their own racial or ethnic group compared with the district schools of exit.[37]

In California, the percentages of white students entered charter schools with lower percentages of white students than in the district schools they left. Black students self-segregated into charter schools, and Hispanic students attended charter schools with fewer Hispanic students.[38]

The Concern over Racially Isolated Charter Schools

Contrary to the admonitions about white flight, minority students have self-segregated into charter schools. Consequently, the concerns over charter schools and racial segregation have shifted from the advantages white students would share if congregated in charter schools to how the separation of minorities into charter schools affects the quality of education these students receive. In the absence of evidence that charter schools improve academic achievement relative to district schools, some observers remain skeptical that minority students are receiving a quality education in racially isolated charter schools.[39]

The paramount consideration is to weigh the academic benefits of attending a charter school against the potential consequences that arise from the congregating of minority students into racially isolated charter schools. On academic achievement, there is no consistent evidence that charter schools improve academic achievement above district schools. Also, no evidence indicates that minority charter school students fare better academically in charter schools than they would have in a district school. In the research on charter school academic achievement, most of the differences between charters and district schools are modest, and the implications of these results for any future expansion of charter school are contested.[40]

What, then, about the potential consequences of the congregating of minority students in racially isolated charter schools? When students enter charter schools, they further restrict themselves from exposure to students from other racial and ethnic groups, compared with the district schools they left. Limited interracial exposure among students in charter schools lends credence to concerns about the lack of diversity and how increased segregation in American public education could compromise students' abilities to engage in and maintain a democratic society.[41]

The reasons that minority students chose to enter segregated charter schools remains a worthwhile topic for further research. Parents may prefer that their student attend schools with students from their same racial or ethnic group despite the lack of quality information on academic achievement to inform their decision, or possibly in conflict with such information. The answers have critical implications for understanding the role of parents as consumers and schools as producers in the education quasi-markets where charter schools both respond to and shape parental preferences.[42]

Finally, there are mounting concerns about the resources available to racially isolated charter schools. Funding disparities could exacerbate historic trends in which racially segregated schools have received fewer resources and students are presented with diminished academic opportunities. As in other circumstances, charter school funding presents a contradiction that challenges traditional models of calculating funding disparities. Previous research relied on differential tax bases at the local level to measure funding disparities. Charter school funding formulas, however, are not dependent on local tax yields; each student receives the same per-pupil amount to attend a charter school. An all-white charter school would receive the same state funding as that received by an all-black charter school.

When local funds are factored into the analysis, funding disparities that disfavor charter schools become apparent.[43] But other funding sources, such as private contributions or corporate partnerships, which are less transparent than public funding, also need to be factored into the disparity equation. Unfortunately, the private portion of the charter school pie remains a mystery because many charter schools are affiliated with privately held companies with no requirements to provide the public with financial information, despite the fact that these schools are funded with public money.[44] In the end, the funding debates would be enriched by greater access to information about what happens inside charter schools; such information would help the public understand the quality of education that minority students receive in racially isolated charter schools.[45]

FROM CREAM-SKIMMING TO DUMPING GROUNDS

The initial charges against charter schools held that they would cream-skim academically talented students and leave district schools as dumping grounds for unwanted students. There are few studies on cream-skimming in charter schools, but the preponderance of the available evidence indicates that charter schools do not enroll a larger percentage of academically talented students than do district schools.

In most literature on cream-skimming, academic ability is rarely measured directly. Academically disadvantaged students are defined according to a combination of student demographic variables such as race or ethnicity, free- or reduced-lunch status, and academic program membership (special education and English language learner [ELL] status). These variables are used as proxies for academic characteristics that are associated with a student being more difficult to educate than others.

For example, Natalie Lacireno-Paquet and colleagues examined cream-skimming in Washington, D.C.[46] Charter schools were considered to cream-skim if they enrolled lower percentages of LEP, SPED, and free- or reduced-lunch (FRL) students. Overall, charter schools enrolled similar percentages of SPED and LEP students and a higher percentage of FRL students than district schools did. The authors concluded that there was no evidence of cream-skimming by charter schools: "On the contrary, in the aggregate charter schools are serving a population that has many characteristics associated with educational disadvantages."[47]

My work has compared the demographic and academic characteristics of students prior to attending a charter school with the characteristics of students who chose other types of schools. The analyses broadened the operational definition of a "disadvantaged" student to include a direct measure of academic achievement. The research has yielded two findings of note: (1) charter schools do not stratify students by academic ability, and (2) charter school students, on average, enter schools at a greater academic disadvantage than district school students.

If charter schools cream-skim academically talented students, then one would expect academically talented students to be disproportionately represented in charter schools. According to this standard, there was no large-scale evidence of cream-skimming in Arizona charter schools. Parents did not exit district schools to congregate into schools with high concentrations of high-achieving students. Actually, students entered elementary charter schools where high- and low-achieving students were exposed to each other at the same levels as the district schools they exited. Overall, students exited elementary district schools where the average student in the top quartile attended a school with 15 percent of students from the bottom quartile. They entered a charter elementary school where the average student in the top quartile was exposed to 17 percent of students from the bottom quartile. Note that despite choosing not to stratify into charter schools by academic ability, elementary school parents chose to enroll students in charter schools that were more racially segregated than the district schools from which students exited.

Upon entry into high school, however, charter school students entered more heterogeneous academic environments with more exposure between high- and low-achieving students than in district schools. On average, students entered charter high schools where the average top quartile student was exposed to 9 percent more bottom-quartile students than in the district elementary schools the students had exited.[48]

In other Arizona research, elementary students who made an optional transfer into a charter school from a district school had the lowest mean achievement score of any group prior to entering their respective schools. In 2003, students who entered charter schools were 23.7 scale score points lower in mathematics and 17.1 points lower in reading than students who remained in the same district school for two years, after controlling for student background characteristics. In mathematics, the differential between the prior academic levels of students entering charter schools and district school students was comparable to the achievement gap between white and Hispanic students (24.38 scale score points).[49] With key student demographic differences held constant, Hispanic students who entered charter schools were on average 48.44 mathematics scale score points behind their white peers who remained in district schools.[50]

The ability to test the cream-skimming hypothesis directly allows for an empirical evaluation of the charter school specialization theory. In cases where school choice has increased the degree of racial segregation, school choice advocates have retorted with the charter school specialization theory and argued that racially segregated schools are the result of parental preferences to attend specialized schools. Thus far, the charter school specialization theory has been perpetuated with scant empirical evidence to test it.[51]

I created hypothetical racial and academic patterns by type of charter school according to the assumptions of the specialization theory and compared the actual student body composition of charter schools to the hypothesized patterns. According to the Arizona results, the weak and sometimes inconsistent relationship between academic and racial segregation outcomes and charter school type provides little compelling evidence to support the charter school specialization theory uncritically. In some cases, such as in "back-to-basics" charter elementary schools, students attended racially segregated schools where there was no a priori reason to expect high levels of segregation based on the academic specialization of the school. These schools may be attracting or excluding students for reasons other than the academic focus of the school. In fact, "back-to-basics" charter schools are the most segregated type of charter school and are a driving force for the segregated conditions in Arizona elementary charter schools.

The student attendance patterns were not one-directional, however, and point to the complexity of parental school choice decisions. Parental choice did not result in universal racial segregation among all charter schools in Arizona. For example, students who chose charter schools with broad themes, such as traditional and Montessori schools joined a student body that was more diverse than the district schools they exited.[52]

Subtle Ways That Charter Schools Stratify

The growing recognition that charter schools do indeed serve academically disadvantaged students has allayed concerns that charter schools would become bastions for academically privileged students. Accordingly, the stratification critique has become more nuanced over time.

In a *Harvard Educational Review* article, Amy Stuart Wells and colleagues regard charter schools as a postmodern paradox where existing definitions of segregation and stratification are of limited utility to explain the implementation of charter schools.[53] From one perspective, charter schools can be viewed as a liberating force for those disenfranchised by the modern American interpretation of the "one best system" of public education. Yet, charter schools have failed to achieve their emancipatory goals and can even establish more subtle means of reinforcing existing inequalities. Thus, Wells and colleagues argue, existing methods to capture segregation (i.e., the division of students by racial or ethnic categories) may lack the sophistication necessary to capture the new ways in which students are segregated or otherwise stratified in charter schools: "Rather than simply looking at the race, class, and gender of students enrolled in charter schools, research must also ask what the other ways in which charter and noncharter students within the same local context differ."[54]

The argument of Wells and her other colleagues in *Teachers College Record* is equally applicable to the traditional means by which cream-skimming has been measured.[55] Do charter schools find subtler means of admitting students who are best positioned to succeed academically? For example, Natalie Lacerino-Paquet and Lacireno fellow researchers argue that instead of creaming, some charter schools "crop" students by enrolling lower percentages of students with manifest academic challenges.[56] The cropping argument contends that market-oriented charter schools—those with stronger business or entrepreneurial inclinations—enroll lower percentages of LEP and SPED students than non-market-oriented charter schools and district schools.

Similarly, charter schools are now accused of stratifying disadvantaged students by educating the "deserving poor" or the most advantaged of the disadvantaged. This charge holds that charter schools tend to deny admission to "students whose parents are absent or uninvolved" and to exclude SPED and ELL students.[57]

Does this more nuanced conceptualization of stratification, however, miss a larger point? Charter schools have many incentives to target academically talented and otherwise advantaged students who are less costly to educate and probably have higher test scores. Yet, charter schools have not overtly cream-skimmed because district schools offer a more comprehensive educational experience to the academically-advantaged student than charter schools can provide.

THE INFLUENCE OF STATE POLICIES ON THE RACIAL COMPOSITION OF CHARTER SCHOOLS

Market theories remain useful to understanding individual and institutional behaviors under charter school laws. Over time, however, the initial conceptualization of charter schools as market-driven entities that operate largely free from state regulations has given way to the realization that state policies can influence the racial composition of charter schools. As a result, academics have expanded their conceptualization of charter schools to regard them as public school choice options with greater attention to how state policies can be leveraged to promote racial integration. As a public school choice policy, charter schools are now considered more analogous to the community schools and magnet programs that preceded them.

This perceptional shift can be credited to increasing evidence that differences in the racial composition of charter schools are associated with variability in state laws. In short, state policies matter. As such, these same policies can be engineered to promote racial integration. Policy makers can use the elements of school choice policies (admissions, funding, and information) to influence the racial composition of charter schools.[58]

One universal lesson from the charter school research over the last two decades is that grouping charter schools under a single label is fraught with pitfalls. States have crafted specific laws, and charter schools from different states often share little more than a common name. Charter schools are as unique as the states that created them. Each state has leveraged the charter school idea of quasi-public schools of choice to different policy ends.

On segregation, the racial-balance provisions of many states or their requirements to serve at-risk students influence the student body compositions of their charter schools. State racial-balance provisions arose out of the precise concern that charter schools would become enclaves for white students. Currently, nineteen states have adopted policies requiring that the racial composition of charter schools reflect the racial characteristics of a geographical region near the charter school.[59] An additional twelve states have statutes that provide chartering authority for charter schools that serve at-risk or minority students.[60]

State racial-balance provisions designate the geographic region that defines the set of district schools with which charters are to be compared and the racial-balance standards that charter schools must maintain. Many state laws use district schools within the same district boundaries as the point of reference to assess the degree of racial balance in charter schools, and the racial-balance standards range from specific percentages to more general descriptors.[61] For example, Nevada and South Carolina require the charter school population to be plus or minus ten percentage points "from the racial composition of pupils who attend public schools in the zone in which the charter school is located."[62] North Carolina, on the other hand, requires that charter schools "reasonably reflect" the racial and ethnic composition of the general population.[63]

Two important points serve as backdrop for the following synthesis of the research. First, charter schools are to be held accountable to their authorizing body through their charter as well as to parental preferences. Charter school authorizers, however, have been criticized for lax implementation in holding charter schools accountable to the conditions of their charter.[64] More particularly, in states with racial-balance provisions, authorizers may effectively ignore these provisions as they carry out their oversight responsibilities.[65]

Second, even if racial-balance provisions work as intended and the composition of charter schools reflects the composition of other schools within the same district boundary, one would still expect segregated schools. The degree of segregation in charter and district schools overall may remain unchanged. If district schools are segregated, say Nathalis Wamba and Carol Ascher, as is the case in many urban districts, then reflecting the racial balance of the local district schools would result in segregated charter schools as well: "In many instances, successful efforts at emulating school district levels of diversity mean continuing a high degree of racial segregation."[66]

The research evidence indicates that the racial composition of charter schools in states with racial-balance provisions differs from charter schools in states where state laws are silent on racial issues. The charter schools in states with racial-balance provisions enroll 5 percent more black students, on average, than states without such a provision. This increase remains robust even after controlling for school-level characteristics that may also influence the racial composition of schools, such as the school curriculum and location. The results point to the influence of state laws on racial composition of charter schools, despite the criticism that such schools are not held accountable to racial-balance provisions in practice.[67]

Kelly Rapp and Suzanne Eckes tested the relationship between the content of state statutes and the racial composition of charter schools.[68] States were divided into four categories according to the content of their charter school laws: states that must comply with desegregation decrees, states with provisions that charter schools reflect a specified racial balance, states with laws that promote diversity, and states with no racial-balance provisions. In half of the twelve states with no racial-balance provisions, charter schools enrolled a higher percentage of minority students. In these states, charter schools enrolled 23 percent more minority students, on average, than district schools, an indication that white flight was not evident even in cases where state laws are silent on racial balance. Of the seven states with desegregation decrees, charter schools in six of these states enrolled an average of 26 percent more minority students than district schools. Finally, of the ten states with racial-balance provisions, charter schools in seven of those states enrolled a higher percentage of minority students than district schools. On average, the charter schools in these seven states enrolled 27 percent more minority students than did district schools. By comparison, in states with racial-balance provisions and where district schools enrolled a higher percentage of minority students than charter schools, the average difference never reached above 11 percent.

In Florida, charter school laws influenced the type and composition of its charter schools. According to Florida law, charter schools are allowed to limit the enrollment process to target specific student populations, such as at-risk students and students who meet reasonable academic or artistic eligibility standards.[69] As a result, a large percentage of Florida charter schools are devoted to nontraditional students such as at-risk and ELL students and resemble magnet schools that enroll students with particular academic, vocational, or artistic interests. Also, a higher percentage of Florida charter schools than district schools were classified as racially segregated.[70]

Certainly, racial provisions alone should not be credited with the degree of racial balance observed across states. Other state policy features also influence the racial composition of charter schools. For example, states where students are not provided transportation to attend charter schools enroll a considerably lower percentage of FRL and minority students than do states that provide transportation. Transportation can become a barrier to prevent some families from exercising their school choice options to attend a charter school.[71] Also, charter schools in states that provide additional funds for at-risk students enrolled a higher percentage of low-income students, on average. Finally, in states where local school districts are the only authorizer, charter schools enrolled a lower percentage of FRL and minority students.[72]

From Markets to Structured Choice Policies

Gary Orfield, in a viewpoint largely unnoticed among those critical of school choice when charter schools first emerged, lamented that charter schools represented a lost opportunity to promote racial integration.[73] Rather than using a market-oriented analogy, he compared charter schools to magnet schools:

> One might well think that charter schools would have a better chance to be integrated than public schools. Like magnet schools a generation earlier, charter schools offer distinctive curricula and the opportunity to create and manage schools with freedom from many normal constraints in large districts. Unlike magnet schools, charter schools have the added advantages of even greater freedom to innovate and for the most part, are not tied to geographically fixed attendance boundaries in residentially segregated communities as are neighborhood public schools but can draw from wherever interested students can be found (in some places where school districts grant charters, they are limited to the school district boundaries).[74]

As the preceding research indicated, state laws can influence the composition of charter schools. Thus, researchers have expanded their consideration of charter schools to include the possibility that all school choice policies operate within a defined structure that dictates the rules under which schools operate. These structures must be taken into account when evaluating any policy, says Terry Moe: "It usually makes little sense to ask whether vouchers or charter schools in some generic sense, have particular effects. Their effects depend on the specific structures in which they are embedded, and they can only be understood and evaluated in that way."[75] To that end, there is now greater attention to how charter school laws can be structured and implemented to promote racial segregation.

Some school choice policies, particularly unrestricted choice, are likely to lead to segregation by race and stratification by ability. Charter schools do not appear to be of the same ilk. Many of the comparisons to open-school choice laws in other countries or domestic voucher programs are of limited utility as a framework to understand charter schools. Most states have either mandated or provided incentives for charter schools to enroll minority or at-risk students and achieve socially desirable ends.

Future research may be dedicated to distinguishing features of charter school laws that are associated with greater racial integration in charter schools. Advocacy groups, such as the Center for Education Reform, have long graded state charter school laws according to the extent to which they promote unfettered school choice. These grading systems have only recently come under academic scrutiny, but one could conceive that more progressive groups may pay greater attention to the importance of communicating how charter school laws promote or hinder socially beneficial outcomes over promoting individual preferences.[76]

CLOSING

Despite the trends identified in this chapter, some charter schools have been used to stratify students to the advantage of white or more privileged students.[77] Also, this chapter is not intended to imply that concerns about the influence of market forces in charter schools have dissipated. Legitimate concerns remain about the detrimental effects of unregulated school choice and the encroachment of privatization into public education. Nevertheless, the sweeping generalizations that once characterized charter schools should be tempered by the realization that they have not materialized as neatly as either opponents or proponents had envisioned.

The charges for and against charter schools continue in earnest, particularly in the mass media. The recent report by the American Federation of Teachers on the academic achievement of charter schools and the subsequent responses are evidence that charter schools remain coveted high ground for those with a stake in influencing public opinion of school choice.[78]

In states across the country, beneath the fray, charter schools have given parents far greater school choice than ever before realized in American public education. Since the introduction of charter schools, a broader cross-section of parents now has a larger set of school choice options. The choices that become available to parents and the schools they eventually choose are influenced by a convergence of state laws, local preferences, and market forces. The outcomes have proven to be more contrarian than first imagined and continue to challenge the traditional notions of racial segregation and school choice.

Charter School Legislation and the Potential to Influence Student Body Diversity

Suzanne E. Eckes

As of March 2010, there were five thousand charter schools operating in the United States.[1] Forty states and the District of Columbia have passed charter school laws.[2] These laws generally cover policy and legal areas such as charter development, school status, fiscal obligations, students served, staffing, labor relations, instruction, and accountability.[3] State laws make the existence of this type of public school possible, but federal law plays an important role in charter school governance as well.[4]

The fact that charter schools are governed by state statutes, which are written by state legislatures, results in wide variation from state to state.[5] For example, one state may wish to encourage student body diversity in charter schools and thus will incorporate language into the charter school law to influence this outcome, while another state's law may intentionally remain silent on this particular issue. Certainly, the political context of a particular state may account for these differences as well.[6] Accordingly, these variations in the language of charter school legislation may have different impacts on charter schools across the nation.[7]

Additionally, even identical charter laws may have different impacts because these laws are enforced to varying degrees across states. Specifically, despite the legislatures' intentions, it is not always clear how charter laws are implemented through charter school policy.[8] Also, once they are implemented, laws may be amended by the legislature or challenged in court for various reasons. Thus, charter schools and the laws governing them are in a nearly continual state of flux.

One area of charter school law that is always evolving is state statutory language focused on student body diversity. Though federal law prohibits charter schools from discriminating against students according to race or ethnicity, socioeconomic status (SES), and academic ability, state statutory language regarding recruitment and admissions can still vary widely. [9] To be certain, the wording of a state's charter school law has the potential to influence charter school admissions and recruitment practices and thus the makeup of a charter school's student body.[10] Specifically, the various state laws may lead to charter schools with varying missions that impact the diversity of the student body.[11] Just as state legislation shapes charter schools, so does litigation challenging these state laws.[12] For example, when a state charter school law is challenged in court, the statutory language may need to be amended to align with constitutional requirements.

This chapter highlights the differences among state charter school laws within the area of student body diversity and, further, demonstrates how legal challenges may influence state statutory language on charter school diversity with regard to race, SES, and ability. The chapter also discusses the current reality of segregation in charter schools despite the intentions of state legislatures. Indeed, an analysis of state statutory language and legal issues will assist researchers, school leaders, parents, and policy makers in determining the influences of various goals of charter legislation over the past two decades and in predicting how the laws will continue to evolve. The chapter concludes that there is still much to learn about whether and how state laws influence student body diversity.

STATE CHARTER SCHOOL LAWS: STUDENT BODY RACIAL DIVERSITY

Since the U.S. Supreme Court *Brown v. Board of Education* decision in 1954, states have adopted various tactics to achieve racially integrated schools. The *Brown* decision made it an American ideal to give "all students the benefits of an education in a racially integrated school and to maintain a community commitment to the entire school system."[13] Unfortunately, in spite of more than fifty years of work toward racial integration, many public schools remain racially segregated.[14]

When charter school legislation was initially introduced, some observers cautioned that this form of school choice might lead to further racial and ethnic segregation.[15] Others went on to make an even bolder claim that school officials would use charter schools to help white parents escape from racially desegregated public schools.[16] These claims appear not to have come to fruition.[17] Current research suggests that few charter schools have a disproportionately high percentage of white students.[18] In fact, data on charter schools reveal that a median 60 percent of students in charter schools are minorities.[19] Though suggesting that "white flight" to charter schools has not happened, studies on charter school student bodies have revealed a tendency for charter schools to be slightly more racially segregated than traditional public schools.[20] For example, in an Arizona study, Casey Cobb and Gene Glass reported that Arizona's charter schools were more racially segregated than traditional public schools.[21] In a nationwide study, Erica Frankenberg and Chungmei Lee found higher levels of racial segregation in many U.S. charter schools.[22] Other more localized studies found similar trends among charter schools.[23]

These findings are all the more troubling because several states, through their statutes, encourage charter schools to maintain a racially integrated educational environment. Specifically, some state laws permit charter school leaders to enroll students from across traditional school district boundary lines, while other laws encourage charter schools to ensure that the racial and ethnic makeup of their school population mirrors that of the community that the school serves.[24] Thus, one might expect charter schools to be less segregated than traditional public schools, but this has not necessarily been the case.

Sample Statutory Language Regarding Racial Diversity

In an attempt to avoid racial segregation in charter schools, nineteen states have created specific racial and ethnic balance enrollment guidelines for their charter schools.[25] Other states have enacted more general legislation, often including regulation of recruitment and admissions processes at charter schools.[26] These laws permit charter schools to create schools that are more racially and ethnically integrated, encouraging diversity to varying degrees: while some states specifically require diversity, others simply suggest it.[27] Of course, one of the motivations behind these laws is to help charter schools avoid becoming white enclaves.[28]

For example, North Carolina's statute clearly provides for increased student body diversity:

> The school shall reasonably reflect the racial and ethnic composition of the general population residing within the local school

administrative unit in which the school is located or the racial and ethnic composition of the special population that the school seeks to serve residing within the local school administrative unit in which the school is located. The school shall be subject to any court-ordered desegregation plan in effect for the local school administrative unit.[29]

New Jersey's law also includes language about diversity and requires that "the admission policy of the charter school shall, to the maximum extent practicable, seek the enrollment of a cross section of the community's school age population including racial and academic factors."[30]

Minnesota's law has a similar statement:

A charter school may limit admission to: (1) pupils within an age group or grade level; (2) people who are eligible to participate in the graduation incentives program under section 124D.68; or (3) residents of a specific geographic area where the percentage of the population of non-Caucasian people of that area is greater than the percentage of the non-Caucasian population in the congressional district in which the geographic area is located, and as long as the school reflects the racial and ethnic diversity of the specific area.[31]

Thus, it appears that the statutory language in Minnesota, New Jersey, and North Carolina encourages some consideration for student body diversity within charter schools because the statutory language indicates that the charter school population should attempt to mirror the population of traditional public schools. South Carolina's law goes even further: "the enrollment of the school is similar to the racial composition of the local school district in which the charter school is to be located."[32] South Carolina's law also notes that if the racial composition of the charter school differs from that of the local school district by more than 20 percent, the school district board of trustees will examine recruitment efforts and the diversity of the applicant pool.[33]

Nevada's law discusses a specific percentage as well, requiring that the racial makeup of a charter school's student body should "not differ by more than 10% from the racial composition" of the surrounding school district.[34] Unlike South Carolina's law, Nevada's law seems to provide very little flexibility in encouraging racial diversity in its charter schools. Although Nevada's law would prevent the establishment of predominantly white enclaves for those students returning to the public school system, the law is the most legally problematic of the few discussed. Specifically, Nevada's law may be open to legal challenge in light of a recent U.S. Supreme Court case, *Parents Involved Community Schools v. Seattle School District No. 1*.[35] This decision makes it difficult for K–12 public schools to consider race and ethnicity in student assignment plans. The *Parents Involved* case will be discussed more in depth in a later section of this chapter.

Note also that although state laws may allow charter schools to increase diversity in the student body, some charter schools must follow additional federal guidelines. Specifically, schools that receive funds from the federal Charter Schools Program (CSP) or Title I must hold a lottery or other random selection process if they have more applications than slots available.[36] Currently, 61 percent of charter schools receive CSP start-up funds.[37] For those newer charter schools that receive CSP funds, giving preference to certain types of students is allowed in some instances, but not in others. For example, a weighted lottery may be held when necessary to comply with the following: Title VI of the Civil Rights Act of 1964, Title IX of the Education Amendments of 1972, Section 504 of the Rehabilitation Act of 1973, the Equal Protection Clause of the U.S. Constitution, or applicable state law.[38] Separate lotteries may not be held for males and females, although schools are allowed to make "additional recruitment efforts toward male or female students."[39] Of course, if a school district is under a court-ordered desegregation decree, more leeway would be permitted in considering race in student assignment plans.[40] For charter schools that do not receive CSP or Title I funding and are therefore exempt from the additional guidelines, diversifying a student body may be possible if permitted by state law. As Jonathan Dolle and Anne Newman suggest, further studies on charter schools' admissions programs are necessary.[41]

Influence of State Statutes

Interestingly, little is known about the influence of state statutory language on the actual racial makeup of a charter school. In one study, Kelly Rapp and Suzanne Eckes analyzed the state statutory language of the thirty-two states enrolling over one thousand students in charter schools during the 2002–2003 school year. They coded the statutes into three categories according to their content: statutes that specified that charter schools must comply with any desegregation decrees, statutes that specified that charter schools must reflect the racial balance of their districts or communities, and statutes aimed at promoting diversity or combating racial isolation.[42] The authors found that statutes aimed at promoting diversity or combating racial isolation yielded the greatest contrast in percentage of minorities in charter versus noncharter schools. However, the authors caution that it is misleading to report trends in charter school enrollment by statutory language in the aggregate, as unique state factors interact with this language to create individual differences. For example, though Missouri and South Carolina have very similar statutes requiring that charter schools' student population reflect the racial balance in the district or community, Missouri has the largest discrepancies in minority enrollment between charter and traditional public schools (68.9 percent), while South Carolina has the smallest (0.9 percent).

The discrepancy between these states in the Rapp and Eckes study may very well be explained by the unique differences that exist in each state.[43] For example, Missouri's legislation limits the establishment of charter schools to metropolitan or urban school districts.[44] South Carolina, on the other hand, has recently faced litigation regarding charter school admissions, which may have made schools wary about allowing the proportion of minority students in charter schools to stray too far from their public school counterparts.

Robert Bifulco and Helen Ladd's study of charter schools in North Carolina revealed that black students are enrolled in charter schools with higher percentages of black students than the public school that they had formerly attended, and white students are enrolled in charter schools with fewer black students than the public school that they had previously attended.[45] Furthermore, Bifulco and Ladd found that of the ninety-seven charter schools in operation during the 2000–2001 school year, thirty were more than 80 percent minority, and twenty schools had higher percentages of minority students than did the neighboring traditional public schools.[46] The researchers noted that charter school families in North Carolina tended to choose charter schools with similar racial and socioeconomic backgrounds to those of their own children.[47] As a result, the charter schools in North Carolina tended to be more racially segregated. Such evidence suggests that North Carolina's statutory language focused on maintaining a diverse student body is not achieving its desired effect.

The situations in North Carolina and other states with similar laws are puzzling and help illustrate the difficulties in determining the exact influence statutory language is having on the racial and ethnic diversity of charter schools. A more thorough understanding of the unique factors influencing segregation in each state is needed.

State Charter Law: Litigation Involving Racial Diversity in Charter Schools

In addition to the influence of state legislatures, litigation may also play a role in shaping state laws focused on diversity either by enforcing or by challenging existing statutes. Robin Miller contends that although courts have already been asked to intervene in a variety of issues, litigation involving charter schools has only just begun.[48] The majority of the cases decided thus far have included challenges related to the constitutionality of state statutory provisions, specifically regarding language on admissions policies interpreted to favor minorities. For example, individuals pursuing lawsuits over student admissions have alleged that charter school laws violate the Equal Protection Clause of the Fourteenth Amendment.

As mentioned previously, states have passed legislation requiring that the racial composition of charter schools not differ from that of the local district by a certain percentage. At one time, South Carolina had passed legislation requiring charter schools to maintain a population that did not differ from the local district by more than 10 percent.[49]

This legislation was the focus of a legal challenge in *Beaufort County Board of Education v. Lighthouse Charter School Committee*.[50] In this case, the Lighthouse Charter School's petition for a charter was partly denied because the petition did not describe the intended racial composition of the school. The charter school challenged the petition's denial, and a South Carolina state trial court judge on remand found that the charter school legislation containing racial balancing provisions was unconstitutional.[51]

In *Beaufort*, the judge focused on the language of the state statute and found that its racial and ethnic balance provisions resulted in an admissions plan that relied too heavily on race.[52] The judge further reasoned that it was unconstitutional under the Fourteenth Amendment's Equal Protection Clause for a charter school to use race as a primary factor in its admissions process. At the time of this case, the South Carolina charter school statute stated: "under no circumstances may a charter school enrollment differ from the racial composition of the school district by more than ten percent."[53] During an appeal to this case, the statute was amended to state: "it is required that the racial composition of the charter school enrollment reflect that of the school district or that of the targeted student population which the charter school proposes to serve, to be defined for the purposes of this charter as differing by no more than twenty percent from that population."[54]

The court found that the amended version "changed the character of the racial composition requirement by injecting a fact-based determination regarding discrimination rather than mandating a straightforward racial quota."[55] As a result of the statute's new language, the issue was considered moot on appeal.

State statutory law has been amended several times throughout the past two decades—often as a result of legal challenges. Indeed, litigation may force state legislators to more carefully craft such language. To avoid litigation altogether, it would be prudent to avoid using strict percentages in charter school admissions and instead rely on more flexible language. It will be interesting to observe if state legislatures are amending their legislation in light of these lawsuits.

More recently, seven parents challenged a Washington, D.C., charter school law in *Save Our Schools v. Board of Education*.[56] In this case, a group of minority parents alleged that a D.C. charter school did want not its student body to be "too black" and therefore enrolled a higher percentage of white students than existed in the rest of the Washington, D.C., public schools. The parents who filed the lawsuit argued that the charter school at issue had a student body that was very different from other schools in Washington , D.C. Specifically, this charter school was 40 percent African American, and the Washington, D.C., public school system was 84.4 percent African American.[57] Thus, the parents argued, the racial disparity between student bodies was a result of the charter school's discriminatory admissions policy. D.C.'s law states that it

> prohibits any educational institution from discriminating based on, inter alia, race, religion, sex, age, familial status, or source of income. By its terms, this section of the District of Columbia Human Rights Act applies only to educational institutions, which are defined as institutions in which professors or teachers, using instructional material, follow a curriculum resulting in the increased skill or knowledge of their students.[58]

To establish de facto segregation, the seven parents who filed the lawsuit needed to demonstrate that the charter school's actions had an impact on a meaningful portion of the school system. Claims of discriminatory purpose at only one school did not meet this standard, however. The court found that the parents were not able to bring a lawsuit based on a discriminatory admissions policy because they did not intend to apply and have their children attend this particular charter school. Specifically, they could not bring this claim, because the charter school had not "injured" any of the parents, since none of their children were technically denied a spot at the school. Unfortunately, this decision did not provide a lot of guidance to charter schools in D.C. that may not enroll a student body that mirrors the student body of D.C. public schools. Nevertheless, the case highlights potential future litigation regarding the consideration of race in student assignment plans.[59]

As noted above in the discussion of Nevada's charter school legislation, a recent U.S. Supreme Court decision will certainly affect state legislatures' attempts to racially diversify student bodies in charter schools and traditional public schools in the future. In the 2007 *Parents Involved Community Schools v. Seattle School District No. 1* decision (the *PICS* decision), the U.S. Supreme Court made the consideration of race in K–12 student assignment plans more difficult. This may place several states' charter school statutes that still contain language about maintaining racial and ethnic diversity in charter schools at risk of litigation. In the case of the *PICS* decision, Louisville, Kentucky, and Seattle, Washington, had independently implemented voluntary integration plans to confront de facto segregation. The school boards in Louisville and Seattle had adopted school assignment plans known as "managed" or "open choice" to promote racially integrated and more equitable schools and to try to reflect the racial diversity of the community at large.

In Louisville, where the K–12 public schools were at one time racially segregated by law, the school board developed a managed-choice plan for assigning students to the public schools. One of the goals of the Louisville plan was to provide "substantially uniform educational resources to all students" in a "racially integrated environment."[60] Jefferson County (in which Louisville is located) school officials sought to provide a form of managed choice in student assignment. The district adopted a student assignment policy that combined neighborhood school assignment, school choice, and assignment based on race. Specifically, the board designated geographic attendance areas, called "residence areas." Each student was assigned to a "resides school" according to his or her address.[61]

In the 2002–2003 school year, 57.5 percent of students attended their "resides school." In addition to choice of geographic location, the plan allowed students to choose among varied specialized schools and programs (e.g., magnet schools, career academies). A student could apply for admission to any of the specialized schools regardless of his or her "re-sides" area. Racial guidelines then applied to maintain a black population of between 15 percent and 50 percent in each school in the public schools. The director of school assignment for the county said that 95 percent of families received their first or second choice of school. In its brief to the Supreme Court, the school district wrote that the student assignment plan was helping to prevent any resegregation that would result from the community's segregated housing patterns. The school district hoped to create the following benefits: "(1) a better academic education for all students; (2) better appreciation of our political and cultural heritage for all students; (3) more competitive and attractive public schools; and (4) broader community support for all JCPS [Jefferson County Public Schools] schools."[62]

While there was never de jure (mandated) segregation in Seattle, de facto segregation was widespread. At the time of the *PICS* lawsuit, the total public school enrollment in Seattle was 40 percent white and 60 percent nonwhite. However, the student bodies of many schools did not reflect this overall racial proportion, with most of the district's white students attending schools in the historically affluent neighborhoods north of downtown and a majority of the nonwhite students living and attending schools south of downtown. In 1998, the Seattle School Board adopted a student assignment plan in an effort to promote greater racial balance in each of Seattle's ten public high schools.[63]

The Seattle School District's plan allowed for some choice. Students applied to schools, and a series of tiebreakers was used when the pool of applicants was greater than the school's capacity. First, preference was given to applicants who had siblings already attending the school. The sibling tiebreaker was used between 15 and 20 percent of the time in admissions decisions for ninth-grade students. The district next used a racial tiebreaker if the racial makeup of the school differed by more than 15 percent from the population of the district. During the 2000–2001 school year, about 300 of the 3,000 student applicants (10 percent) were denied their first choice because of the racial tiebreaker. In fact, only three of the ten public high schools considered race in their admissions decisions at all. In the third tiebreaker, students were given preference based on the proximity of the school to their home. The final tiebreaker was a lottery.[64]

The student assignment policies in both Louisville and Seattle were intended to keep schools from segregating along neighborhood lines. Although the students were assigned to schools using a variety of factors, parents took issue with the fact that race was one of those factors and filed lawsuits contending that the consideration of race in the student assignment plans was unconstitutional.[65]

In the *PICS* decision, the Supreme Court clarified the extent to which the Equal Protection Clause of the Fourteenth Amendment to the U.S. Constitution allows school districts to use race-conscious student assignment plans to counteract resegregation or to maintain integration. Prior to this decision, only lower court cases had examined whether race could be considered in student assignment plans and—these cases offered mixed results.[66]

Although the Supreme Court in *PICS* reaffirmed that student body diversity is a compelling state interest, the Court reasoned that the Louisville and Seattle plans were not narrowly tailored because the plans relied too heavily on race.[67] Specifically, the Court ruled that public schools in Louisville and Seattle could not explicitly take race into consideration to achieve student body integration. In essence, the Court reasoned that both the Louisville and the Seattle school districts failed to carry the heavy burden of demonstrating that the diversity they sought to achieve justified the means they had chosen.[68]

As a result of this decision, state statutory language about diversity in charter schools should encourage race to be taken into consideration in a very holistic way. Because of the *PICS* decision, a state law mandating that 30 percent of a charter school's population be composed of students from a targeted racial or ethnic background would very likely be open to legal challenge. On the other hand, a state law that simply encourages charter schools to mirror the racial and ethnic makeup of the surrounding community may be more likely to escape legal challenge. Beyond the language itself, charter schools' interpretation of legislation will also be important in determining the legality of diversity initiatives.

In this decision, Justice Anthony Kennedy provided some guidance about instances in which diversity initiatives might pass legal challenge. Even though Justice Kennedy appeared deeply skeptical of the Louisville and Seattle programs in the *PICS* decision, he left the door *slightly* open for those who believe race should be considered in K–12 student assignment plans.[69] Specifically, he suggested a few legally permissible ways to maintain racial and ethnic diversity in public schools. First, in his opinion, Justice Kennedy noted that schools may use race in a very restricted way, stating that he would permit school districts to "narrowly tailor" plans that would assist in "avoiding racial isolation."[70] Charter schools that have adopted voluntary desegregation programs or that are considering a plan will need to carefully consider whether their policy relies too heavily on race.[71] Thus, some of the state statutes discussed earlier, such as Nevada's, which offers little flexibility in the racial makeup requirement, may need amending to reflect this most recent U.S. Supreme Court decision.

Indeed, it appears that Justice Kennedy is inviting schools to take a more individualized approach in assigning students to schools. The problem with this route, however, would be that in public school settings, students are not competing against each other on an individual basis. Thus, it is difficult to imagine how a school district would consider race more narrowly than Louisville and Seattle had done. The legal terrain of considering race in student assignment plans is complicated. Different groups have interpreted the *PICS* decision's impact in different ways (e.g., the Office for Civil Rights has interpreted the case differently than how the National Association of the Advancement of Colored People interpreted it). How state legislatures respond to this decision will be an important trend to observe.

Opportunities to Increase Racial Diversity of Charter Schools

Despite the litigation in this area, there are still opportunities for charter school leaders to increase the racial diversity of their student bodies. Charter schools can increase student body diversity by drawing students from across traditional school district boundary lines.[72] In this way, the schools may be able to exercise more control over their student body composition through recruitment measures.[73]

If a state statute does not encourage racial diversity through its recruitment or admissions language, a school leader who is interested in a more integrated charter school could strategically open a school in an area to draw from a more diverse area of students or even attempt to rezone or gerrymander the existing districts to increase student body diversity. Additionally, the No Child Left Behind Act (NCLB) may inadvertently offer school districts the opportunity to increase racial integration. Specifically, under NCLB, schools that are deemed in need of improvement must allow students to transfer to other schools within the district, which could arguably lead to greater racial integration if the race of students leaving poor-performing schools is different from that of students in the higher-performing schools to which they transfer.[74] Unfortunately, one 2004 study by the Government Accountability Office found that less than 1 percent of the students eligible to transfer under the NCLB provision have decided to do so. Future studies could explore why parents are not choosing to exercise these options.[75]

Another study suggests that even school leaders with good intentions are not relying on state statutory language to increase racial diversity in their schools. Suzanne Eckes and Anne Trotter examined the admissions and recruitment practices at eight charter schools to uncover the circumstances in which charter school leaders negotiated state statutes to create a racially diverse student body.[76] The researchers found that even when charter school leaders recognized the benefits of racial integration and were aware that state law permitted them to racially diversify the student body, some leaders did not attempt to create racially diverse learning environments. The school leaders in this study made it a priority to serve students from impoverished backgrounds. Although the leaders embraced racial and ethnic diversity, a racially diverse student body was not their first priority. Thus, despite the attempts of some legislatures to diversify the student bodies of charter schools, not all charter schools embrace these laws. Few studies, however, explore this relationship. Additional research on the influence of state statutory law on charter school policy is needed.

On a related note, some charter school leaders *intentionally* fail to racial and ethnic integration. Instead, they target students from a particular ethnic background. These charter schools are often referred to as *ethnocentric* charter schools. Nina Buchanan and Robert Fox define ethnocentric charter schools as those whose mission is "the promotion and study of one ethnic group as a means of providing students with a link to their cultural heritage, sometimes including language."[77] Such charter schools adopt ethnocentric or culture-oriented themes in their curriculum and may recruit a specific student population. Cultural identity may play a role in the establishment of charter schools, as seen in ethnocentric schools established to address the educational needs of African American students. Buchanan and Fox suggest that the notion of "separate but equal" may be evolving to the belief that only through ethnocentric schools can "true equity emerge."[78]

The *Milwaukee Journal Sentinel* reported in March 2004 that over 200 Afrocentric schools have opened in the United States since 1996.[79] Elissa Gootman suggests that 113 existing charter schools feature cultural themes in their mission statements.[80] Wendy Parker explains that in Lansing, Michigan, African Americans make up 33 percent of the school district, yet the Afrocentric charter school is almost completely African American.[81] Likewise, in Saginaw, Michigan, only 13 percent of the students in the school district are of Latin American heritage, yet the charter school student body is overwhelmingly Latino and Latina.[82] Minnesota has over twenty ethnocentric charter schools that serve predominantly Native American, Hmong, Latino, and African American students.[83] Instruction in some ethnocentric charter schools in Hawaii is conducted almost all in Hawaiian.[84]

Ethnocentric charter schools may contribute to the higher proportion of minority students attending charter schools. Although there could arguably be some post–*Brown v. Board of Education* legal challenges, such ethnocentric charter schools have gained much support.[85] Some minority parents who choose to send their children to schools where they will feel more comfortable have embraced the choice movement.[86] Indeed, parents may prefer that their children attend schools with students of similar socioeconomic or racial backgrounds, thus increasing racial segregation.[87] Nevertheless, these schools present new legal challenges that need additional examination.

STATE CHARTER SCHOOL LAWS: OTHER FORMS OF STUDENT BODY DIVERSITY

In addition to charter school laws focused on racial and ethnic diversity, there are other charter school laws aimed at integrating students according to socioeconomic status (SES). SES is often measured by how many students attending a particular school receive free or reduced lunch.[88] Charter schools with many low-income students tend not to perform as well as schools with wealthier children, because low-income families often lack access to health care, may have difficulty meeting their children's nutritional needs, and face other obstacles that can impede learning.[89] Thus, some state legislatures attempt to integrate charter schools by SES to help level the playing field for this group of disadvantaged students.

Charter school laws may also be written to prevent segregation by student ability. On the other hand, some state charter laws do not prohibit this kind of segregation, leading to the creation of charter schools designed specifically for students with disabilities or for gifted and talented students. Little research has been done on this type of student body diversity, but it is an important aspect of charter school statutory language nonetheless.

Socioeconomic Status (SES)

Several school districts (e.g., Wake County, North Carolina; Cambridge, Massachusetts; La Crosse, Wisconsin) are pursuing integration based on

SES because of legal considerations.[90] Some of these schools have received much media attention not only because focusing on SES is an alternative approach to focusing on race, but also because integration based on SES has led to high student achievement levels.[91] More school districts are considering student assignment according to SES for legal reasons, because integration based on SES, whether the policy is based on state statute or school district policy, can withstand legal challenges more easily than can race-based diversification efforts.[92] Specifically, courts use a more relaxed test of constitutionality when SES is considered in charter school admissions. Under the law, for the state (e.g., a public school district or charter school) to treat people differently according to SES, school officials must demonstrate that there is a rational reason to do so. This is a much easier standard to meet than the standard for the treatment of individuals according to race. As noted earlier, the courts require that a *compelling* reason be proven when the state treats people differently because of race. Some school districts may be using SES as a backdoor attempt to achieve racial integration in charter schools because of the strong correlation between race and poverty. This may also explain why several state legislatures have written laws focused on SES.

One example of a state statute that clearly discusses SES is from Rhode Island:

> The makeup of the charter public school must be reflective of the student population of the district, including but not limited to special education children, children at risk, children eligible for free or reduced cost lunch, and limited English proficient students. No charter shall be authorized for a school with a student population that does not include students eligible for free or reduced cost lunch, students with limited English proficiency, and special education students in a combined percentage which is at least equal to the combined percentage of those student populations enrolled in the school district as a whole.[93]

In light of the *PICS* decision discussed above, more state legislatures are likely to move toward considering SES instead of race. Despite the more relaxed legal standard, charter schools that choose students on the basis of SES or an at-risk status are still open to legal challenges, however. To illustrate, parents in Colorado challenged a provision in the Colorado Charter Schools Act (CCSA) stating that thirteen of its charters were to be reserved for the education of at-risk pupils.[94] The Colorado law defined "at-risk pupils" as those "who, because of physical, emotional, socioeconomic, or cultural factors, [are] less likely to succeed in a conventional educational environment."[95] The parents claimed that by targeting at-risk students, the charters were creating race-based classifications based on "culture," which are unconstitutional under the Fourteenth Amendment. As evidenced in this case, race and SES are often correlated because students from low-income families are disproportionally minority.[96]

The court upheld the Colorado Legislature's intent of the CCSA to educate all children within Colorado's public education system, finding that Colorado's law required that enrollment be open to any child within the district and that the law was nondiscriminatory. In other states besides Colorado, chartering agencies are allowed to give special preference to the charter applicants that wish to serve at-risk students.[97] All such states should ensure that, through their charter school statutory language, they are not violating the Equal Protection Clause of the Fourteenth Amendment.

Research is mixed on whether charter schools are more segregated than traditional public schools with regard to SES. Roslyn Mickelson, Martha Bottia, and Stephanie Southworth contend that charter schools do not tend to segregate according to SES more than traditional public schools do.[98] David Garcia suggests that the charter school sector enrolls a smaller percentage of students who are eligible for free and reduced lunch, especially in urban and rural areas.[99] Frankenberg and Lee argue that more analysis is needed to learn about the numbers of students from low-income backgrounds who enroll in charter schools.[100] They note that the numbers can be skewed because many charter schools do not participate in free- and reduced-lunch programs.

Student Ability

At the same time that state statutory language addresses enrollment based on race and SES, some state charter school laws address the integration (or in some cases segregation) of students with disabilities. Students with disabilities have a history of being segregated from other students in the public school system.[101] The Individuals with Disabilities Education Act (IDEA), formerly called the Education for all Handicapped Children Act, gives students with disabilities legal protections from such discriminatory segregation.

When charter schools were still relatively new, some commentators suggested that these schools might skim the more talented students away from the traditional public schools, leaving students with special needs behind.[102] Thus, state statutes in accordance with federal law specifically prohibit charter schools from excluding students with disabilities. For example, North Carolina's law has this provision:

> Except as otherwise provided by law or the mission of the school as set out in the charter, the school shall not limit admission to students on the basis of intellectual ability, measures of achievement or aptitude, athletic ability, disability, race, creed, gender, national origin, religion, or ancestry.[103]

Overall, charter schools tend to attract fewer special-needs students than do their surrounding traditional public schools.[104] In an earlier national study, researchers found that the enrollment of students with more significant disabilities in charter schools is relatively rare (except when charter schools are specially designed for students with disabilities).[105] Other researchers have suggested that charter schools tend to enroll students with mild to moderate disabilities.[106] These researchers note that charter school employees may be counseling students with disabilities, especially students with more needs, away from attending their school.[107] This counseling may occur at charter schools with college prep curriculums, or at charter schools with specific missions to serve students that are more high-achieving.

The low enrollment numbers of students with disabilities are somewhat puzzling, however, as some studies suggest that students with disabilities who do enroll in charter schools receive more individualized attention than they did at their former school.[108] Julie Mead found that charter school officials reported that parents of special-needs students are attracted to the small teacher-to-student ratio offered in many charter schools and that parents appreciate that their children are in school with peers who relate to their learning struggles.[109] One explanation for the lower numbers of students with disabilities reportedly enrolled in charter schools could be related to parents' failure to disclose their child's disability to the charter school.[110]

Indeed, excluding students with disabilities from charter schools is a violation of both federal and state law.[111] To meet their legal obligations and to provide appropriate support for students with disabilities, charter schools should be connected to a special education infrastructure. In so doing, charter school leaders would have access to people with expertise that would help ensure compliance with the law.[112] Fortunately, one recent study found that as the charter school movement has grown, charter school leaders have become more familiar with special education requirements.[113]

While some charter laws clearly state that students cannot be segregated on the basis of ability, other charter schools recruit only students with disabilities, and a few states have special statutory language that promotes this type of segregation based on disability. Mead has completed a comprehensive study on state statutory language designed to create charter schools for students with disabilities.[114] Currently, seventy-one charter schools have been specifically designed to serve children with disabilities.[115] These schools are located in thirteen states and the District of Columbia, as not all states permit charter schools designed specifically for students with disabilities.[116] Ohio and Florida have the most charter schools designed for students with disabilities, and it appears that many of these schools are designed to serve students with autism.

Only one state's law, that of Ohio, very explicitly includes information regarding charter schools designed for students with disabilities:

> The governing authority may establish a school that simultaneously serves a group of students identified as autistic and a group of students who are not disabled, as authorized in section 3314.061 of the Revised Code. However, unless the total capacity established for the school has been filled no student with any disability shall be denied admission on the basis of that disability.[117]

Mead notes that in addition to Ohio's law, Florida also provides for charter schools aimed at serving students with disabilities.[118] Florida's law requires that charter schools

> collaborate with municipalities, state universities, community colleges, and regional educational consortia as cosponsors for FSE [Florida Schools of Excellence Commission] charter schools for the purpose of providing the highest level of public education to low-income, low-performing, gifted or underserved student populations. Such collaborations shall:
>
> Be used to determine the feasibility of opening charter schools for students with disabilities, including, but not limited to, charter schools for children with autism that work with and utilize the specialized expertise of the Centers for Autism and Related Disabilities established and operated pursuant to s.1004.55.[119]

Such statutes may be open to legal challenge because under the Individuals with Disabilities Education Act, students with disabilities must be placed in the least restrictive environment. According to Mead, charter schools that serve students with special needs and that restrict admissions "do not ensure that each child needs the level of restrictiveness that characterizes the school, [and] they risk violating the dictates of the IDEA."[120] In other words, a segregated school may not be the least restrictive environment for students attending a charter school that enrolls mostly students with disabilities.

In addition to a possible violation of IDEA, charter schools that are segregated by disability may be violating the U.S. Constitution. As noted earlier, under the Equal Protection Clause of the Fourteenth Amendment, the state must have a compelling reason to treat students differently because of race and a rational reason to treat students differently because of SES. Unlike race or SES, however, the state needs merely a good reason to treat students differently on the basis of disability. This analysis is often referred to as *midlevel scrutiny.* It is easier to consider SES and disability in admissions or student assignment plans than it is to consider race. Thus, if states adopt laws that encourage the development of charter schools that cater exclusively to students with disabilities, they may be able to withstand legal challenge more easily than charter schools that consider race. Despite the somewhat easier standard to meet, there will most likely be legal challenges both against the charter schools that do not include students with disabilities and against the charter schools that serve almost entirely students with special needs. More research on the legality of such schools is necessary.

At the other end of the ability spectrum, some charter schools have also been formed to specifically serve gifted and talented students.[121] Additionally, some charter schools market their gifted and talented programs, as is the case in San Antonio and Tucson. The first California charter school with a gifted and talented curriculum was granted a charter in 2006. This school will also admit students who have not been identified as gifted and talented.[122]

Interestingly, gifted and talented charter schools tend to be disproportionately white.[123] Approximately 30 percent of charter schools have gifted and talented themes.[124] Indeed, some would argue that segregation based on ability is a roundabout way of segregating by race and SES.[125] Very little attention has been given to charter schools that gear their curriculum toward gifted and talented students. This issue could certainly be expanded in future research. As more charter schools focused on serving gifted students enter the scene, more research on this underdeveloped area will be needed.

CONCLUSION

State charter school laws are often the source of state-by-state differences in charter schools. While some state legislatures have crafted state laws intended to diversify a charter school's student body, other states have attempted to allow for greater segregation of students. Both types of charter school laws present legal challenges. To provide maximum clarity and to avoid unnecessary legal challenges, state legislators seeking to maintain a diverse student body should consider policies that do not rely too much on race, as required by the *PICS* decision. State legislatures that aim to integrate the student body on the basis of SES and disability will have an easier time avoiding legal challenge because of the lower legal standard required under the Fourteenth Amendment, but they are not immune.

Charter schools that seek to segregate—either intentionally or unintentionally—according to SES or ability need to ensure that they have a rational reason to treat students differently based on SES and a good reason to treat student differently based on ability. As state charter statutes continue to be challenged in court, it is likely that state statutory language will continue to evolve. When state legislatures consider enacting charter school legislation or amending current legislation, they should be aware that legal issues can be avoided through an understanding of the law and carefully crafted language.

Research on the impacts of state statutory language on student body diversity needs to be continued. The majority of studies have been conducted on the influence of statutory language on racial diversity, but separating the impacts of charter law and other factors within a state (i.e., previous segregation history) is difficult. Although charter schools appear to enroll a greater number of minorities than do traditional public schools on the whole, future research should examine disaggregated data at the state and local levels, perhaps utilizing ethnographic methodologies.[126] Also significant would be an examination related to how different political contexts produce different charter school laws and policies.[127]

As SES becomes a more popular proxy for racial diversity—and one that is less easily challenged legally—more research is needed in this area to determine whether state statutes aimed at increasing socioeconomic diversity end up having an impact on racial diversity. Finally, an in-depth study of the impacts of state statutory language on charter school diversity with regard to student ability is lacking. Since some state statutes prohibit segregation by disability and some statutes encourage it, a comparison of how these differing laws on charter school composition affect students with disabilities is warranted. A comprehensive study of charter schools serving gifted and talented students would shed light on this little-studied area of diversity as well.

For all types of student body diversity, researchers should consider the impacts of litigation on state statutory language. Of interest is whether more legal challenges will arise on the basis of segregation by SES and student ability and, further, how these challenges might shape relevant charter law. States' legislative response to such challenges will be an area ripe for future research. The nexus of legal and educational research techniques is sure to uncover many patterns in statutory influences on student body diversity and, in turn, the impact of litigation on statutory language regarding student body diversity.

CHAPTER 4

Performance of Charter Schools and Implications for Policy Makers

Gary Miron

INTRODUCTION

Although charter schools were designed to be highly accountable, after nearly two decades of existence, there is still no clear consensus among researchers regarding how charter schools' performance compares with that of traditional public schools. Some observers claim there is still insufficient evidence, a notion that contradicts, or at least questions, whether these schools are in fact accountable. This chapter will provide an overview of the evidence and draw summative conclusions based on this evidence. Additionally, this chapter will examine factors that suggest charter schools would outperform traditional public schools and the likely factors that explain charters' current performance levels.

There are essentially three forms of accountability for charter schools (1) *regulatory accountability*, which refers to such things as compliance with relevant state and federal laws and regulations; (2) *market accountability*, which refers to accountability to consumers such as parents and students who enroll and remain in charter schools; and (3) *performance accountability*, which refers to the extent to which charter schools fulfill their missions and meet academic targets.

Charter schools are designed to be held accountable by public authorizers under a *charter agreement*: a performance contract detailing, among other things, the school's mission, program, goals, and means of measuring success. Charters are usually granted for three to five years by an authorizer or a sponsor (typically state or local school boards). In some states, public universities or other public entities may also grant charters. Authorizers oversee charter schools' compliance with applicable state and federal regulations (regulatory accountability) and hold the schools accountable for meeting their goals and objectives related to their mission and academic targets (performance accountability). Schools that do not meet their goals and objectives or do not abide by the terms of the contract can have their charter revoked or—when it comes time for renewal—not renewed. Because these are schools of choice and they receive funding according to the number of students they enroll, charter schools also are accountable to parents and families who enroll their child in them or leave for another school (market accountability).

As originally intended, performance accountability covers a commitment to the terms of the charter contract between the charter holder and the authorizer. Charter schools are mission-driven schools; as originally conceived, performance accountability was to be based on the extent to which charter schools were fulfilling their unique missions. The charter agreement was expected to describe the school's program, goals, means of measuring success, and measurable objectives related to the mission. Performance accountability also refers to the extent to which a charter school meets state standards measured with standardized tests. In the 1990s and prior to No Child Left Behind (NCLB)—which increased demands for testing and pressure to meet state standards—charter school accountability was more closely linked to a school's fulfillment of both its unique school mission and the terms of the contract with its authorizers or sponsors. Over the past decade, however, the emphasis on performance accountability for charter schools has shifted to meeting state standards. This shift has had implications for the ability and willingness of charter schools to innovate and has put them under the same pressure that traditional public schools have to "teach to the test."

Why Charter Schools Are Expected to Perform Better

Charter schools, by design, receive more autonomy in operations in exchange for being held more accountable than other public schools for student outcomes. Charter schools use this autonomy to create their own schools, select their own governing boards, design educational interventions appropriate for students' unique needs and learning styles, and hire and fire teachers more freely. In turn, the enhanced autonomy granted to charter schools was expected to result in better performance of students enrolled in them.

The use of market mechanisms whereby funding followed students and contractual relationships with authorizers were intended to make charter schools more accountable for performance. If parents were not satisfied, they would not enroll or they would leave, which could eventually bankrupt the school. If the authorizer did not believe the school was living up to its mission and agreed-upon contract, the contract or charter could be revoked or not renewed after it expired. When the poorly performing charter schools are removed from the ranks, the aggregate results of the remaining charter schools go up. (Results for traditional public schools, on the other hand, are often weighted down by a number of poorly performing schools that are not easily closed or remedied.) These sorts of accountability mechanisms also suggest why charter schools were expected to outperform traditional public schools.

REVIEW OF EVIDENCE

Large differences in performance levels exist within and across states. While it is important to look at single schools and single states, this chapter focuses more on larger policy questions: Does the provision of greater autonomy via charter school reforms result in higher levels of student achievement and greater improvement over time? Because few studies have systematically reviewed the evidence related to fulfillment of mission, the focus of our review is on student achievement.

This chapter examines current knowledge about the impact of charter school attendance on student achievement. This overview and summary of research has several limitations. First, student achievement is not the only relevant "output" of charter schools, or any other school. A full assessment of charter schools' effectiveness and overall desirability must examine other outcomes such as equity, student and parent satisfaction and market accountability, regulatory accountability, curricular quality and relevance, and instructional effectiveness.[1] Moreover, even if student achievement were the only goal of charter schools, standardized test results are only one of many ways to assess it. Few, if any, experts would endorse evaluating a school or student on the basis of standardized tests alone.

Charter school laws, in general, require charter schools to meet the same standards and to take the same achievement tests as those taken in noncharter public schools.[2] The provisions of the No Child Left Behind Act have made this requirement ever more prominent.[3] These testing requirements suggest that there would be numerous evaluations of charter schools' impact on achievement. As we shall see, there have actually been relatively few studies of student achievement in charter schools, although the body of evidence has grown substantially and improved in overall quality over the last decade.

Evolution of the Body of Evidence

The body of research on charter schools has clearly improved over the roughly eighteen years that they have been in existence. Initially, most of the writing on charter schools was rhetorical and theoretical more than empirical. In the mid-1990s, this research largely focused on start-up issues and the degree to which these schools were innovative or how much they promoted segregation. By the end of the 1990s, more of the evaluations of charter schools addressed student achievement. The following factors have led to improvements in the research on student achievement and charter schools:

- Charter schools have now been operating for more years, so there are more schools available with multiple years of data to track.
- As charter schools grow in size, more schools pass the threshold at which their data can be made public.[4]
- Fewer states are changing the tests they use. When testing changed more frequently between 1995 and 2003, the ability to equate test results from year to year was hindered.
- State assessment systems are expanding and improving over time. All states have been adding more grades to be tested, and several states are making greater efforts to equate results from year to year. Also, a few states are developing and allowing access to individual student data with unique identifiers that allow researchers to link students from year to year.
- Finally, the overall sophistication of the charter school research has improved over time as researchers adapt and create more rigorous methods of measuring growth in charter schools, even when only less-than-ideal data are available.

The earliest studies of student achievement in charter schools came out of California, the District of Columbia and Michigan.[5] These studies were eventually supplanted by newer studies with larger samples, better designs, and more appropriate outcome measures.

In 2001, Gary Miron and Christopher Nelson synthesized the evidence on student achievement and charter schools and found fifteen studies of charter school achievement across eight states. Half of these were of limited scope. Using similar selection criteria for studies in 2008, Miron, Stephanie Evergreen, and Jessica Urschel identified and synthesized the evidence from forty-seven studies.[6] While this represented a large increase in the number of studies, many of these are still of limited scope; also, they only cover twenty-three of the forty states (plus the District of Columbia) with charter schools.[7]

Although the body of evidence is improving, we can expect still more improvements in the next few years. With more years of data and larger numbers of charter schools to consider, for example, we can expect the overall quality of studies to continue improving. We can also expect better test data to become available as states strengthen their accountability systems, rolling out more assessment programs and expanding the testing of students. A growing number of states are also moving to value-added accountability models that will yield stronger or more reliable results.

It is common to find in all the state studies evidence that some charter schools are exceptional in terms of student achievement. Similarly, some evidence suggests that results are better in some states than others. Nevertheless, the overall answer to the question of how charter schools perform has not changed with time: Charter schools perform at levels similar to those of comparable traditional public schools.

Variations in Design and Quality of Studies

Evidence about charter school performance is often disputed because of the designs and overall quality of studies used. Studies of charter schools require comparative data from the states covering all schools; most states, however, do not permit access to student-level data. The majority of existing studies, therefore, depend on less-than-ideal data sources that undermine more rigorous designs. Since 2001, however, several researchers have secured student-level data from a handful of states, allowing more rigorous study designs. In more recent years, researchers have simulated random assignment by comparing charter school students with students who applied but did not obtain a place in the school after a selection lottery. In this section, I will discuss the array of designs used to study student achievement in charter schools as well as the evidence resulting from these studies.

Generally speaking, the designs of charter school student achievement studies can be grouped in the following categories: cross-sectional, longitudinal with group-level data, longitudinal with student-level data, and random assignment. There are, of course, many variations of these designs, since they differ in the nature and number of controls used and in the overall scope of the studies (e.g., number of schools or states covered, number of years included, number of grades and subjects included).

Cross-sectional studies of student achievement

Interestingly, some of the most widely discussed and debated studies of student achievement in charter schools have been among the weaker ones in terms of design. In the autumn of 2004, the American Federation of Teachers (AFT) released a report that included a cross-sectional analysis comparing charter schools to traditional public schools using the National Assessment of Education Progress (NAEP) data.[8] The findings showed that charter schools had lower performance levels in reading and math. Because this study received front-page coverage in the *New York Times*, there was a strong backlash by charter advocates, who criticized this study because of its cross-sectional design.[9] Shortly after the release of the NAEP findings by the AFT, Caroline Hoxby released her own national cross-sectional study based on state assessment data, comparing charter schools with nearby traditional public schools.[10] Her study found that charter schools had higher test scores than traditional public schools.[11]

Although these cross-sectional studies provided a snapshot of how charter schools were performing at a single point in time, both attempted to provide some controls for differences in populations. The studies based on the NAEP data blocked and compared subgroups of students by ethnicity, family income (i.e., free or reduced-price lunch [FRL] status), and special education status. The Hoxby study made an assumption that neighboring schools would be demographically similar.

Two further studies were conducted using the NAEP results.[12] These studies both employed hierarchical linear models to examine the difference between charter schools and traditional public schools while taking into account differences in student and school characteristics. Henry Braun, Frank Jenkins, and Wendy Grigg found that charter schools were performing at levels noticeably lower than traditional public school in both reading and math at the fourth-grade level. These differences were statistically significant. Sarah Theule Lubienski and Christopher Lubienski looked at mathematic results in both grades 4 and 8. They found that charter schools performed at levels lower than traditional public school at grade 4—a finding that was statistically significant. At grade 8, the charter schools had slightly higher results, but this finding was too small and was not found to be statistically significant.[13] Aside from the national studies noted above, a few states have also relied on cross-sectional designs to evaluate charter schools.

Although not considered suitable to measure change or impact, cross-sectional designs have often been used by the media and advocacy groups to assemble quick and easy comparisons of student achievement in charter schools relative to traditional public schools. The strength of some of these cross-sectional studies is scope. For example, the studies using the nationally representative NAEP data provide an excellent overview of the performance of charter schools. This is something no other single study has been able to do. These studies can answer such questions as "What are charter schools' performance levels relative to comparable traditional public schools?" The cross-sectional studies cannot, however, answer questions such as "Are charter schools improving or adding more value over time?" Examining effectiveness and impact requires a longitudinal design that examines findings over two or more years.

Longitudinal studies with group-level data

Most available studies of student achievement in charter schools employ longitudinal designs with group-level data. Data for these studies are readily available from state assessment systems. The data can be sorted by grade and subject and are reported for whole groups within each school as well as by subgroups divided by race and ethnicity, free and reduced-price lunch status, special education status, and so forth. The longitudinal design is employed when school- or group-level results are compared over two or more years.

Typically, studies in this category compare successive groups of students at the same grade level over time. For example, reading results for fourth-graders in 2001 are compared with reading results for fourth-graders in 2002. This design allows group comparisons between charter and non-charter public schools. This is a common approach because only a handful of states allow access to individual student data. Until recent years, state assessment systems tested and reported data at only a few grade levels, which made following the same groups, rather than successive ones, over time more difficult. The key assumption in this design is that students in successive years will have more exposure to the treatment (i.e., charter school). Another key assumption is that the schools attract and enroll students with similar background characteristics each year, so that changes in student performance are not affected by shifting demographics over time. Unfortunately, these assumptions do not always hold true: Mobility rates in charter schools can be high, and when charter schools are fully implemented, they may attract students with differing characteristics than they did during the start-up phase.

Same-cohort studies refer to those that follow the same groups of students over time. For example, the reading scores of a group of students would be tracked in grade 4 in 2003, then in grade 5 in 2004, and so on. As states expand assessment systems to more grades, it is increasingly possible to follow a single cohort over time rather than successive cohorts. Calculating gain scores on same-cohort groups is preferable to consecutive cohorts, although there is still the possibility that students leave or are added to the group over time, which cannot be controlled for without individual student data.

Studies in this category vary considerably, depending on whether and how well they control for demographic differences between the charter and noncharter public schools being compared. Some studies use blocking of data and compare subgroups of students according to ethnic background, FRL status, Title 1 funding status, special education status, and so on. Other studies have controlled for differences using regression analyses, which take into account all of the same demographic characteristics.

Although studies in this category are most often state-specific, Tom Loveless used statistical adjustments to combine and compare results across ten states.[14] In this study, charter schools were performing at lower levels than were traditional public schools, but were improving more rapidly than traditional public schools over time.

I have used two unique methodological approaches in the category of longitudinal studies with group-level data in state evaluations and in multistate studies. The methods—residual-gains analysis and odds-ratio analysis—are among the more rigorous approaches available for working with group-level data.[15] These approaches compare each charter school with a set of demographically and geographically similar noncharter public schools. Variables used to create comparison groups are obtained from state and federal databases and include income, race, special education status, limited English proficiency, and urbanicity.

The residual-gains methodology has been applied in a number of state evaluations, and in 2007, this approach was used to study five-year trends in student achievement in six Great Lakes states.[16] This study represented one-quarter of the nation's charter schools. Key findings from this large-scale study include the following:

- Charter schools in the Great Lakes states are not currently outperforming demographically similar, traditional public schools.
- Trends indicate that generally, charter schools are making notable gains in achievement over time, especially in the states with relatively newer charter school laws, where charter schools are further behind traditional public schools.
- As performance levels of charter schools in more mature states improve and approach the level of demographically similar traditional public schools, the levels tend to flatten out and remain similar to the performance level of traditional public schools.

Over time, the studies that rely on group-level data have become larger in scope and more sophisticated in their efforts to match charter schools with traditional public schools. Although studies using group-level data are the most prevalent, they are not as reliable as studies that can examine impact based on student-level data.

Longitudinal designs with student-level data

An increasing number of charter school studies are based on individual-student data that can link test results for students over time to measure gains or changes in performance. Student-level data allow analysts to match charter and noncharter students on a few or several demographic characteristics and then track their relative performance over time. The first study of student achievement in charter schools that used a matched-student design was completed in 2001 for Arizona.[17] Since then, several other states have studies based on student-level data; these include California, Delaware, Florida, North Carolina, and Texas.[18]

In order to measure the impact of charter schools, these studies need to collect data on charter school outcomes while also measuring what the outcomes would have been without charter schools. Experimental designs do this by dividing students at random into two groups, one receiving the intervention and the other not. Quasi-experimental studies cannot do this, so they seek to match students receiving the intervention with similar students who do not.

Matched-student designs vary considerably in quality. Although all use student-level data, the better studies include more schools, as well as more grades and subjects. Also, the better studies will examine changes over more years. The overall quality of these matched-student designs also depends on the procedures and controls used to match students. Several quasi-experimental designs have developed, and many of them use creative statistical methods to control for differences in the nontreatment group. For example, some designs account for nonresponse error due to attrition of students or because some students are held back and dropped from the analysis. Two increasingly common designs include propensity-score matching and regression discontinuity.

Matched-student designs are the most promising development in research on student achievement in charter schools. The costs are reasonably low, and researchers can conduct large-scale studies with relatively strong controls. One considerable obstacle, however, is that only a handful of states are making student-level data sets available to researchers.

Randomly controlled experiments

Conducting a randomly controlled experiment with charter schools involves randomly assigning students to either a charter or a traditional public school. This is a very complex and difficult design to implement because it requires the recruitment of participating families willing to abide by the decision to enroll in the school to which they are assigned (either charter or noncharter). In reality, families who are dissatisfied with their local public school and apply for a place in a charter school are likely to seek other options if that application is denied. For example, many will apply again to the charter school the next year; some might even move their children to private schools. This is only one example of why such studies are complicated to implement. Using such designs in clinical settings or for more narrowly defined interventions is more practical.

Attempts have been made to use students who apply, but do not gain access, to an oversubscribed charter school as a control group. This represents a simulation of random assignment. Hoxby and Jonah Rockoff conducted one study in a small group of Chicago charter schools and found that charter school students outperformed those who did not gain a place through the lottery system and who had to continue in district schools.[19]

While questions have arisen regarding the scope and incomplete nature of the technical report for this study, Hoxby and Sonali Murarka conducted a similar study in New York City, and Atila Abdulkadiroglu and colleagues completed a similar study for seven of Boston's charter schools, all with positive findings in favor of charter schools.[20]

Using waiting lists for simulating random assignment is a promising idea, but a number of limitations need to be considered. As voucher research has shown, there is often considerable attrition in control groups constructed from waiting lists.[21] Moreover, my fieldwork in charter schools suggests that charter school waiting lists are often insufficient for a randomized experiment. In many cases, such lists are out of date or contain an accumulation of names over a number of years. In the most extreme cases, these lists cannot be produced for review when requested and may exist only in the minds of school administrators. Aside from questions about the validity of these waiting lists, it is nearly impossible to assess whether students on the lists had subsequently enrolled in other charter schools or had been exposed to other educational reforms. Some students who are accepted into a charter school may not have enrolled, because of things like transportation problems or difficulty with the requirement that parents volunteer at the school. Using the waiting lists to simulate random assignment first requires a review and an audit of the waiting lists, and greater efforts must be made to identify and track students who do not enroll at the charter school or who do not return to their traditional public school.

The charter schools with sufficiently large waiting lists and a willingness to participate in such studies are among the higher-performing and more sought-after schools. Because of the more selective nature of these schools, and because few schools are included in these simulated random-assignment studies, these results cannot be generalized to other charter schools that did not participate or that do not have waiting lists.

The U.S. Department of Education has funded a large and expensive, randomly controlled study of student achievement in charter schools, conducted by Mathematica Policy Research, Inc. No progress reports have been released, although indications are that the study has been negatively affected by attrition of participants and other factors. If or when this study is released, it will probably have limitations of its own. Despite the $5 million price tag of the Mathematica experimental study, it will reportedly cover only forty charter schools. In light of our own work, around one hundred statewide matched-student studies could have been funded for the cost of one large random-assignment study.

In practice, many of the sophisticated approaches are not applied, because of cost and time restrictions and sometimes because methods elaborated on paper are undermined by unforeseen lapses in data quality that do not become apparent until the study is under way. Some of these unforeseen data limitations include (1) missing or incomplete background data for experimental or control groups, and (2) large proportions of students in either the experimental or the control groups that do not take the test, switch schools, or are retained and retake the same test in consecutive years.

Although randomly controlled experiments are commonly perceived as the gold standard for study design, these are very difficult to implement when evaluating policies as broad as charter school reforms. The lack of a single successful study of this sort on charter schools underlines the difficulty involved in implementing such designs for evaluating large-scale reforms.

Synthesis of Findings Across Studies

Policy makers want definitive answers regarding the success of education programs and new school reforms such as charter schools. Although charter school reforms have existed for eighteen years, and even though these schools were expected to be highly accountable, we still do not definitely know whether they are leading to improved student achievement. Some observers argue that we will not have a definitive answer until we can conduct a randomized experiment. Others recognize that a randomized study is still likely to have limitations of its own. Others, including myself, have attempted to provide an answer to policy makers by summarizing or synthesizing the existing body of research on the topic. Ideally, these efforts to synthesize the research would use a meta-analytical approach or at least a best-evidence approach; however, these approaches require a more sophisticated set of studies that calculate and report effect sizes.[22] There are a number of more rigorous studies now available. Unfortunately, the scope of many of them is limited, representing only a small portion of the states with charter schools.

Given the limitations in data available for research on charter schools, it is not always possible to calculate and synthesize effect sizes. Therefore, it has been difficult to provide systematic and rigorous summaries of the research. Julian Betts and Y. Emily Tang have used effect size to synthesize the evidence from value-added and experimental studies of student achievement in charter schools.[23] Unfortunately, the selection criteria resulted in a narrower examination of the evidence from the more rigorous studies, which in the end comprised only fourteen studies covering seven states and single urban school districts in two other states. The median effect size across these studies was barely distinguishable from zero (i.e., 0.00519).[24] This overall finding, however, masks the fact that the Betts and Tang meta-analysis found effects that were more positive in favor of charter schools at the elementary level, especially in reading, and increased likelihood of negative effects at the high school level.

Together with colleagues at Western Michigan University, I have been involved in efforts to synthesize the growing body of research on charter schools.[25] Our approach has been to construct a picture from the diverse studies available, even though many of these studies rely on group-level data with relatively less rigorous study designs. Each new study on student achievement in charter schools brings the picture into greater focus. Our approach to synthesizing the research involves the following four steps:

1. Inclusion and exclusion criteria are set to determine which studies will be considered (e.g., we only include studies with technical reports, and if a study has been supplanted by a more recent or more comprehensive study, we include only the most recent version).
2. Next, the selected studies are categorized by the nature of the impact on student achievement (i.e., very negative, negative, mixed, positive, and strongly positive).
3. The studies are then weighted by the quality of the design and the scope and duration of the study.
4. The final step involves weighing and synthesizing the results to calculate average state and national performance levels.

A recent update using this approach synthesized the evidence across forty studies.[26] Figure 4-1 illustrates how the findings vary by state, by the nature of their impact (i.e., either positive or negative), and by the overall quality of the study. Each study is charted on a horizontal axis according to its relative quality and along a vertical axis according to its impact rating for a particular model. For the state-specific studies, we use state abbreviations to designate the studies. The other studies are national or multistate and are marked with a "US." The figure illustrates three important facets: (1) breadth and scope of available research, (2) the broad range in the overall quality of research, and (3) overall concentration of findings in terms of impact ratings.

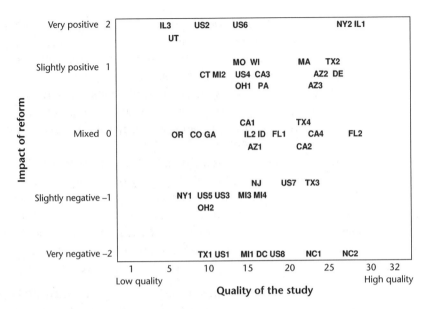

FIGURE 4-1   Quantity and impact ratings for studies of student achievement
in charter schools

Source: Gary Miron, S. Evergreen, and J. Urschel, "The Impact of School Choice Reforms on
Student Achievement, " Education and the Public Interest Center Education Policy Research
Unit, Arizona State University, Tempe, 2008.

Close examination of figure 4-1 reveals that studies vary widely in impact and design quality. Overall, nineteen studies had positive findings,
twelve studies had mixed findings, and sixteen had negative findings. The
mean impact rating for charters was +0.04. The weighted mean (adjusted
for quality of studies) was +0.1. These findings indicate a mixed effect. Although not a strong or significant correlation, there is a very slight tendency for the studies with more rigorous designs to conclude that charter
schools were outperforming their comparison groups.

This chapter examines both the relative scope and the relative quality
of empirical research on charter schools and student achievement. The
conclusions that can be drawn from the body of evidence include the
following:

- The overall picture indicates that charter schools perform at levels
similar to those of traditional public schools.

- Although charter schools perform similarly to traditional public schools, there are large differences in performance both within and among states.
- The design quality of the research on charter schools varies considerably; for about half of the studies, relatively weak quality is due to the absence of—or inability to obtain—student-level data.
- The inclusion of relatively lower-quality studies did little to change the overall findings.
- National and multistate studies tend to have findings that are more negative. Studies that cover single schools or small numbers of schools tend to be more positive.
- Studies prepared or funded by advocacy groups are all positive or slightly positive in favor of charter schools. A single study prepared by the American Federation of Teachers—a group seen by many to be an opponent of charter schools—had negative findings.[27] Studies by independent researchers tended to have a wide array of outcomes, with some positive, but most with mixed or slightly negative findings.
- The general conclusions that could be drawn from the evidence ten years ago is the same one that can be drawn from the evidence today. The difference is that the summative conclusion today is much more sound and clear, whereas a decade ago, there were still too few studies.

DISCUSSION AND CONCLUSION

There are a number of possible explanations for the observation that charter schools are not performing at noticeably higher levels than are traditional public schools. These possible explanations include but are not limited to the following:

- *Lack of effective oversight, and insufficient accountability.* Charter authorizers are expected to oversee the charter schools they sponsor. Many authorizers, however, lack funds for oversight, and some are unprepared and, in some cases, unwilling to sponsor charter schools. A key factor undermining effective oversight is that objectives in charter contracts are vague, incomplete, and not measurable. In recent years, more attention has been given to the role and importance of authorizers, which may have an impact. Without rigorous oversight, the poorly performing charter schools cannot easily be corrected or closed. Overall, closure rates for charter schools remain relatively low, and most charter schools that are closed do so because of financial mismanagement, rather than poor performance.

- *Insufficient autonomy.* Re-regulation and standardization driven by NCLB and state assessments are limiting autonomy. Because of requirements to administer the same standardized tests and have the same performance standards as traditional public schools, charter schools cannot risk developing and using new curricular materials. The original plans for charter schools assumed more autonomy.
- *Insufficient funding.* The financial viability of charter schools is dependent on the state, on how facilities are funded, and on the particular needs of the students served. Some charter schools maintain large year-end balances because they serve students who are less costly to educate, the schools have extensive sources of private revenues, or both. Some charter schools are clearly underfunded for the types of students they serve, and many charter schools lack the social capital to attract outside resources to supplement revenues. Funding formulas vary by state, but if charter schools are expected to innovate, they need more funding, not just greater autonomy.
- *Privatization and pursuit of profits.* Nationally, around one-quarter of all charter schools are operated by for-profit or nonprofit educational management organizations (EMOs). The increasing numbers of private operators may bring expertise or experience, but they also glean high management fees and tend to spend less on instruction. Further, reports continue to show that EMO-operated schools perform worse than non-EMO-operated schools. Some emerging nonprofit EMO models may prove more effective. While advocates claim that EMOs can make charter schools more effective, others have questioned whether EMO-managed schools retain their "public" quality and produce the results they promise.[28] While charter schools were originally intended to be autonomous and locally run schools, increasingly we are finding charter schools being started by EMOs, rather than community groups, and steered from halfway across the country.
- *Strong and effective lobbying and advocacy groups.* For charter schools, these strong groups can quickly reinterpret research and shape the message to fit their needs rather than the long-term interests of the movement. Attacking evidence that questions the performance

of charter schools, these groups offer anecdotal evidence, rarely substantiated by technical reports, in rebuttal. Such lobbying has undermined reasoned discourse and made improving charter schools more difficult.

- *High attrition of teachers and administrators.* Attrition rates ranging from 15 to 30 percent lead to greater instability and lost investment.[29] Attrition from the removal of ineffective teachers—a potential plus of charters—explains only a small portion of the annual exodus.

- *Growth in school size and class size.* One of the unique and attractive features of charter schools has been small school and class sizes. The school and class sizes of charter schools are growing and approaching the sizes found in traditional public schools. School size is largely increasing because existing schools are adding classes as their oldest cohorts of students progress to the next grade. We have also seen that the average size of new start-up schools has increased over time. A driving force behind these trends is likely to be financial pressure for economies of scale.

- *Rapid growth of reforms.* In states that implemented and expanded their charter school reforms too quickly, charter schools have faced a backlash as shortcomings in oversight and other neglected aspects of the reform become apparent. The states that have carried out their reforms more slowly have been able to learn from early mistakes and establish better oversight mechanisms.

While advocates claim that less restrictive charter school laws would result in more successful charter school reforms, Miron and Nelson found no relationship between student performance and the permissive or restrictive nature of the laws.[30]

Building Consensus Around the Evidence

The cause of educational reform is best served by careful and honest consideration of the evidence. This, in turn, requires policy makers to sort through the mountains of evidence and separate rigorous, independent research from anecdotal accounts and pseudoresearch lacking empirical procedures and technical reports.

Independent and impartial research is particularly important in view of the highly polarized context in which charter schools are being implemented. "Independence" is difficult to observe in practice. However, a few general rules of thumb can be used to determine whether a given evaluation or research study is independent. First, independence requires that the evaluation or research is conducted by a third party—some organization other than the charter schools and the agency or organizations overseeing the charter schools. Second, independent evaluations must include data other than those self-reported by the schools.

A third rule of thumb is to ensure that those conducting the research are impartial. Here, one can ask questions about whether the research is being conducted or sponsored by an advocacy or opposition organization. Also, it is good to consider whether the authors of these studies have ever released findings counter to their current results. Lead researchers of these studies typically have extensive experience, and the odds—for example, that someone would never have a finding that was in support of traditional public schools, or vice versa—speak loudly about the nature and underlying purpose of their work.[31] That is not to say that research commissioned by partisan groups will always result in positive or negative findings. Nevertheless, the body of evidence reveals that not one study released by groups advocating for charter schools found that charter schools had a negative impact on student achievement.

Given that charter schools represent a highly politicized reform, there are many attempts to influence policy with sensational and sometimes unfounded claims about student achievement by advocacy or opposition groups. Typically, these claims allude to empirical research. Press releases with data charts and talking points appear in papers or on Web sites. Earlier reviews of the existing research have had to weed through piles of these pseudostudies. Most such studies were not included in any synthesis of evidence, because they lacked technical reports with details on methodology. While technical reports may take many forms, the public should be aware that when technical details are not included in a study, the study's findings cannot be verified and replicated and, therefore, the conclusions cannot be justified.

Sound policy formation needs to consider the broader body of evidence, not the sensational stories of successful or unsuccessful charter schools. The stories of the exceptional charter schools are certainly worth studying and understanding better, but it would be wrong to build policies based on such evidence, especially when the larger body of national evidence indicates that charter schools perform at levels similar to those of comparable traditional public schools.

Questions Policy Makers Should Be Asking

Policy makers should be asking three key questions regarding charter school performance:

1. Can we create better public schools through deregulation and demands for greater accountability?
2. How are charter schools using the opportunity provided them?
3. Are there better uses for public resources than charter schools, for example, smaller class size, increased teacher remuneration or incentives, increased oversight of public schools, and support to restructure struggling or failing district schools?

The answers to these questions require comprehensive reviews of the evidence. Claims that every charter school is its own reform and should be looked at separately are not relevant in answering them. While the preceding questions deal with the outcomes of charter schools, policy makers should also consider questions about improving charter schools, such as how charter school laws can be revised to create schools that are more accountable, or how incentives and regulations can be used to ensure that poorly performing charter schools will be closed.

Action Needed

A sound initial step for improving charter schools would involve a cap on their number. This should include restrictions on an increasingly common practice in which existing charter schools open new schools or campuses under the same charter. Caps are not the same as a moratorium, since closing poorly performing schools would allow more charters to be granted.

Second, authorities should to move more aggressively to close poorly performing charter schools. This will strengthen charter school reforms in three ways: lifting the aggregate results for charters that remain; sending a strong message to other charter schools that the trade-off of autonomy for accountability is real; and redirecting media attention from a few scandal-ridden schools toward successful charter schools. Once independent evaluations establish that charter schools are successful in pursuing the intended goals, and when, as a whole, they are performing better than demographically similar traditional public schools, caps can be lifted.

Although these suggestions may be seen as antagonistic by the charter school establishment, they would help improve and strengthen charter schools in the longer run. The charter school idea was to create a better system of schools, not divide limited public resources across parallel systems that perform at similar levels and suffer from similar breaches in accountability. Charter schools can be returned to their original vision: to serve as a lever of change, spurring public schools to improve both by example and through competition. But if charter schools are to do so, they must perform better than traditional public schools and must be held accountable for their performance.

The beginning of the chapter described the diverse forms of accountability for charter schools. While this chapter covers performance accountability, the evidence presented and discussed has focused solely on test data from standardized tests. However, student achievement as measured by standardized tests is only one component of performance accountability.

Charter schools were originally designed as mission-driven schools. As such, they were to be held accountable for the measurable goals and objectives included in the charter contract. While some of these objectives deal with performance on standardized tests, many others are unique and specific to the school. Over time, performance on standardized tests has pushed aside the use of mission-specific outcomes. This has happened for many reasons. One is the increasing demand to use of standardized tests under NCLB. Another, however, is that authorizers and charter were not putting measureable and realistic objectives related to those other, mission-specific outcomes in charter contracts, and charter schools were not collecting and reporting on them. If policy makers wish to return to the original charter ideal, considerable effort must be reinvested in establishing oversight mechanisms that consider outcomes other than test performance. If such an effort is made, charter schools will need to be proactive and work harder to demonstrate accountability according to a diverse array of outcomes, so that oversight agencies do not revert to the easier-to-interpret test results.

CHAPTER 5

The Competitive Effects of Charter Schools on Public School Districts

Yongmei Ni and David Arsen

INTRODUCTION

The U.S. system of K–12 public education has been subject to widespread criticism over the last quarter century for failing to educate children well despite ever-increasing expenditures. Critics point to stagnant test scores, low graduation rates, and poor international comparisons, among other things. These developments suggest a productivity problem in American public schools. Formally, school productivity, also referred to as efficiency, is defined as student achievement (or other desired outcome) per dollar spent, controlling for the incoming achievement of students. Proponents of school choice policies assume that the prevailing educational system is not as efficient as it could be, and they point to the benefits of competition in the private sector to argue that market-based reforms in education would generate improved student outcomes without substantially increasing public expenditures. Importantly, advocates predict that choice policies will benefit both students who actively choose their school (the direct effect) and nonchoosers who remain behind in their assigned public schools (the systemic effect). Both predictions have been forcefully advanced in policy debates concerning charter schools, the fastest-growing form of school choice. This chapter assesses the systemic effect hypothesis in light of available research evidence. We do not address the numerous studies of student performance in charter schools, but focus instead on the effects of charter school competition on traditional public schools (TPSs), that is, on the students who are not active choosers.[1]

The theoretical arguments underlying the prediction that charter schools will benefit nonchoosers have always been less clear-cut than the arguments regarding benefits to choosers. If one assumes that students would only attend a charter school if it were better or a better match than their assigned public school, then the achievement of students who actively choose charter schools ought to be superior to what it would have been had they stayed in the public school. The cumulative effect of these choices, in turn, ought to be an improvement in the education system's overall efficiency.[2] By contrast, discussions of how choice will affect students who remain in TPSs have been dominated by two opposing arguments. Choice advocates maintain that if charter school policies offer parents expanded choices and tie funding to enrollment, then TPS educators will have an incentive to compete and increase their efficiency by working harder and implementing educational improvements. Critics of school choice, on the other hand, argue that a more competitive education system will not benefit all students, but rather create winners and losers relative to the status quo, increasing academic, racial, and ethnic stratification while further concentrating many of the most disadvantaged students in schools depleted of the personnel and resources needed for improvement.

The proposition that competition will spur public schools to perform better is now familiar to most Americans and self-evident to many. It is a compelling idea. In his acceptance speech before the Republican Party National Convention in August 2008, presidential nominee Senator John McCain brought the delegates to their feet with this pronouncement:

> Education is the civil rights issue of this century. Equal access to public education has been gained. But what is the value of access to a failing school? We need to shake up failed school bureaucracies with competition. Empower parents with choice.

It is but one measure of the charter movement's success that both major parties support an expansion of charter schools.

As charter schools proliferate, it is clearly important to gain a better understanding of how they affect the performance of the public school system for better or worse, since, in the short term, the vast majority of students will remain in TPSs. U.S. charter schools have expanded in an era of dramatically heightened expectations that the effectiveness of education policies and practices will be established by research. Yet studies of charter schools' competitive effects have not been possible until recently, because they require sufficiently high rates of charter school participation over a long enough period to elicit TPS responses. In recent years, several rigorous studies have emerged to begin filling in our understanding of how charter schools affect the performance of the pubic school system.

While the literature of rigorous quantitative studies is still taking shape, the initial results offer little evidence that charter schools will improve outcomes in TPSs. The existing research indicates that charter schools' competitive effects are quite mixed and generally small. Participants in the emerging market for schooling have a variety of rational responses to charter school policies that may either benefit or harm students who remain in their assigned public schools. Thus far, available research provides only a rudimentary understanding of which responses are most likely to emerge in a given setting and why.

This chapter is organized into several sections. In "How Charter Schools Might Improve, or Harm, Students in Traditional Public Schools," we summarize theoretical arguments about how charter schools may have positive or negative impacts on nonchoosers in district-run schools. In "How Traditional Public Schools Respond to Charter School Competition," we draw on qualitative and case study research on school districts' organizational responses to choice competition to present a conceptual framework of potential responses. We then turn to examine the quantitative research. "Why Charter Schools' Competitive Effects Are Difficult to Measure" presents a methodological discussion of why reliable estimates of the competitive effects of charter schools are difficult to obtain, and "Evidence on the Competitive Effects of Charter Schools" reviews the existing quantitative research. This body of research has been extremely helpful both in dispelling overly strong predictions concerning the systemic effects of charter school choice and competition, and in posing more refined questions about factors that may be responsible for the muted and disparate impacts observed thus far. In "The Rules and Local Context Matter," we discuss these conditioning factors, focusing on features of charter school policy design (the rules) and the states or local contexts in which policies are implemented. The final section,

"Implications for the Charter School Policy Debate," distills some larger implications for the debate.[3]

HOW CHARTER SCHOOLS MIGHT IMPROVE, OR HARM, STUDENTS IN TRADITIONAL PUBLIC SCHOOLS

Discussions of charter school competition are often cast in terms of simple economic theories of supplier and consumer behavior in markets. A notable prediction derived from such theories is that competition will compel public school personnel to improve their performance lest their schools lose resources as students choose schools that are more efficient. In fact, however, this is just one of many possible outcomes, since households and schools have a wide range of potential responses to charter schools. Charter school critics have emphasized ways that charter schools could harm nonchoosers. In this section we briefly summarize these accounts of how charter school competition could benefit or, alternatively, harm children who remain in their assigned public schools.

How Charter Competition Could Improve Traditional Public Schools

The conventional argument that charter schools will benefit children who remain in their assigned public schools is fundamentally a story of incentives. Proponents of this view start by assuming that public schools are not as efficient as they could be. This inefficiency, in turn, is due to the absence of appropriate incentives that would encourage better performance by school employees. According to this logic, public schools are overly bureaucratic and complacent. Since children are assigned to attend their local neighborhood school, parents typically have limited options for publicly funded schooling once they choose where to live. Public school personnel, therefore, operate in relatively protected or monopolistic markets. They have little incentive to strive to serve their students, because their employment and compensation are not dependent on their performance or that of their school. If, however, policies offer parents and students expanded educational choices and tie school funding to enrollment, then educators will have an incentive to work harder and use resources more effectively.

The predicted benefits for nonchoosers turn on a specific set of anticipated responses by households and schools. On the demand side of the market, students (and families) are expected to select higher-quality schools, generally defined as schools that more efficiently produce desired student outcomes.[4] On the supply side, this reasoning implies that high-quality (efficient) schools, including charter schools, will attract students and resources while low-quality schools will be spurred to improve or will lose students and resources. How will the improvement in low-quality schools come about? This is seldom specified in much detail. The most common suggestions are that school employees will exert greater effort in performing their jobs while also striving anew to identify and implement administrative and instructional improvements. In the search for better practices, charter schools themselves may provide examples that TPSs could adapt. If they fail to improve, however, low-quality TPSs will continue to lose resources and eventually be forced to close.

How Charter Competition Could Harm Traditional Public Schools

Some observers are skeptical about the predicted benefits of charter competition, instead arguing that children who remain in their assigned public schools are harmed. The most prominent of these arguments fall into four categories.

First, the improvement predicted by charter school proponents will only happen if active choosers take the first step of selecting schools that are more efficient. Families' choices have to be based on schools' academic quality. Yet we know that families choose schools for a variety of other reasons, including their student racial or socioeconomic composition, extracurricular activities, safety, or proximity to home.[5] In fact, parents often lack good information on schools' academic quality, and in such situations, they may use more visible features, including student demographics, as a proxy for school quality. Unlike the textbook model of perfect competition, where producers supply homogeneous goods and services to the market, the educational services of alternative schools are distinguished on many dimensions that matter to families aside from their efficiency. Insofar as choices are based on considerations other than school quality, charter schools can create the wrong type of competition, encouraging schools to change in ways—increasing advertising, extracurricular activities, or ethnocentric curricula—that potentially diminish their overall efficiency.

Second, charter schools will ordinarily cause a resorting of students across schools, which will generate externalities in the form of peer effects on students who remain in TPSs. Whether these peer effects are positive or negative is theoretically uncertain. Nevertheless, students remaining in TPSs are most likely to suffer negative peer effects when parents select schools according to peer characteristics, thereby increasing socioeconomic and ability stratification across schools. If low-achieving students benefit from attending schools with higher-achieving classmates, and active choosers are disproportionately higher achieving, then disadvantaged (high-cost) students may become ever more concentrated in low-end TPSs, where they suffer negative peer effects.

Third, while choice advocates celebrate the prospect of shaking up conventional schools, the associated turbulence can also diminish school quality and efficiency. Student mobility and turnover pose serious challenges for urban schools serving low-income students. Charter schools, by design, increase student mobility among schools. While low levels of mobility to and from charters could perhaps blend into the background noise characteristic of urban schools, higher levels aggravate an already-turbulent educational setting, undermining teaching and learning by interfering with the establishment of stable rapport between students and their teachers. Increased turbulence may also undermine school morale, prompting quality teachers to leave heavily affected TPSs for more manageable jobs in more stable schools.

Fourth, charter schools may hinder efficiency in TPSs that are losing students if the traditional schools are forced to underutilize their capital facilities or personnel. Since many school expenses are relatively fixed in the short to medium term, average per-pupil costs will ordinarily increase in TPSs that are losing students. Schools may rationally hesitate to lay off teachers or close buildings until it is clear that enrollment declines are permanent. More generally, however, depending on the structure of a state's funding system, revenues might decline more rapidly than costs in declining-enrollment TPSs, obliging these schools to make expenditure reductions that diminish the quality of educational programs available to nonchoosers who are left behind.

Each of these potential advantages and disadvantages of charter competition on nonchoosers is plausible and supported by at least some anecdotal accounts. At this stage, we lack a clear sense of the relative weight and intensity of these conflicting influences in actual settings characterized by meaningful charter competition. Thus far, quantitative studies of charters' competitive effect, which we will review later, only capture the net effect of these and other systemic adjustments on TPS performance.

And as we will see, the balance between positive and negative effects could easily vary from one local setting to another.

HOW TRADITIONAL PUBLIC SCHOOLS RESPOND TO CHARTER SCHOOL COMPETITION

While households and the public school system can, obviously, respond to charter schools in ways that produce dramatically different consequences for nonchoosers, to date our knowledge of this complex behavior, especially the supply-side adjustments of TPSs, is very incomplete. With early empirical studies showing little evidence that charter schools improved TPS performance, people have become more interested in understanding what determines how districts respond to charter schools. There is reason to anticipate future progress on this count. Economists, after all, have developed a vast array of theoretical models of strategic behavior under alternative competitive conditions, but so far, very little of this research has been applied to the analysis of competition among schools. This section sets a more modest objective, drawing on available case study and anecdotal accounts of school system behavior to outline a conceptual framework for the analysis of TPS response to charter school competition.

Interview and case study data clearly point to the diversity of TPS responses to charter competition. Many of these responses bear little resemblance to the educationally beneficial changes predicted by charter school proponents. In many cases, charter competition clearly elicits little or no school district response at all. In an analysis of five urban school districts, Paul Teske and colleagues conclude that the link between charter competition and public school response was "tenuous as best."[6] Reviewing studies covering multiple districts, Frederick Hess notes a common finding that the majority of school systems display no response to competition.[7] When districts do respond, among the ways they do so is by changing school leadership, opening magnet schools, and creating new programs consistent with parents' preferences.[8] Other district responses include launching add-on programs, such as all-day kindergarten, after-school child care, and extracurricular activities. Several researchers have noted an increase in district marketing initiatives. Some observers have also noted efforts by TPSs officials to vilify charter competitors or otherwise obstruct their opening and operations.[9] Thus far, however, there is little evidence that choice competition stimulates significant change or innovation in TPS instructional practice.[10] On balance, while some of the reported responses of TPSs to charters can be viewed as enhancing school quality, many plainly cannot.

In trying to give some conceptual structure to the welter of school district responses to charter competition, it is useful to highlight three distinct stages in the process (figure 5-1). To have an impact, charter *competition* must change the *perceptions* of public school personnel, particularly administrators, who then change their *behavior*. There are a number of reasons, however, why this process can break down at the first of these linkages. If TPS personnel do not make the effort or are unable to monitor families' choices or why they are making them, these educators lose the ability to translate mobility patterns into useful signals about the changes that families want in their schools. Where district enrollment is growing despite the appearance of charters, educators may not even recognize the impact of choice. Alternatively, administrators may recognize the loss of students to charter schools, but conclude, correctly or not, that students are leaving for reasons (e.g., student racial composition) that they cannot respond to. Insofar as any of these possibilities apply, school improvements will not be forthcoming with the introduction of charters.

There remains a good deal of uncertainty regarding how much competition is required to change the perceptions (and behavior) of public school personnel. Analysts generally presume that the greater the charters' market share, the greater the competitive threat and incentive for TPSs to respond. It is also possible that threshold levels of charter competition must be reached before beneficial (or harmful) systemic effects are observed. Currently, however, we know little about what this critical market share (or other indicator of competition intensity) might be. Caroline

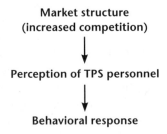

FIGURE 5-1   Three distinct stages in public school districts' responses to charter school competition

Hoxby, for example, drawing on empirical analysis of Michigan charter schools and districts, identified the threshold charter market share as 6 percent.[11] Meanwhile, other observers have taken the extreme theoretical position that true competition in the education system requires an approximation of the textbook conditions for perfect competition.[12]

Consider now the second link in Figure 5-1—possible responses of school personnel who correctly perceive the actual or potential adverse financial impact of charter competition. Table 5-1 identifies three major categories of responses: accommodate entry, compete, and create barriers to entry.

Accommodate entry. One response to new competitors is passive. District schools may accept a smaller market share as students move to charter schools. This inaction may be purposeful, as in cases where current district enrollment exceeds capacity or where the district is content to let charter schools draw away certain students, for example, high-cost, special-needs students. In certain cases, a district may strike a collusive arrangement with a charter school to formally segment the market or fix market shares, for instance, an agreement that the charter school only provides alternative education services. Accommodation, however, may also be the default response for school districts that are incapable of marshaling a coherent reaction to the challenge of new competitors. The prospect for charter schools to spur improvement depends on the quality of TPS administrative leadership. If leadership is weak, politically divided, and subject to rapid turnover, a school or district will have limited capacity to respond effectively to competitive pressures.[13]

Compete. Unlike most private-sector markets, where price competition is an essential dimension of strategic firm behavior, price competition by public schools is generally not feasible. Instead, school districts have

TABLE 5-1 Responses of public school districts to charter schools

Accommodate entry	Compete	Create barriers to entry
Passive	Improve school quality	Fill product space
Collusion	Product differentiation	Political actions
Incapable of effective response	Marketing strategies	Restrict access to networks

to compete with new competitors through efforts to improve service quality, product differentiation, or marketing. Efforts to improve school quality—the response highlighted by charter school proponents—might include, for example, initiatives to improve teacher quality, to link instruction to assessment, to improve student discipline, or to enhance administrative effectiveness. Product differentiation strategies may be particularly appropriate if specific segments of a district's market are vulnerable to competitors. Schools may develop or upgrade services in specific areas such as transportation or after-school, vocational, or academically talented programs. Competition for students through marketing strategies may entail advertising and public relations initiatives in local media (radio, television, and print), direct mailing to parents, and open houses.

Create barriers to entry. Some strategic responses seek to prevent new entrants from entering an incumbent producer's market or to handicap the new schools' ability to compete. There are many examples of such barriers to entry. A school district could establish its own charter school in an effort to fill the product space that a potential independent charter school might move into. Districts might engage in political actions to oppose the placement of a new charter school in their community by organizing opposition among elected officials, the chamber of commerce, the PTO, or realtors. Alternatively, established school districts could work collectively to deny new charter entrants access to networks such as athletic leagues, superintendents' roundtable, or professional or legislative associations.

While all of the school district response noted in Table 5-1 have been observed in the case study literature, it is difficult to assess the relative frequency of alternative actions. Indeed, any given district might engage in multiple, even conflicting responses that could change over time with the evolution of market conditions. Nevertheless, among the possible TPS responses, those that can be reasonably expected to improve school quality and efficiency are clearly but a small portion of the total. This observation ought to bring a little circumspection to charter school policy debates. A better understanding of which responses are most likely to emerge in any given setting, and why, is clearly needed. Models of competitive behavior developed by industrial organization economists may eventually provide helpful insights in this regard.

Although case study research offers enlightening insights regarding the variety of schools' organizational responses (and nonresponses) to charter competition, we cannot gauge, using such studies, competition's overall impacts on school quality. This is the objective of the quantitative studies to which we now turn.

WHY CHARTER SCHOOLS' COMPETITIVE EFFECTS ARE DIFFICULT TO MEASURE

Despite the demand in policy circles for simple and clear answers, measurement of charter schools' competitive effects is complicated. These methodological challenges account in large measure for why the available evidence remains limited and contentious despite the widespread implementation of charter school policies. There are two general criteria for judging the quality of studies of charter schools' competitive effects. The first is *internal validity*, which is achieved when changes in the outcomes of TPSs facing charter competition can be solely attributed to that competition. The second criterion is *external validity*, or whether the competitive effect found in one study can be usefully generalized to charter schools in other settings. Preferably, studies should have both high internal and external validity. In this section, we focus on threats to internal validity in competitive-effect research; we take up issues related to external validity in a later section.

The ideal way to ensure internal validity would be through experimental methods, where researchers randomly assign TPSs to one of two conditions: facing charter competition or not facing charter competition. After a certain period, if outcomes differed between the two groups of schools, the difference must be due to the only thing that differed between them—whether they faced charter competition. In reality, however, such an experimental study would be virtually infeasible. Consequently, thus far all empirical studies of charter schools' competitive effects have been observational, examining charter competition in natural settings rather than through random assignments.

Observational studies that seek to identify a causal relationship between charter school competition and TPS outcomes must overcome a number of key threats to internal validity. First, charter school location is not randomly distributed across local communities, but rather is probably influenced by the past performance of local public schools. Second, students who move to charter schools are self-selected so they are not a random subset of TPS students and their departure can change student composition in TPSs. Third, the effects of any given level of charter competition may vary significantly across local public schools in a region or state, depending on a variety of extraneous factors. Finally, the most basic element of competitive-effect research, the specification of an appropriate measure of the intensity of charter competition, is fraught with ambiguity. Given these methodological challenges, it is nearly impossible for observational studies to fully isolate charters' competitive effects. Researchers, however, seek to control for these problems through the use of sophisticated statistical methods to improve internal validity.

Nonrandom Charter School Location

Why does the lack of randomness in charter location pose a methodological problem? Suppose charter schools are drawn to areas where families are the least satisfied with local public schools. Now suppose researchers find that higher levels of charter competition correlate with lower public school outcomes. It is possible that low public school quality encouraged more charters to locate, or, alternatively, that charter competition lowered public school performance. Reliable estimation of the competitive effect, therefore, requires researchers to address this chicken-and-egg problem.

One method to address this problem is *propensity score matching.* Researchers match TPSs exposed to charter competition with TPSs that were not exposed to charter competition but that have a similar likelihood, or propensity, of facing charter competition, in light of observable characteristics. Then the difference in student outcomes between the two groups of TPSs can be regarded as the competitive effect. By removing TPSs from the sample that have no obvious counterpart among the schools exposed to competition, internal validity should be improved because these TPSs are likely to differ in ways that could bias estimates. However, matching cannot remove all the bias if the likelihood that a TPS would face charter competition is related to unobservable or unmeasurable factors such as parents' motivation and their involvement in their child's education.

Another way to address the charter location problem is through *school fixed-effects estimations*, which have been widely used in competitive-effect studies. This approach relies on multiyear data to track the progress of the same school over time while implicitly controlling for unobservable historical influences on the likelihood of its attracting charter competition. The school fixed-effects strategy, however, will not fully eliminate all bias if charter school location is responsive to *trends* in local schooling conditions, including changes TPSs make in response to charter competition.[14] One possible, but not foolproof, alternative utilized in several competitive-effect studies is an *instrumental variable* (IV) estimation strategy, a statistical method that provides a consistent estimate of the competitive effects of charter schools as long as an IV can be found that is correlated with charter location, but not correlated with the unexplained variation in student achievement.[15]

Student-Self-Selection Problem

Students who participate in school choice may differ systematically from those who remain in their assigned public schools in terms of their socioeconomic background, past performance, or parental motivation.[16] For this reason, self-selection could significantly change TPS student composition and student performance trends. If, for example, charter schools tend to attract lower-performing students, the average performance of students remaining in TPSs would automatically increase, even without any competitive effect. In addition, student self-selection could be related to parents' perceptions of any competitive effects.[17]

The problem of student self-selection can be addressed in two ways. One is to explicitly control for charter-induced changes in student composition by including school-level measures of student characteristics in the estimation. This approach, however, may not remove bias associated with unobserved student characteristics such as parental motivation or perceptions. The second approach, *student fixed-effects* estimation, can correct this bias, in cases where longitudinal student-level data are available, as long as these unobservable characteristics remain constant over time. Unfortunately, multiyear student-level data are still unavailable for many states with charter school policies.

Distributional Effects

The statistical techniques mentioned thus far, including fixed-effects and IV methods, only estimate the *mean* effect of charter competition on TPS student outcomes. However, there is reason to expect dissimilar responses to competition among TPSs, even within a given state. Indeed, school choice advocates predict as much when they suggest that competition will prompt schools to improve their quality, while other schools that fail to improve will be driven out of business and close. Accordingly, one might wonder whether there are systematic differences in competitive effects across different types of TPSs. For example, do charter schools have the same effect on public schools in low-income, urban areas and middle-class, suburban areas, or on schools both with abundant resources and with scarce resources? While these are certainly important considerations in evaluating the consequence of charter competition, they are methodologically difficult to investigate, and researchers so far have made only limited progress in doing so.[18]

Measure of Competition

Although any estimate of charter school competitive effects requires researchers to measure the level or intensity of competition faced by TPSs, there is no unambiguous way to do so. Past researchers have conceptualized competition in two distinct ways: either (1) in terms of the potential threat charters pose to draw away students or (2) in terms of the actual loss of students to charters schools (reduced market share).[19] Under the first conception, researchers typically use the number of charter schools within a given radius of public schools or the distance of a public school from the nearest charter school to measure the intensity of competition. Under the second conception, researchers use the percentage of students who have exited to charter schools. Some market-share measures assume that all charter school students left the local public school district where the charter school is located. However, since many charter school students attend schools outside the district where they live, a preferable competition measure expresses districts' enrollment loss as the share of resident students who depart to charter schools whether those schools are located inside or outside the district.

Taken as a whole, none of these alternative competition measures is unanimously considered better. Nor is there yet much insight on the implications of using one measure versus another. Accordingly, some researchers have used multiple measures of competition to assess the robustness of their results. Whatever the measure of competition, policy makers would also benefit from better information on the thresholds for beneficial or harmful competition and the effects of variations in competition duration (short term versus long term).[20]

Finally, in light of the preceding discussion of alternative strategic responses available to TPSs, it is worth noting that all of these measures reflect the existence of multiple schooling options, not, strictly speaking, the intensity of competition or whether and how schools or districts compete.

EVIDENCE ON THE COMPETITIVE EFFECTS OF CHARTER SCHOOLS

Research on the impact of charter school competition on TPS student outcomes is still not very extensive. We identified eleven studies on the topic, most of which were completed since 2000. All studies focused on individual states or large school districts within a single state. One study looked at Arizona and Michigan; two studies looked at just Michigan, two each looked at Texas and North Carolina, and one each California, Florida, Ohio, and an anonymous urban school district. Among the eleven studies, six relied on district- or school-level data, and five used student-level data. All studies used longitudinal data, most of which allow for fixed-effect estimations. Most of the studies controlled for other variables, such as student characteristics that are correlated with educational outcomes. The outcome variables were mainly math and reading test scores, and in some cases gain scores. Since most charter schools have been established recently, none of the studies focused on long-term outcomes like graduation rates or employment and earnings. Charter competition was measured in many ways, either at the district or the school level.

Table 5-2 summarizes our analysis of the studies. Among the three studies on Michigan, Hoxby analyzed trends in school-level performance between the school years 1992–1993 and 1999–2000 through detrended difference-in-difference methods that controlled for each school's initial productivity. She found that achievement and productivity in Michigan's TPSs increased once charter school competition reached at least 6 percent of district enrollment. The estimated achievement increase was largest in the fourth grade, about 0.13 standard deviations in reading and 0.16 standard deviations in mathematics.[21] In the same study, Hoxby also found similar positive effects of charter school competition in Arizona. The major qualification in assessing Hoxby's findings is that she did not control for student composition and other TPS characteristics that may change as charter schools enter the educational system. Eric Bettinger analyzed school-level Michigan data from school year 1996–1997 to school year 1998–1999, incorporating controls for student characteristics.[22] He also employed IV estimations to control for the possibility that charter location is influenced by the performance of public schools. In contract to Hoxby, his results showed no significant competitive effect of charter schools on test scores in nearby TPSs.

Both Hoxby and Bettinger's studies were conducted at an early stage in the development of Michigan's charter schools policy. Using eleven years of school-level data, Yongmei Ni analyzed the evolution of charter schools' competitive effect over time.[23] She refined Hoxby's measure of charter competition and controlled for several student and school characteristics. Based on multiple estimation strategies, including fixed effects, Ni's results show that charter competition exceeding 6 percent of district enrollment hurt student achievement and school efficiency in Michigan's TPSs. This effect was small or negligible in the short run, but became more substantial in the long run (after five years of sustained competition). In the long run, for schools in districts where charter schools had drawn away a significant share of students, charter competition decreased math and reading test performance in the range of 0.2 to 0.5 standard deviations.

The two studies of North Carolina yielded contrasting findings. George Holmes, Jeff DeSimone, and Nicholas Rupp used longitudinal school-level achievement data in a variety of models, including cross-sectional regressions and IV panel models. The researchers found that exposure to charter schools improved TPS test scores by approximately 1 percentage point, about one-quarter of the average yearly growth.[24] Robert Bifulco and Helen Ladd, on the other hand, examined a student-level panel dataset for grades 3–8 from 1996 to 2002 and controlled for individual-student fixed effects.[25] They found no significant competitive effects on reading or math scores in nearby TPSs. Bifulco and Ladd attributed the difference in findings between the two studies to their ability to better control for shifts in student composition through the use of student-level data.

Texas is the only state in which two studies have found consistent, overall positive effects of charter school competition. John Bohte used a pooled time series regression analysis on district-level data for 1996–2002 and found that a 1 percentage point increase in countywide charter school enrollment was associated with a 0.1 percentage point increase in district test pass rates.[26] In another study, Kevin Booker and his colleagues used student-level data over eight years for grades 4–8 in fixed-effects regressions.[27] They found that the presence of nearby charter schools generated a small but statistically significant increase in test scores in Texas

TABLE 5-2 Summary of research on the impact of charter competition on student outcomes in traditional public schools

Location	Author(s) (Publication year)	Unit of analysis	Student outcome measure	Competition measure	Estimation methods	Results
Arizona	Hoxby (2003)	School level	ITBS and Stanford 9 test from 1992–1993 to 1999–2000	Whether charter enrollment accounts for 6 percent of total district enrollment	School-fixed effects	Schools facing charter competition raise fourth-grade math and reading scores by 2.31 and 2.68 national percentile points and seventh-grade math by 1.59 points. No effects on seventh-grade reading.
California	Buddin and Zimmer (2005)	Student level	1997–1998 to 2001–2002 Stanford 9 reading and math scores	Distance to charter school; presence of charters; number of charters; percentage of students switching to charter schools within 2.5 miles	Student- and school-fixed effects	For elementary schools, a nearby charter reduces reading scores by 0.75 SDs, but no effects on math achievement. Middle school math scores increase by less than 0.1 SDs if a charter is present. High school reading scores increase by less than 0.05 SDs if a charter exists within 2.5 miles.
Florida	Sass (2006)	Student level	FCAT-NRT for third to tenth graders from 1999–2000 to 2002–2003	Enrollment share of charter schools; presence of charter schools; and number of charter schools within 2.5-, 5-, and 10-mile radius	Student- and school-fixed effects	Charter competition is associated with unchanged reading scores and 3 percent of annual gains in math.

(continued)

TABLE 5-2 (continued) Summary of research on the impact of charter competition on student outcomes in traditional public schools

Location	Author(s) (Publication year)	Unit of analysis	Student outcome measure	Competition measure	Estimation methods	Results
Florida	Sass (2006)	Student level	FCAT-NRT for third to tenth graders from 1999–2000 to 2002–2003	Enrollment share of charter schools; presence of charter schools; and number of charter schools within 2.5-, 5-, and 10-mile radius	Student- and school-fixed effects	Charter competition is associated with unchanged reading scores and 3 percent of annual gains in math.
Michigan	Bettinger (2005)	School level	1996–1997 to 1998–1999 fourth-grade math and reading MEAP satisfactory rates	Number of charter schools within a 5-mile radius of a TPS	Difference-in-difference; lagged dependent variable specification;IV estimates	Difference-in-difference estimates show test scores in TPSs near charter schools are 0.01–0.02 SDs higher than other TPSs. Lagged dependent variable approach shows no effect on math and about 0.01 SD positive competitive effects. No competitive effect in the IV estimates.
Michigan	Hoxby (2003)	School level	Annual change in fourth and seventh math and reading MEAP scale scores from 1992–1993 to 199 9–2000	Whether charter enrollment accounts for 6 percent of total district enrollment	School-fixed effects	Schools facing charter competition increase 1.2 and 1.1 scale points in fourth-grade reading and math, 0.96 and 1.4 points in seventh-grade reading and math.

TABLE 5-2 (continued)　Summary of research on the impact of charter competition on student outcomes in traditional public schools

Location	Author(s) (Publication year)	Unit of analysis	Student outcome measure	Competition measure	Estimation methods	Results
Michigan	Ni (2009)	School level	1994 to 2004 fourth and seventh grade math and reading MEAP satisfactory rate	Whether a district loses more than 6 percent of its resident students to charters	School-fixed effects; random-trends modeling	If charter competition persists more than five years, TPS satisfactory rates decline by 0.2 SDs in math and 0.5 SDs in reading.
North Carolina	Bifulco and Ladd (2006)	Student level	EOG reading and math scale scores for five cohorts of third-grade students in 1996–2000	Number of charter schools within 2.5, 2.5–5, and 5–10 miles; the distance to the nearest charter school	Student- and school-fixed effects	Charter competition reduces reading (but not math) test score gains by 0.01 SDs in TPSs located within 2.5 miles of a charter school. No effect is found for TPSs 2.5 miles and more away from charter schools.
North Carolina	Holmes, DeSimone, and Rupp (2003)	School level	1996–1997 to 1999–2000 state standardized tests on math, reading, and writing	Distance from a charter school	IV panel models	Test scores increase by about 0.25 SDs in TPSs facing charter competition.

(continued)

TABLE 5-2 (continued)   Summary of research on the impact of charter competition on student outcomes in traditional public schools

Location	Author(s) (Publication year)	Unit of analysis	Student outcome measure	Competition measure	Estimation methods	Results
Ohio	Carr and Ritter (2007)	School level	Fourth and sixth grades proficiency rates in 2002–2006	Presence of charter school in a district; number of charter schools in a district; percentage of district enrollment in charters	Pooled time series regressions	An increase of one charter school in a district is associated with an 0.3 and 0.55 percentage point decrease in reading and math passage rates.
Texas	Bohte (2004)	District level	Grade 10 TAAS pass rates for 1996–2002	Presence of charter schools in a county; total number of charter schools in a county; percentage of county enrollment in charter schools	Pooled regression with year dummies	A 1 percentage point increase in charter enrollment rate increases student achievement by 0.10 percentage point.
Texas	Booker et al. (2005)	Student level	TAAS scale scores in math and reading for students in grades 3 through 8 for 1995–2002	Percentage of district enrollment in charters; percentage of students leaving a school to enroll in a charter	Student- and school-fixed effects; IV estimates	A 1 percentage point increase in charter penetration raises reading by 0.02–0.11 SDs and math by 0.02–0.07 SDs.

TABLE 5-2 (continued)   Summary of research on the impact of charter competition on student outcomes in traditional public schools

Location	Author(s) (Publication year)	Unit of analysis	Student outcome measure	Competition measure	Estimation methods	Results
Large urban school district	Imberman (2007)	Student level	National NPR examination test scores from 1998 to 2004	Percentage of students within a specified radius who are in grades covered by the district school but attend a charter school	Student- and school-fixed effects; IV estimates	FE estimates show no effects in levels models, but positive effects in gains models. A 10 percent increase in charter share is associated with an 0.46 and 0.76 NPR increase (about 0.5–0.9 SDs) in every exam subject. IV estimates show that a 10 percent in charter share within 1.5 miles generates 1.9–3.8 NPR drop on each exam.

Abbreviations: AZ, Arizona; EOG, end of grade; FCAT-NRT, Florida comprehensive assessment test norm-referenced test; FE, fixed effects; ITBS, Iowa Tests of Basic Skills; MEAP, Michigan Educational Assessment Program; MI, Michigan; NPR, national percentile ranking; SD, standard deviation; TAAS, Texas Assessment of Academic Skills; TPS, traditional public schools.

public schools. The two Texas studies, however, disagree on who benefits from the charter school competition. Both studies reported positive effects on TPS students in schools performing below average before the appearance of charter schools. However, Booker and colleagues, unlike Bohte, found a small negative impact on students in high-performing schools.

A feature of the Texas charter school policy may influence these results and their applicability to other states. Since roughly half of the Texas charter schools were authorized as "at risk" charters, they drew away low-income TPS students by design.[28] The exit of high-cost, at-risk students could have positive peer effects on nonchoosing at-risk students and could also free up resources for gifted and talented programs that benefit higher-performing students left behind. So far, these are the only two studies to examine the distributional effects of charter competition. Given their inconsistent findings, it would be premature to draw any firm conclusions about what kinds of students or schools benefit most from charter competition.

Results are also mixed in studies focusing on other states. Researchers have found charter competition to have a positive impact on TPS student achievement in Florida, no effect in California, and a negative effect in Ohio. Tim Sass analyzed student-level Florida data for grades 3–10 over a three-year period with fixed-effects regressions and found a small significant positive competitive effect on TPS math achievement, but no effect on reading. The positive results on math were robust under alternative measures of charter competition.[29] Richard Buddin and Ron Zimmer also used student-level fixed-effects regressions, combined with propensity-score matching, to analyze data from six large California school districts between 1997–1998 and 2001–2002.[30] They found that charter school competition measured in a variety of ways had no consistent effect on TPS outcomes. Matthew Carr and Gary Ritter used a pooled time series regression analysis of Ohio data and found a slight negative competitive effect: a 1 percentage point increase in charter school enrollments was associated with an 0.46 percentage point decrease in reading passage rate and an 0.60 percent decrease in math passage rate.[31]

Finally, Scott Imberman employed both fixed-effects transformations and IV estimates to examine the impact of charter schools on TPS achievement in an anonymous urban school district.[32] He found moderate gains in TPS test scores when using fixed-effect methods, but negative effects when using IV procedures. The study serves as a useful reminder that research findings are sensitive to methodology when selection bias exists.

In sum, the results of the eleven studies are mixed, with three studies finding negative competitive effects, three no effects, and five positive effects. Where positive effects have been found, they are generally quite small. Among the studies focusing on the same states, mixed results are reported in Michigan and North Carolina. Although two studies found overall positive effects in Texas, they differed on who benefits from the competition. Even when the studies are organized by methodology, no consistent patterns emerge. Regardless of the measure of competition, level of data aggregation, or estimation strategy, the results are mixed.

Since all these studies are nonexperimental, they are bedeviled by their inability to totally remove student-self-selection bias. If peer effects are important, then the estimated effects are at best the combined effect of charter school competition and student sorting.[33] So in cases where charter schools attract low-ability students, nonchoosers remaining in the regular public schools probably will benefit from the departure of these students, and the estimated competitive effects will be biased upward. Alternatively, if charter schools attract relatively high-performing students, the estimated competitive effects will be biased downward. In fact, several authors have noted that the estimated competitive effects they obtained might be confounded by student-self-selection problems. For example, although Bettinger found no significant relationship between charter school competition and test scores in nearby regular schools, he noted that the competitive effect could actually be negative since charter schools attract students who are performing worse on average than the nonchoosers in neighboring regular public schools.

While we have focused on issues of internal validity in charter school competitive-effect research, there are also important questions of external validity. All past studies have analyzed charter competition within a given state. Given interstate variations in public school systems and charter school policies, however, it is risky to extrapolate findings from one state to others. Researchers are already appealing to possible state-specific factors to account for the disparate patterns of empirical findings. We turn now to briefly consider these factors.

THE RULES AND LOCAL CONTEXT MATTER

School choice policies initiate a complex set of adjustments among participants in educational systems that both theory and available evidence suggest can have either positive or negative results. The likelihood of either depends on features of charter school policy design (the rules) and the state and local context in which the policy is implemented. The administrative organization and regulation of charter school policy varies tremendously from state to state. Consequently, studies of charter school competitive effects for any given state may have limited external validity. We offer some examples of how local context may influence competitive effects, and then propose examples of charter school policy features that should help to preserve the benefits of choice policies while diminishing the potential harm.

Consider how a given charter school policy could elicit diverse effects in different states or local contexts. The rate of population growth or decline in a region, for example, will strongly affect the competitive pressures of charter school policies. In rapidly growing areas, the competitive threat is greatly muted. Public schools may even welcome the departure of students to alleviate enrollment pressure. In areas with declining population, however, choice is more likely to generate strong competitive pressure on TPSs, especially in states where districts lack the ability to raise additional funding locally. This combination of circumstances also poses the greatest risk that choice will touch off a downward spiral in at least some TPSs. Accordingly, a study of competitive effects in a rapidly growing state may have limited external validity with regard to a declining-enrollment state.

Another dimension of the state or local context that affects choice outcomes is the degree of preexisting inefficiency in public schools, which itself may be a function of the range of private or public school choices historically available to families. Charter schools may bring about greater adjustments in states with large, county-wide school districts and few private schools than in states where families already have extensive choices between private schools, local school districts, and interdistrict open-enrollment options. Alternatively, suppose that families tend to pick charter schools with students having similar demographic characteristics to their own. Then the likelihood that choice policies will generate either positive or negative peer effects on students remaining in TPSs will decrease in settings characterized by high levels of preexisting racial and socioeconomic segregation in the public school system.

Consider now the ways in which charter schools' competitive effects on nonchoosers in any given setting will vary according to features of the charter school policy itself. We focus on three categories of policy features: (1) financial arrangements, (2) regulations, and (3) policy implementation.

Financial arrangements. The nature of competition between schools depends critically on the link between student flows and school funding. If resources are not at stake, schools are unlikely to compete for students. The share of per-pupil funding that schools lose when students depart to charter schools varies greatly across states, depending on the structure of their funding systems. Moreover, it is difficult to get the financial incentives right. If the loss of revenue when a student leaves is less than the marginal cost of educating that student, then the TPS actually benefits financially when students move to charters. But if, on the other hand, revenues decline faster than costs when students leave, schools losing students have difficulty avoiding cuts to existing programs; still less are they able to marshal the resources necessary to improve services.[34] A more promising way for policy to address this tension is to phase in the full per-pupil funding loss over a period of years.

In addition, student funding must be adequately adjusted for higher-cost students (such as special versus regular education students or those in secondary versus elementary school); otherwise, charter schools have an incentive to compete for the cheapest and easiest students to educate.[35] Insofar as charter schools are successful in enrolling low-cost students and excluding high-cost students, they reduce their own average cost. They accomplish this not by increasing their efficiency, however, but by increasing the average cost for TPSs that continue to enroll high-cost students.[36]

Regulations. The regulations governing choice policies strongly influence the incentives and constraints that market participants face and therefore how they respond. The predicted benefits of school choice for nonchoosers apply only if students choose schools, not the other way around. To reduce the risk of harmful effects on students who remain in TPSs, rules prohibiting formal and informal selective admissions practices at charter schools are essential and must be enforced. Rules that establish a uniform process for enrollment at charter schools decrease the opportunity to enroll or exclude students on the basis of cost or other student characteristics.

Other regulations regarding curriculum, teacher preparation, or testing in charter schools are more contentious. On the one hand, the potential scope for educational innovation by charters will be narrowed if they face the same regulations in these areas as do TPSs. On the other hand, parity between the two sectors in the rules faced in these areas serves to channel competitive actions into other activities that pose less risk to choosers and nonchoosers alike.

Policy implementation. How a state's charter school policy is implemented will affect outcomes. TPSs are more likely to benefit from charter schools when public agencies rigorously oversee charter school proposals, operations, and outcomes. Public schools are also more likely to benefit when the policy framework includes technical assistance for TPSs in need of improvement. All of these requirements are easier to meet when the number of charters in a state expands at a moderate pace.

Parents typically lack complete information on the quality of alternative schools, and all schools have incentive to present only favorable information. Policies that ensure that families receive information on application procedures and academic programs of available schools help parents make sound choices. Moreover, these policies help schools learn from one another and encourage widespread adoption of best practices.[37]

The competitive effects of charter schools on students who remain in TPSs are not set in stone. They will vary across settings and be influenced for better or worse by the policy rules and their implementation. Further research is needed to clarify the competitive effects of specific policy features in conjunction with given local conditions to minimize the potential harmful effects of choice competition on some students.

IMPLICATIONS FOR THE CHARTER SCHOOL POLICY DEBATE

Research on charter schools' competitive effects remains at an early stage. The weight of existing evidence, however, fails to indicate that the competitive threat posed by charter schools induces consistent or substantial improvements in public school districts. The current research is conspicuously at odds with strong claims regarding the beneficial, systemic effects of charter schools. Neither does it sustain sweeping claims of harmful impacts. If the existing research has one thing to say to participants in the charter school policy debate, it is to be more circumspect—to turn down the volume.

Charter school competition is a very blunt policy tool for bringing about needed reforms in urban schools. Although it represents a compelling idea, it is also a long shot. Participants on both the demand side and the supply sides of the market for schooling have many feasible responses (and nonresponses) to charter school policies, and only a subset of them will benefit nonchoosers who remain in TPSs. While the design and implementation of charter school policies can be undeniably improved, policy makers should remain wary about suggestions that large, systemic improvements would result from major increases in the number of charter schools.

The state of current research recommends a wait-and-see position in the charter school policy debate. It is too early to draw firm conclusions on the systemic effects of charter schools. With the passage of time, researchers will be better able to assess whether the long-run, competitive impacts of charter schools on the public school system are any more positive and stronger than those observed thus far. As charter schools mature and become more established, their effectiveness may improve in ways that would benefit TPSs. On the other hand, researchers will move beyond analyses of average effects to rigorously test the proposition that charter schools harm certain types of schools or settings. Moreover, with additional time, we will be able to observe whether charter schools induce improvements in long-run TPS outcomes such as graduation rates, college continuation rates, or future wages. One can only hope that the wait-and-see position prevails and that research progressively shapes and better informs charter school policy. As it stands, popular policy debates concerning charter schools' competitive effects have a lot of catching up to do with available research.

Because education policy debates are neither static nor patient, the wait-and-see position may become obsolete before conclusive evidence on charter schools' competitive effects is available. Existing evidence provides little basis for anticipating that charter schools on their own could be the catalyst for dramatic improvements in the educational outcomes of the neediest students who remain in the public school system. Unless this evidence changes, interest in charter schools' competitive effects will eventually wane, as attention focuses on other aspects of charter schools (e.g., perhaps the benefits to active choosers), and researchers and policy makers look elsewhere for policies to bring about significant improvement in urban public school systems. Examples of this alternative position are already evident.

In an insightful study of school districts' organizational responses to choice competition, Fredrick Hess argued that the muted effects of choice policies were due not to their small scale or relatively recent inception.[38] Instead, he said, they were due to structural and cultural factors in the public school system that would continue to produce outcomes at odds with the predictions of choice proponents: "In and of themselves, markets are not an elixir and they will not magically improve schooling." He concluded: "The lesson is not that markets cannot drive more profound change in education but that such effects will require changing the institutional and organizational contexts of urban schooling."[39] For Hess, that could entail changes in school governance and teacher certification and compensation, and the establishment of enhanced authority and performance incentives for school administrators. More recently, as the accumulating evidence on school choice has become no more hopeful, Hess, currently director of education policy studies at the American Enterprise Institute, has celebrated the transformative potential of an expanded role for profit-seeking entrepreneurs in developing talented educators and effective instructional programs in U.S. public schools.[40]

Others will draw different conclusions about alternative and more promising strategies to improve outcomes in low-performing urban public schools, if the beneficial systemic effects of charter schools remain elusive.

CHAPTER 6

Charter School Finance

Seeking Institutional Legitimacy in a Marketplace of Resources

Luis A. Huerta and Chad d'Entremont

INTRODUCTION

This chapter examines how charter schools identify, acquire, and use public and private resources to support educational programming. Previous evidence suggests that charter schools receive proportionally less funding per student than do traditional public schools.[1] For example, charter schools receive limited funds for costs unrelated to instructional services, such as building maintenance, and may be denied access to state categorical aid. Charter schools must also devote considerable resources to operational expenses that are either unfamiliar to traditional public schools or typically addressed at the district level. These expenses include school start-up costs, legal and financial advisement, and marketing. As a result, charter schools face a difficult choice: (1) commit fewer dollars to instructional services; (2) increase operational efficiency; or (3) gain access to new revenue sources.

Fundamental to the theory of charter school reform is that competition for students along with increased autonomy from state regulations sparks entrepreneurial thinking. School leaders are expected to respond to limited budgets by finding innovative ways to acquire and use resources rather than risk sacrificing critical programs and services. In our own research of New York charter schools (detailed below), we have uncovered numerous examples of charter schools' pursuit of nontraditional resources.

These resources range from intangible, in-kind assets, such as voluntary human services provided by parents or community-based organizations (CBOs), to hard fiscal resources gained through capital fund-raising, foundation grants, or partnerships with educational management organizations (EMOs).[2]

However, we have also uncovered institutional factors that constrain charter school decision making and their subsequent use of nontraditional resources. Principally, charter schools function within an *active central state* that encourages and rewards particular norms of practice. In other words, while the emphasis of charter school reform is on innovation and competition, these schools are still expected to satisfy state standards and accountability measures. Schools that openly defy accepted public schooling practices may face fierce resistance and, ultimately, be viewed as illegitimate by authorizers. As a result, we have found that charter schools generally pursue resources and adopt practices that explicitly support and expand on established educational programs and services, such as remediation, college prep, or extended-day programs.[3] This behavior, referred to as *organizational isomorphism* by neo-institutional theorists, serves to increase support for charter schools among state and local bureaucratic agents, as well as a larger body of policy actors and funders (e.g., CBOs, private foundations, and for-profit companies) invested in the dominant education system.

In the pages that follow, we examine more closely how charter schools acquire and use resources. Our goal is to increase understanding of emerging conflicts between the principles of charter school reform and the increased role of state governance of public education. Using institutional theory as an analytical lens, we argue that although market incentives may prompt charter schools to aggressively compete for new resources, the potential for this behavior to substantially alter current schooling practices is limited. To enhance their own standing as effective schools, charters appear more likely to rely on new resources to fulfill the requirements of nascent state accountability systems. To be clear, we are not suggesting that such behavior is inappropriate. Ensuring that all public schools achieve specific educational goals provides important public benefits, and charter school supporters may rightfully point out that fostering local discretion within an overarching quality framework is an expressed purpose of reform.[4] But, at points of intersection between state governance and local action, particularly when considering the downward flow of education funding, imbalances in institutional power have a substantial effect on school behaviors. As charter schools continue to grow in popularity, it is important to determine their potential impact on our larger educational system. Changes in school governance and finance may do little to prompt innovation or offer solutions to stubborn educational problems if larger institutional factors that influence school decision making are not taken into account.

SCHOOL FINANCE AND CHARTER SCHOOLS

After almost forty years of school finance litigation, plaintiffs who have challenged the equity of state funding formulas have prevailed in twenty-eight of forty-five cases that reached a judicial decision.[5] The debates in these cases focused primarily on disparities in the distribution of per-pupil revenues at both state and local levels. Charter schools are subject to the same strains in school funding that traditional public schools must face. However, as this section will reveal, important differences in how charter schools are funded (in many states) potentially exacerbate the issues linked to funding equity. These challenges are contextualized in a wider debate that focuses not only on whether charters receive equal levels of resources, but more importantly, on whether charters provide the same level of services and serve the same types of students as traditional schools.[6]

In examining equity in charter school financing, we must consider both *interdistrict* and *intradistrict* disparities. In states where interdistrict disparities persist, charters are subject to the same inequities in the distribution of per-pupil expenditures (most commonly tied to local property values) as those faced by traditional public schools, unless state laws provide charters with additional revenue to supplement the local revenue they receive. Where intradistrict disparities persist, and where the allocation of revenues to schools within a district is unequal, charters are subject to the same local governance decisions that lead to funding disparities among traditional schools. For example, within a district, schools that employ teachers with greater experience may receive a disproportionately higher level of funding to pay for higher salaries. In addition, school districts may have capital plans that distribute facilities revenues on a per-pupil basis, regardless of differences in regional or local costs or student populations served. As a result, the distribution of revenue may not be equitably linked to the actual costs of providing an educational program.

More recent debates have focused on disparities that move beyond the distribution of equal revenues. These disparities are linked to policy solutions that attempt to align school funding systems with an adequate level of resources necessary to meet both constitutional minimums (determined by education clauses in the state constitutions) and the outcomes demanded by state accountability systems.[7] The charter school model may extend the definition of adequacy by demanding that states recognize differences in the costs associated with funding and operating charter and traditional schools. For example, start-up costs, including funding for new facilities, teaching materials, and furnishings, are seldom provided by either state or local governments for new charters schools. In addition, costs associated with operating smaller schools that are independent from local districts and may not easily tap into economies of scale can tax charter school budgets even when funding is equal. These costs may include transportation, cafeteria services, library, and legal and insurance fees. Understanding the larger economic context in which charter schools operate is important in examining the challenges charters face in acquiring resources from both state and local sources and private sources in the for-profit and nonprofit sectors.

Charter schools, like traditional schools, are principally funded on a per-pupil basis. A set dollar amount is usually linked to the per-pupil expenditures of local districts and is provided for each student enrolled.[8] This system creates a quasi-marketplace where charter schools that attract and retain large numbers of students are well supported, while schools with smaller enrollments may be forced to close.[9] However, previous evidence suggests that charter schools receive less funding per student than do traditional public schools, which charter school advocates claim places an unfair burden on even the most successful schools.[10] For example, data from the 2002–2003 school year indicated that, on average, charter schools in sixteen states received $1,801 less per student than did traditional public schools, a deficiency of 21.7 percent.[11] Similarly, an analysis of eleven states for the fiscal years 1998 and 1999 found funding deficiencies for charter schools ranging from $200 to $1,841 per pupil.[12]

The primary reason charter schools receive less financial support than traditional public schools receive is that charters generally do not receive funding for educational expenses unrelated to instructional costs.[13] In many states, charter schools are not identified as local education agencies (LEAs) and therefore may be ineligible for state categorical aid or participation in special programs and services, such as substance abuse prevention, compensatory education, and universal pre-kindergarten.[14] In addition, school districts may be permitted to withhold public funding that would pay for central administrative services, including transportation, food service, referrals and aid for special-needs students, and school assessments.[15] While potentially justifiable, similar charges are usually not subtracted from the instructional budgets of traditional public schools. It appears that the very autonomy from state regulation that provides charter schools with greater operational freedom can lead to financial hardship. Charter schools cannot raise taxes; they struggle to secure low-interest loans or issue bonds and frequently lack administrative staff with the expertise to take advantage of federal and state grants.[16]

Charter school budgets are also constrained by a range of operational expenses that are either unfamiliar to traditional public schools or typically addressed at the district level. Start-up charter schools must secure a facility, purchase instructional materials, design a curriculum, hire staff and possibly legal and financial experts, and advertise their services—all before opening.[17] For growing schools, moving to a new location or attracting new students may require sacrificing previous investments in facilities, curriculum, or political relationships. As a result, charter schools devote a greater portion of their budgets to facilities costs and administrative services than do traditional public schools.[18] In Michigan, charter schools were found to spend between $435 and $628 per student on business office expenses, compared with only $38 in small elementary school districts.[19] Gary Miron and Christopher Nelson observed that this outcome is not entirely unexpected. Unlike school districts, charter schools are unable to take advantage of economies of scale and disperse costs across multiple schools.[20] Creating a charter school network or contracting with an EMO may alleviate some expenses, but is unlikely to reduce them to district levels. EMOs have been shown to spend up to five times as much on administrative services as is spent by local school districts.[21]

The large amount of money spent by charter schools on administrative costs has raised concerns about whether providing charter schools with increased funding would benefit students. Proponents have argued that charter schools are not intended to replace traditional public schools, but rather to provide alternatives to mainstream schooling practices, which includes finding efficient solutions to limited education budgets.[22] Given this understanding, comparing per-pupil expenditures in charter and traditional public schools may be inappropriate if little information is actually gathered on charter schools' spending patterns. A more relevant question would ask, Do current funding levels create incentives for charter schools to seek new resources, leading to more efficient and innovative school designs?

A review of available evidence suggests two conclusions. First, limited budgets and increased operational expenses lead charter schools to spend less on teaching and learning. For example, charter school teachers are generally lower paid than traditional public school teachers, and are therefore less experienced, less likely to hold a master's degree, and more likely to teach out of their subject area.[23] Research by Miron and Nelson suggests that charter schools emphasize low-cost, basic education programs with minimal support services.[24] These schools tend to enroll fewer low-income and high-needs students, reducing per-student costs, and provide less instructional staff support (e.g., professional development, libraries, audiovisual equipment, and computer-assisted instruction), student support services (e.g., special education, compensatory education, guidance, health, and counseling and social work), and extracurricular programs (e.g., athletics and community outreach).[25]

Second, charter school operators understand that they receive proportionally less funding per student than do traditional public schools and behave accordingly. Respondents to a survey of charter school administrators commissioned by the U.S. Department of Education claimed that limited funding is the most significant barrier to new charter schools.[26] School leaders address budget shortfalls by pursuing widely available, but frequently overlooked revenue sources, often for the express purpose of improving instructional programs. Additional public resources may be provided through in-kind services delivered by public school districts and may include transportation, classroom and library materials, extracurricular activities, personnel services, and school testing.[27] Productive working relationships with local authorizers and traditional public schools may also provide access to preschool, vocational education, and after-school programs.[28] Finally, public support is also available in the form of state and federal grants, many of which exclusively target charter schools. For example, the New York State Department of Education reserved $2 million for the planning and implementation of charter schools from 2007 to 2010, and additional grants of up to $200,000 are available to cover start-up costs and the acquisition, renovation, and construction of school facilities. At the federal level, the U.S. Government Accountability Office estimates that between 1994 and 2003, the Public Charter Schools Program awarded roughly $1 billion in grants.[29]

While gaining access to additional public resources is often essential to covering operational expenses, many of the most fiscally sound charter schools aggressively pursue private resources in the form of direct lending, charitable contributions, or partnerships with private organizations.[30] An increasingly preferable approach has been to raise private capital by adopting strategies employed by independent private schools, such as applying for grants from private foundations or launching capital campaigns.[31] Charter schools have also begun to build networks to share information and partner with charter school associations, nonprofit organizations, and EMOs that provide technical assistance and legal expertise. By working together, charter schools and their supporters have developed a strong voice, effective at advocating for increased fiscal and political support.

However, what remains unclear is whether increased participation in the educational marketplace is a viable funding strategy capable of supporting alternative approaches to public schooling. New dollars and private partnerships may come with restrictions that limit innovation.[32] More importantly, charter schools operate within broader social, cultural, and economic environments that influence their behaviors. For charter schools to succeed in attracting customers and satisfying state authorizers, they must promote educational goals consistent with established definitions of effective schooling practices.

In the next section, we use institutional theory to expand on this observation and explore why an influx of new resources is unlikely to alter approaches to schooling.

CONCEPTUAL FRAMEWORK

Institutional theory provides a valuable lens for understanding how charter school organizations may respond to the broader institutional environment in which they operate.[33] According to institutional theory, effective school organizations are normatively understood to operate as rational systems that tightly coordinate the production of teaching and learning. In reality, however, schools operate as loosely coupled organizations that are responsive to their institutional environment.[34] That is, there is a lack of coordination and control over the technical processes linked to classroom instruction.[35] Institutional theory thus challenges rational conceptions of organizations as internally goal driven and technically efficient. Instead, institutional theorists argue that legitimacy is derived from conformity to the normatively held rules, norms and scripts of the institutional environment, rather than instructional effectiveness; for schools, organizational success thus depends on factors other than technical efficiency.[36] By concentrating on coordinating ritual classifications (e.g., teacher certification, instructional time, class size) rather then the technical aspects of education (e.g., measurable outcomes), schools avoid calling attention to the lack of coordination between instruction and outputs.[37]

Charter schools—like all public schools—face pressure to uphold ritual classifications. Despite evolving among parallel school-reform strategies that call for both market-orientated reform and community-based empowerment, charter schools are still expected to satisfy the demands of rule-based accountability systems advanced by the active central state. The result is the formalization and uniformity of educational services similar to those pressed onto other sectors by Weberian-like governments, ranging from the rationalization of the post office to the standardization of health care or preschool education.[38] The one-size-fits-all approach to bureaucratic oversight is likely to hold charter schools accountable to standards and assessment systems that require them to look more like traditional public schools.[39]

The willingness of individual charter schools to challenge accepted definitions of public schooling, which may include the pursuit of non-traditional resources, is perhaps best explained by their positioning on a public-private continuum shown in figure 6.1. Charter schools are encouraged to work with a range of public and private actors (e.g., local school districts, nonprofit organizations, and for-profit businesses), and these associations directly influence their responses to market pressures and political and bureaucratic demands.[40]

Figure 6.1 identifies three types of charter schools: conversion schools, mission schools, and market schools. This typology is based on past charter school research that explains how the interests and behaviors of public, nonprofit, and for-profit organizations both overlap and vary.[41] For example, David Osborne and Ted Gaebler explain that organizations closely aligned with public norms tend to be less entrepreneurial, but better able to take advantage of local policies and regulations to achieve organizational goals.[42] As organizations become more focused on private goals, such as profits, they become more innovative and responsive to change,

| Public schools | Conversion charters | Mission charters | Market charters | Private schools |

FIGURE 6-1   Continuum of charter school types based on market orientation

targeting clients to increase overall efficiency. More detailed definitions for each charter school type are provided here:

- *Conversion schools.* These are former public schools that frequently result from the desires of school-level administrators, teachers, and parents to play a greater role in shaping educational outcomes. These schools often have established ties to local communities and a strong understanding of the rules and regulations that govern public schools.
- *Mission schools.* These nonprofit organizations developed either in isolation or as part of a larger network of schools. They are often created to serve specific student populations or educational missions and may be most successful at balancing relationships with both public authorizers and private funders.
- *Market schools.* Partnered with for-profit EMOs, market schools have the least amount of interaction with public institutions. They rely primarily on their EMO to help cover operational costs, guide administrative decisions, provide professional development, and conduct student assessments, but they remain accountable to public authorizers.

Evidence is scarce, but suggests that access to public and private resources varies among conversion, mission, and market charter schools. For example, a recent analysis of the 1999–2000 Schools and Staffing Survey (SASS) revealed that conversion charter schools, which are more closely aligned with the habits of traditional public schools, have greater access to public funding.[43] Conversion charter schools, on average, offer higher teacher salaries and employ a greater number of credentialed teachers and fewer part-time teachers than do start-up charter schools (i.e., mission and market charters).[44] Conversion charter schools are also more likely to take advantage of categorical aid. In California, 55 percent of conversion charter schools received funding for transportation, 73 percent for Title I programs, and 83 percent for special education, compared with 4 percent, 34 percent, and 67 percent of start-up charter schools.[45]

In contrast, mission and market charter schools have benefited from alliances with private businesses and foundations to supplement public funding.[46] Again, important differences have emerged. Mission schools appear more likely to build relationships that provide funding and social service arrangements for particular educational programs, whereas market schools rely on EMOs for more comprehensive school management solutions.[47]

Katrina Bulkley observes that the EMOs often function as de facto school districts, guiding administrative decisions, providing professional development, evaluating student achievement, and helping to cover operational expenses.[48]

In sum, decisions to break away from institutional norms through the pursuit of nontraditional resources appear to be influenced by charter schools' organization and market orientation. Below, we present empirical evidence drawn from a study of New York charter schools that begins to explain these complex practices across diverse charter school types.

NEW YORK CHARTER SCHOOLS

Understanding charter school funding patterns requires an in-depth understanding of how school-level actors identify and acquire educational resources. To increase knowledge in this area, we conducted qualitative research in several New York charter schools. This research is part of a wider study that applies quantitative methods to examine the influence of state, district, and school factors on funding disparities in a national sample of charter schools derived from the National Center for Education Statistics Schools and Staffing Survey (2002).[49]

The State of New York approved charter school legislation in 1998 with five schools opening for the 1999–2000 school year. Growth was rapid and quickly reached the state-imposed cap of one hundred charter schools in January 2006.[50] The state provided an appropriate venue to study charter school funding for two reasons. First, similar to most states, at the time of our study, charter schools in New York received less public funding than did traditional public schools. Charter schools were entitled to 100 percent of local operational expenditures, but were prohibited from receiving state categorical aid. Further, charter schools received less funding than school districts for full-time special education services.[51] As a result, funding disparities ranged from $600 to $8,000 per pupil for severely disabled, special education students.[52]

Second, state law provides charter schools explicit instructions to address budget shortfalls through private fund-raising and other entrepreneurial activities. The Charter Schools Act of 1998, Article 56, states, "The board of trustees of a charter school is authorized to accept gifts, donations or grants of any kind made to the charter school . . . private persons and organizations are encouraged to provide funding and other assistance to the establishment or operation of charter schools." New York City has taken additional steps to expand access to public and private resources; these steps include developing charter school networks, supporting public-private partnerships, and granting unprecedented access to public facilities.[53] Entrepreneurship has led to substantial funding disparities among charter schools. For example, the Thomas B. Fordham Foundation reported that in 2002–2003, the average New York charter schools spent $10,881.16 per student, whereas the three best-funded charter schools in the analysis—the Child Development Center, the Harlem Day Charter, and the KIPP Academy Charter—spent between $17,985 and $22,686 per student. Such disparities suggest that New York charter schools have taken a wide variety of approaches to securing additional public and private resources.[54]

Our research, which was focused on a purposive sample of three charter schools in the New York City metropolitan area, was designed to maximize variability across mission orientation, school organization, and location. All three schools had been in operation for at least five years, were reauthorized, which demonstrates a proven track record of success, and are identified with pseudonyms that represented the type of charter school they are:

- *Conversion School.* This former public school is located in one of New York City's outer boroughs where parents, educators, and local community members worked together to achieve charter status.
- *Mission School.* This start-up charter school is located in Manhattan; it has an active board, established political connections, and relationships with a number of successful nonprofit organizations.
- *Market School.* This for-profit charter school is partnered with a nationally recognized EMO and is located within eighty miles of New York City.

We found that each charter school type took a unique approach to identifying, acquiring, and using new public and private resources to address budget shortfalls. Decision making was based on a process of weighing the anticipated benefits associated with new resources against the potential risks to each school's educational vision, a proxy for each schools' need to establish legitimacy within the larger context of the public education system.

Conversion School

Conversion School is a former district school located in an outer borough of New York City. The school has a history of innovative practice and strongly believes that learning is a collaborative process based on the

By resisting the dominant funding strategies of some of the best-known charter schools in New York City, the school has opened itself up to questions about its direction, stability, and legitimacy as a learning institution. During the reauthorization of the school's charter, conflicts emerged when the chancellor's office tried to impose a number of new regulations, including district approval of future board members and expenditures over $25,000, on the school. The authorizer also wanted another $25,000 to be put in an escrow account in case the school was dissolved. Notably, at no time during the reauthorization process was the school found to be in financial trouble.

The school emerged from the reauthorization process battle-weary. The principal noted that the school enrolls a significant number of middle-class students with above-average test scores, and he questioned whether charter schools with different student populations would be able to follow the school's example. The school's codirectors spoke of the necessity of building charter school networks to support similar mom-and-pop operations that were not interested in joining more formal charter management organizations (CMOs). Overall, the school seemed disenchanted with the current direction of the charter school movement. As one codirector observed:

> What's happened in the charter movement was that initially, the movement [was] very pro bringing in outside partnerships because they wanted to bring in outside money. Which is great, but that was at the expense of the grassroots-type schools like [us] that didn't have those big corporate partners and didn't want them. Because it was a group of teachers that started [the school]. The movement is not going to succeed if it's only these corporate-driven partners, even if it's not-for-profit, because people start to say "What is this?" and they start looking at it politically, and then it becomes a Republican movement. So now they're saying, "Okay, we have to have both; we have to allow for the grassroots." What's wonderful is that this year for the first time in five years, they approved another conversion school.

In light of this remark, it is possible to argue that Conversion School will never vigorously pursue private resources, regardless of the sacrifice, because it considers corporate partnerships fundamentally incompatible with the school's mission. This conclusion stands in stark contrast to the opinions and behaviors expressed in Mission School, which we describe next.

Mission School

Mission School is a start-up charter school that originally hoped to locate in a large Dominican community in Manhattan. The school partnered with a local Hispanic community organization and adopted a dual-language curriculum to provide enrolled students with fluency in both English and Spanish. School leaders perceived their charter as an investment in their community and culture. As the school's facilities manager explains:

> I come from a poor family, poor background, from the Caribbean, and I've always wanted to give something back to the community. I've enjoyed helping people, always. I was one of the kids that my mom would take to translate when she needed to go to offices . . . I was the translator. So I would end up translating in front of ten to twenty people when I would go to these places, and so I always enjoyed this. I think it's important that when you receive something and you become something, that you give something back and remember, especially, the place that you come from. It's important, because if we all become professionals and leave [here], where does that leave the kids?

Unfortunately, finding an appropriate facility proved difficult, and the school was moved a few miles south to a largely African American community. Requests to hold separate lotteries for English and Spanish speakers were denied, forcing administrators to immediately change the school's educational program. As the director of the charter school board explains:

> To have a dual-language school, you need bilingual students. We started in [a neighborhood] with an English monolingual student population that made the dual-language program an educational impossibility, and right now, at the end of the day, we continue to get students through word of mouth, the overwhelming majority of our kids continue to come from [the neighborhood] and continue to be monolingual English kids.

In addition, the new location affected the school's interactions with external partners. Few relationships emerged from the local community. Instead, school leaders relied on associations with more distant Hispanic community organizations, including their cofounding partner. At first, familiarity bred trust and flexibility, but over time, informal interactions became more complicated. School personnel found themselves exhausting personal favors in other parts of their life where they were deeply invested. Thus, as a result of distance and necessity, the school's relationships with outside organizations evolved into formal public-private partnerships where specific resources were clearly identified and provided. A prominent immigrant community organization helped support an after-school program and extracurricular activities. The National Council of La Raza, a national non-profit organization that seeks to improve opportunities for Hispanic Americans, offered a consultant to administer professional development to teachers. Opportunities to secure small private grants emerged. The school principal estimated that the school had secured roughly $30,000 from a federation of various Hispanic organizations. These relationships produced vital resources.

As the school matured, school leaders recognized the need to tap into revenue sources outside the Hispanic community. Again, the school's approach was to build external partnerships and pursue increasingly larger private grants. External partnerships provided both indirect and direct benefits. For example, the Center for Charter School Excellence helped the school find and hire its current principal, an individual with significant experience in private fund-raising. External partnerships also made the school more attractive to private foundations reluctant to fund schools directly, alleviating some risk. Of course, it remained entirely possible for the school to devote considerable time and energy to a grant application and receive no payout. The school's principal explains:

> The example I'll give you is the Walsh Foundation. Walsh is here in the city. They fund in New York, they fund in Boston, they fund public and private schools, and they like to fund around facilities. So they went to the [Center for Charter School Excellence], and they said to them, "Get us a listing of some of the schools that you work with . . . " So, we dropped everything we were doing. We submitted all the information, and a couple of weeks later, we came to find out that they decided that we should not be among the schools that should approach them for funding for this round.

However, when the school's efforts were successful, significant risks led to substantial rewards that could greatly improve educational services. The State University of New York's Charter Schools Institute (CSI) reports that from 2000 to 2004, the school received $940,775 in private grants and do- nations, not including funds for capital expenses. At the time of our in- terviews, the school had recently secured a commitment of more than $4 million from the New York City Council to help purchase a second school building and potentially open a middle school. While these funds would be publicly provided, the deal was premised on the school's ability to raise an additional $9 million. School leaders commented that their success in building new relationships and raising private revenues was essential to gaining the City Council's support.

As evidenced above, the school's shift in focus toward private grants and donations did not preclude its acquiring additional public resources to cover costs. Yet, public grants remained less attractive, because they are generally viewed as more time-consuming, less sustainable, and less suit- able to external partnerships. Several administrators commented that fi- nancial and academic success can eliminate important public funding streams. In contrast, private resources, which may also be temporary, are more flexible and easier to incorporate into long-term strategies to build brand recognition and develop lasting partnerships. School leaders looked around the city and noted that the more successful a charter school be- comes, both in academic performance and in financial viability, the easier it becomes to perpetuate continued success. One leader spoke of specific examples:

> There's the KIPP Academy. There's the Harlem Children's Zone. They're two of the more highly recognized and, I believe, more suc- cessful charter schools in the city . . . So, if you have that kind of cachet, and you have the kind of people who are involved in those programs, then, it's my impression—I could be totally wrong—but things come to them. But let's face it, funders, support groups, part- ners; they're all attracted to success and things that are big, things that are successful, things that are shiny.

The school's interest in private fund-raising has arguably provided sub- stantial financial security, but also transformed the school's original mis- sion. In the last few years, the school has removed all vestiges of its original language curriculum, adopted New York City learning standards, and be- gun annual testing, which it initially eschewed. In part, these changes address the legitimate needs of the school's students. They also helped sat- isfy the school's authorizer and facilitate reauthorization. However, these changes have also led to teaching and learning methodologies that are more closely aligned with some of the city's best-known charter schools, including KIPP Academy. In addition, the school has nurtured a high-profile student performance group reminiscent of some of the extracurricular activities at the Harlem Children's Zone.

As a result, the school has redefined its mission to principally focus on the students it enrolls. When discussing their students, administrators and staff frequently evoke references to family and community. However, this passion is no longer easily extended to the larger community beyond the school's doors. To be clear, we are not suggesting that the changes that have taken place at Mission School are inappropriate or will produce negative outcomes. Change may reflect improvements in practice and ultimately benefit students, parents, and staff. We simply observe that a transformation has occurred. The director of the school's board of trustees was asked to reflect on whether the school had changed:

> Oh, my gosh! We stopped being a dual-language school and became a foreign-language school. We abandoned the codirector structure to a head-of-school structure. We totally standardized our curriculum throughout the school, to meet New York State Regent standards. We redid the school.

These changes reflect the trade-offs that most charter schools confront. By attracting private resources, purchasing a building, and implementing a more traditional educational program, Mission School has increased its institutional legitimacy. The school enjoys increased support from its authorizer and finds it easier to attract customers and build external partnerships. At the same time, the school has been forced to narrow its original mission. Its new mission is to teach students, not engage the larger community.

Market School

Market School was founded in partnership with a national for-profit EMO. This relationship has greatly influenced the school's pursuit and use of educational resources, as well as the teaching and learning methodologies it employs. The school relies almost entirely on revenues generated through student enrollments to cover operational costs. Thus, while the school is committed to providing high-quality education, school leaders also view students as important revenue sources and acknowledge the necessity of adopting cost-efficient programs. The school's principal explains the charter school funding:

Again, remembering that the way that charter schools are funded is through tuition . . . so if you have five hundred kids here, you get $5 million. If you've got two hundred kids here, you get $2 million. The more kids you have, then it generates more funds. For example, if three kids give us $30,000, a program for it could cost us $10,000, so you're $20,000 ahead of the game. But if you only had one kid and a program costs $10,000, then you would absorb everything by that one youngster. So, the more kids you have, the more revenue you generate.

The principal's comments reveal that the school's educational programs and practices are unaltered by student enrollment characteristics. In this way, the school stays in good standing with its EMO and takes full advantage of its partnership.

The EMO provides the school with three main resources. First, the school receives a standardized curriculum aligned to state standards and testing requirements, as well as lesson plans, textbooks, and worksheets, and a host of other classroom materials. Second, the EMO administers and interprets a monthly assessment program that tracks student progress. Tests are given and interpretations are immediate, allowing staff to better assist struggling students. Third, the EMO provides professional development for teachers, including on-site training, online training, and national and regional conferences. Programs are offered for both administrators and teachers and cover topics ranging from guided discovery learning to classroom management and discipline to building an inspiring learning environment. The resources provided by the EMO are not additions to school's budget. The school pays for these services. But, staff administrators express confidence that this partnership lowers costs, assures quality, and establishes a level of stability that is generally unavailable to a small, independent school.

The EMO partnership also buffers the school against competition from surrounding local districts. Unlike Conversion School and Mission School described above, Market School is located outside New York City in an area where support for charter school reform is tentative. At times, disputes over educational resources with local districts have become contentious. For example, all school districts within a fifteen-mile radius of a charter school are required to provide public transportation. However, this does not prevent districts from setting up transportation schedules that inconvenience charter school students. Market School's principal explains:

With most districts, we've been able to resolve some of the problems of arrival and departure of our students. But there are still one or two districts who I'll say are playing games with the transportation aspect because when you say to a parent that your child—five, six, seven years of age—has to be up and out of the house and ready to be picked up in order to get to school at 6:30 or quarter of 7 in the morning, that is impacting a great deal. And then you don't get them home again until between 5 and 5:30 in the evening.

Given such conflicts, the school's EMO partnership provides access to resources and a larger network of schools without working through local districts. However, once again, the school's educational focus and interest in resources beyond student generated revenues is limited. The school principally communicates with other EMO-partnered schools and sees little reason to build community relationships.

Thus, an interesting paradox exists within Market School. On the one hand, the school is noticeably isolated from the larger public education system in the community where it operates. In fact, the school attracts low-income and minority parents who feel their children were neglected by their assigned public school. The school takes great pride in providing an alternative to dissatisfied families and children previously placed in low-academic tracks and remedial programs. On the other hand, the school does not see itself as providing an educational program that is any different from that of a traditional public school. The school utilizes the same basic funding, applies a curriculum aligned with state standards, and relies on an EMO, much like a school district, to perform administrative duties. Again, the school's principal comments:

I've said to my board and I've said to my staff, "What makes us any different than any other elementary school?" And while they were trying to answer, I said, "Save your energy: Nothing! . . . Reading, math, science, social studies, phys ed, et cetera, just like the other elementary school."

Remarkably, the school that takes fullest advantage of private partnerships provides the most traditional educational program and devotes little time and energy to locating new funding sources.

ANALYSIS

In the preceding sections, we have examined past research and presented new evidence on the impact of educational funding on charter school behaviors. Our examination of New York charter schools indicates that the identification, acquisition, and use of public and private resources is best viewed as a process of weighing potential benefits against the risks to each school's mission and organization plan. Despite their popularity, charter schools continue to sit on the margins of the dominant educational system, and charter school operators appear sensitive to the influence of school-level decisions on public perception.

The active central state policies that determine, and often limit, charter school funding influence the difficult decisions that charter operators must make. Charter schools must weigh internal school goals and objectives against the institutional legitimacy that is necessary to remain viable in a wider institutional environment of public schools. Specifically, school leaders must account for the risks and benefits associated with seeking additional resources and weigh their decisions in the context of a shifting policy environment that seems to be privileging schools with external partnerships.

This section uses constructs from institutional theory to explain how local actors must weigh both the internal goals of their school and the external demands of their institutional environment, when faced with the decision to seek additional resources in the nonprofit and private sectors. We discuss how school-level leaders operate with an active understanding of the macro-level forces that their schools must confront within their institutional environment. In some cases, these leaders feel micro-level impulses to consciously resist and challenge external forces that are encouraging them to conform to institutional definitions of effectiveness. In other cases, leaders are actively seeking the institutional legitimacy associated with promoting normative definitions of schooling.

Table 6-1 shows how the pursuit of new resources requires balancing the potential yield of institutional legitimacy with the impact on school-level autonomy. Charter schools' mission, organization, and preexisting partnerships are shown to have a direct bearing on the resources they pursue. For example, community-based partnerships that yield only in-kind, intangible resources may have low effects on school autonomy, yield high civic capacity, but low institutional legitimacy in the context of meeting traditional notions of effectiveness. A partnership with an EMO may add a modest amount of capital and much institutional legitimacy but at the expense of building local partnerships that increase civic capacity. Finally, partnerships with foundations and businesses require substantial human resource capacity at the school level to manage grant writing and external

TABLE 6-1   Risks and benefits in the charter school resources marketplace

Resource partnerships	Governance factors		Market factors		Institutional factors
	Effects on autonomy	*Effects on school capacity (HR and staff)*	*Capital yield ($)*	*Civic capacity yield*	*Legitimacy yield*
Community-based partnerships	Low	Low	Low	High	Low
Foundations and business partnerships	Med	High	High	Med	Med
EMO or CMO partnerships	High	Med	Med	Low	High

Abbreviations: CMO, charter management organizations; EMO, educational management organizations; HR, human resources.

partnerships, but may realize a high capital yield and increased institutional legitimacy as a viable school.

The range of available strategies for pursuing new resources suggests that charter schools will focus on forming external partnerships, an approach that effectively balances a potential high yield with the need to establish legitimacy within the larger educational marketplace. In fact, this strategy was evident in the charter schools most interested in expanding their influence and has been aggressively pushed by state and local authorizers. For example, New York City has encouraged charters to engage in formal partnerships (in some cases requiring partnerships as a condition of rechartering). The district accountability system contained within the revised Children First initiative requires all traditional schools in New York City to choose from among three types of school support organizations: (1) the network of already-established empowerment schools, (2) an internal support organization, led by a team of regional leaders, and (3) an external partnership support organization, which includes EMO/CMOs, colleges and universities, and other nonprofit intermediary organizations. The Department of Education's endorsement of EMOs and CMOs and other external partnerships has essentially bestowed institutional legitimacy on one particular school management model, which may be viewed as inconsistent with the spirit of charter school reform.

Not surprisingly, "mom-and-pop" charters with strong community ties feel threatened by state-supported expansion of charters partnered with EMOs or CMOs. From their perspective, the original vision of charter school reform championed new schools as "laboratories of learning" where increased autonomy and a renewed focus on community engagement would help create school environments better able to serve the needs of students, parents, and educators.[56] Participation in the educational marketplace is not inconsistent with this goal, but is viewed as necessary for innovation and for charter schools' ability to effectively compete with traditional public schools. What mom-and-pop charters reject is the privileging of a few select strategies for engaging the marketplace. They view the increasing role of external agencies removed from the daily business of running a school in budgeting and school management decisions as an effort to usurp the movement of community lead schools.

Conversion School exemplifies this emerging conflict between mom-and-pop charters and state and local authorizers who view external partnerships with CMOs or EMOs as a prerequisite for success. This charter school intentionally pursued a path that was risk-averse and sought partnerships with arts organizations, museums, and local universities—partnerships that resulted in low-capital yield, but strengthened the school's internal goals of expanding civic capacity in its community. At the same time, the school remained aware of the changing policy context in New York City and the potential for the chancellor's preference for external partnerships to undermine community-run schools as a viable charter governance and organizational structure. The school has risked its institutional legitimacy by resisting coercive, isomorphic pressures to uphold newly emerging definitions of effective schooling (in this case, newly emerging, institutionalized definitions of effective resource partnerships) and may have essentially jeopardized its long-term sustainability.[57]

In 2007, the mayor and chancellor successfully lobbied the New York Legislature to lift the cap on charters to 250 schools, hoping that over the next three years 50 additional charters could open in New York City.[58] Given the propensity to endorse the involvement of intermediary organizations in managing charter schools and the new requirement for all traditional schools to partner with support organizations, it seems likely that authorizers will give preference to new charter schools that are partnered with an intermediary support organization (e.g., 16 of the 18 new charter schools approved to open for 2008–2009 were partnered schools). These policy decisions pose important implications for how charter schools will continue to evolve in New York City. Specifically, will devolving public authority expand local discretion with the goal of promoting new schooling innovations that can better serve the needs of local communities? Or, will the expansion of intermediary partnerships result in simply devolving bureaucratic oversight of schools to middleman organizations responsive to centralized definitions of effectiveness and accountability?

Our research suggests that charter schools are evolving among parallel reform strategies that call for both market-orientated reform and local-community empowerment within the larger institutional environment that defines public schooling. Despite their decentralized freedoms, charters remain subject to elaborate bureaucratic controls advanced by an active central state. These controls are linked to upholding ritual classifications that shape the actions of students, teachers, and schools.[59] The important point here is that while charter schools are granted autonomy and freedom from most regulations that govern traditional public schools, they are not evolving within a policy vacuum. Charter schools still operate within an *active central state* and are subject to normative definitions of effective schooling—the bureaucratic, hierarchically organized, rule-based accountability structures advanced by the institutional environment.

Walter Powell and Paul DiMaggio suggest that an organization that depends on another for "funding, personnel, and legitimacy" will be more compelled to adopt the organizational structure, culture, and climate of that organization.[60] As charter school reform evolves in New York City, the exclusion of community lead schools and increased reliance on external partnerships with management organizations appears likely to increase the importance of ceremonial conformity in determining newly evolving definitions of school effectiveness. John Meyer and Brian Rowan explain:

> By designing a formal structure that adheres to the prescriptions of myths in the institutional environment, an organization demonstrates that it is acting on collectively valued purposes in a proper and adequate manner. The incorporation of institutionalized elements provides an account of activities that protects the organizations from having its conduct questioned. The organization becomes, in a word, legitimate, and it uses its legitimacy to strengthen its support and secure its survival.[61]

Ironically, it appears that the main currency driving charters in the competitive marketplace is not the creation and promotion of new schooling models, but rather, legitimacy that is linked to upholding traditional notions of effective schooling. As the state continues to prioritize charters schools that partner with CMOs and EMOs, as exemplified by Market School and Mission School, this outcome is only likely to occur more often.

Every market has a commodity that is sold and traded. In the case of charter schools that seek additional resources in the nonprofit and private-sector marketplace, the commodity seems not to be linked to promoting new educational innovations that challenge traditional schooling practices, but rather, ensuring widespread acceptance among authorizers and potential customers. Specifically, charter schools pursue additional resources to fund and reinforce accepted models of public schooling—including teaching and learning, governance, and organizational structures—that ultimately yield increased student enrollments and funding and, most importantly, institutional legitimacy.

CONCLUSION

In this chapter, we examined whether increased competition for resources within the educational marketplace has an impact on the organization and behavior of charter schools in ways that might challenge normative definitions of effective schooling. We explored the assumption, common to charter school reform, that greater fiscal autonomy leads to innovation, prompting charter schools to experiment with applying resources to local needs or unique mission-oriented goals. We also found charter schools willing to partner with external management organizations (e.g., CMOs and EMOs) to help run academic programs, provide technical expertise, or manage business affairs. By exploiting their increased autonomy, charter schools appear to have the potential to make the greatest strides in challenging or redefining institutional practices, offering examples of how to efficiently and effectively achieve desired educational outcomes.

However, our review of available evidence, strengthened by our own original analysis, also demonstrated that increased fiscal discretion does not guarantee innovation, and new resources often fail to produce new schooling practices. Using institutional theory to frame our thinking, we find that school decision making is linked to both internal organizational objectives and the external institutional environment. In other words, charter schools are pressured to adopt schooling practices that mirror "successful" schools as determined by state accountability systems, the expectations of private funders, and widespread public understanding of what a school should look like (e.g., normatively shared beliefs, rituals, and roles of students, teachers, and administrators). As a result, limiting funding for charter schools may not prompt entrepreneurial thinking, but rather may encourage organizational isomorphism. When funding is limited, charter schools may feel additional pressure to conform to dominant public schooling norms to gain access to untapped educational resources.

Further, we suggest that charter schools' decisions about the acquisition and use of new resources are greatly affected by differences in school mission and organizational focus. Somewhat surprisingly, charter schools that are more oriented toward the educational marketplace and willing to engage in external partnerships appear more likely to mirror the practices of traditional public schools. Demonstrating proficiency in programs and services that satisfy state authorizers and match public expectations are key components of running a successful business. Alternatively, charter schools designed to serve specific communities, that is, "mom-and-pop" charters, seem more likely to adopt nontraditional practices suited to local needs.

Ultimately, we can better predict charter school behaviors by understanding the risks and potential yield associated with different resource partnerships. Community-based partnerships pose little threat to charter schools' autonomy and capacity, but provide few benefits outside increased civic capacity. Partnerships with private funders (e.g., foundations) increase charter schools' capital yield, but private dollars divorced from a more substantial network of supports may not be viewed by state authorizers as evidence of a successful operation. Finally, partnerships with EMOs or CMOs greatly reduce charter schools' autonomy, but provide a substantial return by improving their standing as legitimate schools. Given that charter schools must first be accepted by viable schooling options, it appears most likely that they will steadily gravitate toward partnerships with EMOs and CMOs, except in cases where school leaders are devoutly committed to a particular educational vision. This approach has been increasingly accepted by educational officials and school authorizers as a working definition of what it means to be a charter school, potentially limiting the scope and original intent of the reform.

CHAPTER 7

Uncommon Players, Common Goals

Partnerships in Charter Schools

Priscilla Wohlstetter and Joanna Smith

INTRODUCTION

Unlike traditional public schools, which depend on district central offices for resources such as funding, personnel, facilities, administrative support, and curriculum and instruction, charter schools must identify their own sources for these essential goods and services. The need to amass resources on their own poses a significant challenge for charter schools, especially newly established, stand-alone charter schools. Since passage of the first charter school law in Minnesota in 1991, charter school leaders have consistently reported implementation and operational challenges exacerbated by insufficient financial resources, limited expertise, and inadequate facilities. Studies have shown that most charter school failures occur for nonacademic reasons; governance and finance continue to be the two primary roadblocks to creating and sustaining successful charter schools.[1]

Since charter schools cannot look "up" to school districts for assistance and support, they often have to look "out" to other organizations for the essential resources they need to survive and thrive. These operational challenges create incentives for charter schools to form partnerships with outside organizations. Typically described as a "win-win" situation, a partnership is defined as organizations working together to solve issues of mutual concern that are based on the benefits of collective action, addressing needs and problems that are beyond the capacity of either organization to resolve alone.

Exemptions from many district and state regulations enable charter schools to seek partnerships more readily than traditional public schools can, and laws in many states encourage such outside involvement. Well-constructed partnerships can provide a host of needed resources such as facilities, funding, administrative support, and curriculum and instruction, as well as less tangible benefits, such as increased visibility, governance expertise, and help in getting charter school applications approved. In some cases, members of partner organizations participate on charter school boards. In other cases, the organizations provide or supplement the curriculum that forms the focus of the school. In still other cases, partnerships with social services providers offer wraparound resources that help meet the needs of the school's students and their families. At the same time, partnerships with charter schools can help the partner organizations achieve their own goals. Often, these organizations are able to expand the services they provide by partnering with a charter school. For example, museums generally have education outreach functions in addition to their core mission, and partnering with a charter school enables the museum to integrate its programs into a school's curriculum rather than being limited to the peripheral curricular supplements provided to traditional public school students in a once-a-year field trip.

THEORY OF ACTION: WHY PARTNERSHIPS?

To help frame the prevalence of partnerships in the core operation of charter schools, we posit a theory of action (figure 7-1). According to the theory, the charter school context is ripe for attracting new players into public education to meet resource needs. As shown in the figure, state laws create an environment in which resource scarcity interacts with a legislative intent to include outside organizations in the establishment and operation of charter schools. This results in the creation of partnerships between charter schools and community, for-profit, and faith-based organizations.

Partnerships offer an array of resources—financial, human, political, and organizational—to alleviate the challenges charter schools face.

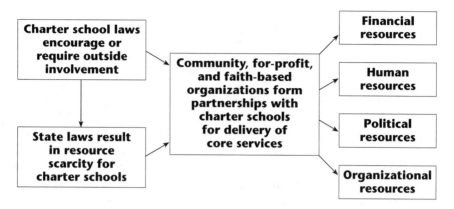

FIGURE 7-1   Partnership theory of action

Financial resources. Many charter school operators face an array of costs not met by their state funding allocation, a problem exacerbated when some states defer funding until partway through the charter school's first year of operation.[2] Funding disparities between charter and traditional schools also contribute to charter schools' inability to meet their financial needs. Tammi Troy found that traditional public schools in New York City were allocated $9,739 per pupil for the 1999–2000 school year, while charter schools received only $6,207, compelling many charter schools to seek additional funding through partnerships with outside organizations.[3] Similarly, Janelle Scott and Jennifer Holme studied six California charter schools. The researchers found that the existing funding formula "leaves partially 'publicly funded' schools starved for resources to pay for fundamental things, such as buildings and equipment . . . Charter schools exist within a policy framework that leaves them no choice but to scramble for private resources."[4] Not at all surprising, Joanna Smith and Priscilla Wohlstetter, in a more recent national study of charter school partnerships, found that financial resources—grants, donations, awards—were provided at twenty-one of twenty-two study sites.[5]

Human resources. In addition to the financial resources provided by many partnerships, outside groups can also provide human resources such as board expertise, back-office support, and tutors and mentors for the school's students. Furthermore, charter schools, which are often founded by teachers, face difficulties in learning the administrative tasks necessary to maintain school budgets successfully.[6] Numerous studies confirm the importance and use of outside organizations to provide expertise, either purchased or donated.[7]

Political resources. Political resources include the credibility to secure a loan, the name recognition to attract students, and the legitimacy to aid in charter school application approval. In interviews with state-level charter administrators, Wohlstetter and her colleagues found that in addition to struggling with resource scarcity, charter schools must stay afloat amid local animosity or skepticism of their stability when applying for loans. Loan applications were made easier when a school partnered with a well-known organization.[8] Partnerships increased the school's credibility in the community during fund-raising and the application process. Moreover, charter schools often benefited from partnering with a community organization that advocated for them.

Organizational resources. Charter schools' organizational needs range from facilities to curriculum, materials, and supplies. The need for facilities is particularly pronounced; numerous studies have found that one of the biggest challenges for charter schools is to locate and finance a facility.[9] In line with this, Smith and Wohlstetter reported that each of their twenty-two study charter schools were either housed in a partner's facility; received capital from a partner to lease, buy, or renovate a facility; or used a partner's facility for special events.[10] In some cases, partner organizations shared the cost of a facility, which often led to greater resource-sharing.

Table 7-1 provides examples of the common resources different types of partners provide.

As the partnership idea has spread, charter school laws have gradually broadened the range of organizations that could be involved in the delivery of public education. As Ted Kolderie observed, "For the new models of school and schooling, we will probably need to look mainly to people new to education and now outside it."[11] Over time, thirteen state laws have included the intention of increasing community involvement as one goal of the charter school law, and some state laws have allowed for-profit organizations to operate charter schools. In several cases, public charter schools are allowed to rent space from faith-based organizations. To wit, by 2007,

TABLE 7-1   Resources partnerships provide

Type of partner	Examples of resources
Community-based	• Name recognition to attract students • Legitimacy to aid in charter school application approval • Board expertise
For-profit	• Grants, donations, and loans • Credibility to secure financing • Back-office support
Faith-based	• Facilities • Fund-raising expertise

nearly all state laws encouraged charter schools to partner with other organizations in one way or another for additional resources.

PARTNERSHIPS IN ACTION: VIEWS FROM THE STATE LEVEL AND ON THE GROUND

With the idea of partnerships in mind, state legislatures have spent considerable time considering how charter schools might or might not partner with outside organizations to enhance their capacity. According to David Osborne and Ted Gaebler, diverse kinds of organizations possess distinct strengths, making partnering across organizational sectors particularly attractive.[12] Organizations in the nonprofit sector, for example, are generally focused on "moral codes and individual responsibility for behavior" and are strong in areas that require "compassion and commitment to individuals."[13] They are particularly successful at meeting client needs and working in areas that "require extensive trust" or need "hands-on personal attention (such as day care, counseling, and services to the handicapped or ill)."[14] Organizations in the for-profit sector are particularly effective at innovating, adapting to rapid change, and performing technical tasks.[15] Furthermore, the for-profit sector brings access to finance and capital, managerial effectiveness and efficiency, and entrepreneurship.[16]

Legislative provisions governing partnerships in charter schools run the gamut from encouraging or requiring partnerships to restricting or prohibiting them. Community involvement is often encouraged before a charter school even opens, with some states requiring evidence of community support in the application stage. In contrast, many charter school laws prohibit or limit certain types of organizations, most notably faith-based organizations and for-profit organizations, from serving as partners.

The information in the remainder of this chapter comes from a review of charter school laws in each state and the District of Columbia—a total of forty-one as of January 2007. Data on grassroots partnerships come from interviews conducted between January and July 2007 in each state within the charter school community to identify common challenges and opportunities. Over one hundred interviews were conducted with charter school stakeholders at all levels of the system: state, authorizer, and school levels. At the state level, respondents included administrators from state departments of education (charter school offices) and leaders of state charter school associations, resource centers, or technical assistance centers.

PARTNERSHIPS WITH COMMUNITY ORGANIZATIONS

State Policies

Charter school laws encourage the formation of partnerships with community organizations in two main ways. Some state laws require partnerships with or support from community organizations in the charter school application. As of January 2007, this was part of the law in fifteen states, with some laws stressing that this support must be available on an ongoing basis, not just during the school's establishment. For example, the Arkansas law specifies: "The State Board of Education shall review the petition for charter school status and may approve any petition that: . . . (3) Includes a proposal to directly and substantially involve the parents of students to be enrolled in the charter school, as well as the certified employees and the broader community, in the process of carrying out the terms of the charter."[17]

The District of Columbia and Pennsylvania laws require, respectively, "a description of how parents, teachers, and other members of the community have been involved in the design and will continue to be involved in the implementation of the proposed school" and "demonstrated, sustainable support for the charter school plan by teachers, parents, other community members and students."[18]

In six states, charter school laws encourage community involvement through membership on the charter school governing board. In Virginia, the charter school law specifies: "A public charter school shall be administered and managed by a management committee, composed of parents of students enrolled in the school, teachers and administrators working in the school, and representatives of any community sponsors."[19] In the District of Columbia, the law requires charter school boards to "have an odd number of members that does not exceed 15 out of which a majority shall be residents of the District of Columbia."[20] In South Carolina, the charter school application must include "the nature and extent of parental, professional educator, and community involvement in the governance and operation of the charter school."[21] Table 7-2 summarizes how state laws have addressed partnerships between charter schools and community organizations.

View from the Ground

In many cases, charter petitions are created by a group of parents or teachers hoping to establish a charter school who approach a community organization to help with the application process. State laws may influence the creation of such a partnership. One interviewee explained what typically happens:

> What happens in many, many cases is you'll have a group of parents and community folks who want to start a charter school, but they don't have standing as an eligible entity under the law. So what they'll do is they'll approach a nonprofit organization whose mission is consistent with the type of school they want to establish, and that nonprofit organization will agree to sponsor the application. Some nonprofit organizations get directly involved in a school. Some just serve as that sponsoring entity, with representation on the board of the school but minimal involvement in the actual operation of the school.[22]

Some state policies have also provided incentives for nonprofit community organizations to establish charter schools as an outgrowth of their organization. For example, one interviewee noted, "There is encouragement [in the state] for charter schools to have relationships with community organizations, and several of our schools have started out of an existing nonprofit that wanted to expand to actually provide a school." In Missouri, where the state law requires community involvement in the application, the Della Lamb Elementary Charter School was founded by Della

TABLE 7-2   How state laws address community involvement

	Include community involvement as one intention of the charter school law	Require community involvement or support in application	Encourage community involvement on the charter board	No relevant provisions
Alaska				X
Arizona				X
Arkansas	X	X		
California	X			
Colorado	X	X		
Connecticut				X
Delaware	X			
District of Columbia		X	X	
Florida				X
Georgia				X
Hawaii			X	
Idaho	X			
Illinois	X			
Indiana	X			
Iowa				X
Kansas		X		
Louisiana				X
Maryland				X
Massachusetts*		X		
Michigan				X
Minnesota				X

(continued)

* Massachusetts law does not require community involvement in charter school applications, but it gives approval "priority to schools that have demonstrated broad community support" (ALM GL ch. 71, § 89(i)).

TABLE 7-2 *(continued)*   How state laws address community involvement

	Include community involvement as one intention of the charter school law	Require community involvement or support in application	Encourage community involvement on the charter board	No relevant provisions
Mississippi		X		
Missouri		X		
Nevada				X
New Hampshire				X
New Jersey		X		
New Mexico	X	X	X	
New York	X	X		
North Carolina	X			
Ohio				X
Oklahoma				X
Oregon	X	X		
Pennsylvania		X		
Rhode Island	X		X	
South Carolina	X		X	
Tennessee				X
Texas				X
Utah				X
Virginia†		X	X	
Wisconsin				X
Wyoming	X	X		

† Virginia law specifies that support during the application phase and involvement on the board is only required if the school is sponsored by a nonprofit organization (Va. Code Ann. § 22.1-212.5).

Lamb Community Services (DLCS), and the school's mission reflects this partnership—a mixture of "educational and academic services in conjunction with supplemental family support services."[23] The charter school was located purposefully near a satellite DLCS social services facility; the school also uses a satellite DLCS gymnasium for the students' physical education classes.

At other times, partnerships with community organizations are created once the school is operational, as the school discovers its resource needs. As one interviewee reported, "Many of our charter schools are very entrepreneurial in entering into partnership agreements with a lot of community service organizations as a way of bringing people from the community into the school." Another interviewee noted, "There's a school that has partnerships with basically everyone in the community: local theaters, local doctors' offices, local nonprofits where the students do their internships."

In other cases, interviewees reported that some nonprofits see the charter law as an opportunity to get more deeply involved in education:

> Some of the longtime service providers for our minority populations that have been doing more of the before-school and after-school care . . . are becoming established enough, in terms of their nonprofit governance structure and their ability to . . . run a business, that they're starting to . . . realize that their next area of development is a school. They've already got good partnerships with local districts . . . The benefits are that the students being served are traditionally the ones who weren't scoring well in terms of state standards and assessments.

In some cases, community involvement occurs as part of a greater neighborhood revitalization initiative. For example, one interviewee described Drew Charter School in Georgia and its partnership with the Cousins Foundation:

> They are one of the biggest real estate developers here in town. He has a foundation set up for charitable purposes, and he built a building for the school back in '98 as part of a large neighborhood revitalization project that included building the charter school, putting in a YMCA, building mixed-income housing to replace public housing that had been there for thirty years, and building a grocery store across the street from the charter school to serve a neighborhood that hadn't had a grocery store within twenty-five miles for the past

fifteen years. And so there's an awful lot of national attention paid to Drew Charter School as a model of how a charter school can be a small piece of a larger neighborhood revitalization.

PARTNERSHIPS WITH FOR-PROFIT ORGANIZATIONS
State Policies

States vary in the extent to which they allow for-profit involvement in charter schools. Some states restrict for-profit organizations from opening or running charter schools, while others give such organizations broad access to charter schools. Still other states are silent on the issue (see table 7-3).

Where laws do address for-profit involvement, states use five common provisions to guide this involvement:

- For-profit organizations are prohibited from applying to open a charter school.
- For-profit organizations are allowed to apply to open a charter school.
- Charter schools are required to report involvement with for-profit entities.
- Partnerships are allowed for facilities.
- Partnerships are allowed for services.

Currently, sixteen states prohibit for-profit organizations from applying to open a charter school. This ensures that although for-profit organizations may provide services, the charter holder is not a for-profit organization. The charter school laws prohibiting for-profit organizations from establishing charter schools often list for-profits among other groups that are ineligible to apply. For example, New Mexico law states: "Municipalities, counties, private post-secondary educational institutions and for-profit business entities are not eligible to apply for or receive a charter."[24]

In Indiana and New York, state law requires charter schools to report their involvement with for-profit entities, giving charter schools the flexibility to partner with for-profit organizations and charter school authorizers the responsibility for monitoring such involvement. In Indiana, the law requires charter schools to submit an annual report listing "the number and types of partnerships with the community, business, or higher education."[25] In New York, the law states: "For charter schools established in conjunction with a for-profit business or corporate entity, the charter shall

TABLE 7-3   How state laws address for-profit involvement

	Prohibit FPOs from applying to open a charter school	Allow FPOs to apply to open a charter school	Require charter schools to report involvement with FPOs	Allow partnerships for facilities	Allow partnerships for services	Workplace charter schools allowed	No relevant provisions
Alaska							X
Arizona							X
Arkansas				X			
California					X		
Colorado		X		X	X		
Connecticut						X	
Delaware					X	X	
District of Columbia	X			X			
Florida		X		X		X	
Georgia	X				X		
Hawaii							X
Idaho	X				X		
Illinois				X	X		
Indiana	X		X				
Iowa							X
Kansas							X
Louisiana	X				X		
Maryland							X
Massachusetts	X			X		X	
Michigan							X
Minnesota	X			X	X		
Mississippi							X

(continued)

TABLE 7-3 (continued)   How state laws address for-profit involvement

	Prohibit FPOs from applying to open a charter school	Allow FPOs to apply to open a charter school	Require charter schools to report involvement with FPOs	Allow partnerships for facilities	Allow partnerships for services	Workplace charter schools allowed	No relevant provisions
Missouri					X		
Nevada	X						
New Hampshire					X	X	
New Jersey	X			X			
New Mexico	X				X		
New York		X	X		X		
North Carolina							X
Ohio							X
Oklahoma							X
Oregon	X			X	X		
Pennsylvania	X			X			
Rhode Island							X
South Carolina							X
Tennessee	X				X		
Texas	X			X			
Utah	X						
Virginia				X	X		
Wisconsin					X		
Wyoming	X			X	X		

Abbreviation: FPOs, for-profit organizations.

specify the extent of the entity's participation in the management and operation of the school."[26]

Thirteen state charter school laws include language allowing partnerships with for-profit organizations that offer charter schools access to affordable, suitable classroom space. In some cases, the charter school law explicitly permits for-profit organizations to provide a facility. For example, the Texas law states: "The State Board of Education may grant a charter . . . to operate in a facility of a commercial or nonprofit entity, an eligible entity, or a school district."[27] In other cases, the law states that a facility may be acquired from "public or private sources" without specifying whether the private sources are limited to nonprofit organizations or include for-profit organizations. For example, the Pennsylvania law specifies: "(a) A charter school . . . [has] the power to: . . . (3) Acquire real property from public or private sources by purchase, lease, lease with an option to purchase or gift for use as a charter school facility."[28] In still other cases, a lack of specificity in the law suggests that a facility may be provided by a for-profit partner, as in Wyoming: "(j) A charter school may negotiate and contract with a school district, the governing body of a state college or university, or any third party for the use of a school building and grounds."[29]

Charter school laws in five states—Connecticut, Delaware, Florida, Massachusetts, and New Hampshire—explicitly provide for workplace charter schools, typically located on the site of the for-profit organization.

In addition to partnerships for facilities, seventeen states allow charter schools to partner with for-profit organizations for the provision of goods and services. In some instances, the organization is a business that "adopts" a charter school, similar to the relationship found in traditional public schools in which for-profit organizations provide in-kind services as part of a charitable giving campaign. In other cases, for-profit education management organizations (EMOs) partner with charter schools to offer curriculum, back-office support, or whole school management and design. Louisiana law states: "A nonprofit organization may enter into a contract with a for-profit organization to manage the charter school and may delegate to the for-profit organization such authority over employment decisions at the charter school as the nonprofit organization deems necessary and proper."[30] In Idaho, the law states:

> No charter shall be approved under this chapter: . . . (b) To a for-profit entity or any school which is operated by a for-profit entity, provided, however, nothing herein shall prevent the board of

directors of a public charter school from legally contracting with for-profit entities for the provision of products or services that aid in the operation of the school.[31]

Another provision included by a few state laws—Colorado, Louisiana, and New York—is to allow for-profit organizations to apply to open a charter school. The Colorado law states: "An 'applicant' may include, but shall not be limited to, an individual, a group of individuals, a nonprofit or for-profit company, an existing public school, a school district, or an institution of higher education."[32] The New York charter school law specifies: "an application to establish a charter school may be submitted by . . . [a] for-profit business or corporate entity authorized to do business in New York State."[33] Louisiana state law allows a for-profit organization to form a nonprofit corporation in order to apply to open a charter school:

> Any of the following may form a nonprofit corporation for the purpose of proposing a charter as provided in this Subsection, provided that the group submitting the charter school proposal includes three or more persons holding valid and current Louisiana teaching certificates: . . . (d) A business or corporate entity registered to do business in Louisiana pursuant to law.[34]

View from the Ground

In the case of partnerships between for-profit organizations and charter schools, practice doesn't always mimic state law. Although only three states allow for-profit organizations to open charter schools, many more states allow EMOs to operate or manage charter schools, if the charter is held by a public or nonprofit organization. A recent report by researchers at Arizona State University and Western Michigan University concluded that about 425 charter schools across the country are EMO-managed.[35] In Michigan, for instance, which has no restrictions in its charter school law around for-profit involvement, 75 percent of the 230 charter schools in the state have some affiliation with an EMO or another for-profit service provider. Nationally, the average is only one in four.[36] As it turns out, benefits and retirement plans for public employees (teachers)—and not the charter school law itself—attract EMOs to Michigan.[37] The partnership between the company and the school allows the EMO to arrange its own private benefits and retirement plans, which are less expensive that the state plans.

Of the three states that do allow for-profits to open charter schools (Colorado, Florida, and New York), Liane Brouillette found that of the first fifty charter schools granted in Colorado, only one was to a for-profit organization.[38]

In another model, for-profits partner to establish a workplace charter rather than holding the charter themselves. In the late 1990s, Florida was the first state to pass such legislation. The Florida charter school law sets forth incentives for businesses to participate; they are exempt from taxes for property that is used for creating worksite partnerships with public schools and public school districts. The JFK Medical Center Charter School in Palm Beach County, Florida, was opened in 2002 and offers priority enrollment for the hospital employees' children. The medical center's board of trustees hoped the new school would help address Florida's high turnover rate of nurses and health-care technicians by enhancing employee morale and retention. The medical center already operated a child development center, a preschool, and an infant day care center for JFK Medical Center employees, so the charter school was viewed as another benefit to help with employee satisfaction.[39]

PARTNERSHIPS WITH FAITH-BASED ORGANIZATIONS

State Policies

Similar to the restrictions around for-profit involvement, many state laws restrict or prohibit partnerships with faith-based organizations. States have limited the involvement of these organizations in several ways. For one thing, fifteen state laws prohibit faith-based organizations from applying to open a charter school (table 7-4).

In many cases, this restriction specifically applies to private schools run by faith-based organizations and prohibits them from converting to charter status. In some cases, the law leaves open the possibility of a charter school's partnering with a faith-based organization for services, facilities, or human resources, while many of the states that include these restrictions around founding schools have additional prohibitions on faith-based involvement with charter schools. For example, in Idaho, the law states: "No charter shall be approved under this chapter: (a) Which provides for the conversion of any existing private or parochial school to a public charter school" and further specifies that "a public charter school shall be nonsectarian in its programs, affiliations, admission policies, employment

UNCOMMON PLAYERS, COMMON GOALS **163**

Table 7-4 How state laws address partnerships with faith-based organizations

	Prohibit faith-based organizations from establishing charter schools	Prohibit involvement with faith-based organizations	Allow partnerships with faith-based organizations for facilities	No relevant provisions
Alaska		X		
Arizona				X
Arkansas		X		
California		X		
Colorado		X		
Connecticut		X		
Delaware	X		X	
District of Columbia	X	X		
Florida	X	X		
Georgia	X			
Hawaii				X
Idaho	X	X		
Illinois	X	X		
Indiana		X		
Iowa		X		
Kansas				X
Louisiana		X		
Maryland	X			
Massachusetts	X	X		
Michigan	X	X		
Minnesota	X	X	X	
Mississippi				X
Missouri		X		
Nevada		X		

(continued)

Table 7-4 *(continued)*   How state laws address partnerships with faith-based organizations

	Prohibit faith-based organizations from establishing charter schools	Prohibit involvement with faith-based organizations	Allow partnerships with faith-based organizations for facilities	No relevant provisions
New Hampshire		X		
New Jersey	X			
New Mexico		X		
New York				X
North Carolina		X	X	
Ohio				X
Oklahoma	X	X		
Oregon		X		
Pennsylvania	X	X		
Rhode Island				X
South Carolina				X
Tennessee	X	X		
Texas				X
Utah	X	X		
Virginia		X		
Wisconsin				X
Wyoming				X

practices, and all other operations."[40] The New Jersey charter school legislation, in contrast, contains only one provision related to the involvement of faith-based organizations: "A private or parochial school shall not be eligible for charter school status."[41] Maryland law states:

An application to establish a public charter school may be submitted to a county board by: (iii) A nonsectarian nonprofit entity; (iv) A nonsectarian institution of higher education in the State . . . A public chartering authority may not grant a charter under this title to: (i) A private school; (ii) A parochial school; or (iii) A home school.[42]

In other cases, states include broad restrictions in their charter school laws against the involvement of faith-based organizations. The language in these twenty-six states tends to take one of two forms. Either the provision says, "A charter school shall be nonsectarian" (e.g., New Mexico and Oregon), or the law specifies that a charter school "must be nonsectarian in its educational program, admissions policies, employment policies, and operations" (e.g., Florida and Virginia).

Although these provisions restricting the involvement of faith-based organizations aim to maintain the separation of church and state, the vague language creates room for some ambiguity about what is and is not allowed. For example, if a charter school is prohibited from being sectarian, the law may leave open the possibility of partnerships with a faith-based organization for facility space, one-on-one tutors, or back-office tasks. Similarly, prohibiting the involvement of faith-based organizations in educational programs, admissions policies, employment policies, and operations may not necessarily prevent involvement in other areas, such as fund-raising or publicity.

The nonspecific nature of these provisions leaves it up to charter school authorizers or the state department of education to interpret the intent of the law. Arlo Wagner reports that in the District of Columbia, seven formerly private Catholic schools converted to charter status in 2007, despite a provision requiring charter schools not to "engage in any sectarian practices in its educational program, admissions policies, employment policies, or operations."[43] According to an article in the *Washington Times*, the schools will remain housed in parish buildings and will "not include religious education but will emphasize 13 values" consistent with Catholic teachings. Five of the twenty-six states with restrictions on partnerships with faith-based organizations are more explicit, specifying that charter schools are not allowed to have any affiliation with these organizations. For example, Louisiana law states: "A charter school shall not: (1) Be supported by or affiliated with any religion or religious organization or institution."[44] Massachusetts law specifies:

> If the charter school intends to procure substantially all educational services under contract with another person, the terms of such a contract must be approved by the board either as part of the original charter or by way of an amendment thereto; provided, further

that the board shall not approve any such contract terms, the purpose or effect of which is to avoid the prohibition of this section against charter school status for private and parochial schools.[45]

These prohibitions would seem to preclude partnerships. North Carolina law states that "a charter school shall not be affiliated with a nonpublic sectarian school or a religious institution."[46] Nevertheless, allowance is made for a charter school to lease a facility from a faith-based organization:

> If a charter school leases space from a sectarian organization, the charter school classes and students shall be physically separated from any parochial students, and there shall be no religious artifacts, symbols, iconography, or materials on display in the charter school's entrance, classrooms, or hallways. Furthermore, if a charter school leases space from a sectarian organization, the charter school shall not use the name of that organization in the name of the charter school.[47]

Delaware law includes a similar caveat for facilities as well as services provided by faith-based organizations:

> A charter school may . . . contract with a sectarian or religious college or university incorporated in the State and operating a program or programs for teacher education within the State empowered to enter into contracts for such property and services, so long as the property contracted for is used in a nonreligious and nonsectarian manner and the services contracted for are provided in a nonreligious and nonsectarian manner and are of a nonreligious and nonsectarian type.[48]

In Minnesota, the law states:

> If the school is unable to lease appropriate space from public or private nonsectarian organizations, the school may lease space from a sectarian organization if the leased space is constructed as a school facility and the Department of Education, in consultation with the Department of Administration, approves the lease.[49]

View from the Ground

In practice, the most common form of partnership between charter schools and faith-based organizations occurs around facility use. This sort of partnership helps charter schools alleviate the high cost of renting, renovating, or purchasing their own facilities. Characteristic of this kind of partnership is Minnesota's Internship Center (MNIC), which has five sites around Minneapolis, one of which is the Shiloh Campus, housed at the Shiloh Temple Church in North Minneapolis. The MNIC Web site (www.mnic.org) also lists several faith-based organizations as community collaborators, including Jordan New Life Church and Urban Hope Ministries.

Faith-based organizations generally use their buildings on weekends and evenings, creating a perfect match for charter schools that need facility space during weekdays. However, interviewees noted that there are both benefits and challenges in this type of partnership. For example, one interviewee noted:

> In one case, the church itself wanted to open [a charter school] and the school district went to the [the church] and said, "You know, let's work on this together. This can be a win-win situation. We can provide the transportation, the food, and the teachers. We need to do more for our at-risk students . . . but we don't have the extra facility; you have the facility." So they came together and submitted an application for a conversion charter. The church is providing the facility and all the utilities; the public school district is providing the teachers, the food service, student transportation, and all of that.

On the other hand, another interviewee noted:

> We have seen schools that have closed because the church providing the facility was too much "in bed with the board." In one case, the authorizer pulled the plug, saying, "This church is charging you exorbitant rent, and the charter school board is not being responsible and has allowed that to happen."

CONCLUSIONS

The charter school movement's early pioneers believed that charters offered opportunities for innovation in who governs and operates public schools. While public schools traditionally have been operated by local school districts, this chapter shows ways in which state charter school laws have opened up the public school sector to organizations other than school districts to start charter schools or to work as partners with charter schools in the delivery of core education services. This is a radical departure from the status quo—a system change. What we've observed on the ground is more incremental. There are pockets of innovation around the entry of new players, to be sure, but there has not been the widespread innovation some expected, and the status quo is more common than innovation in most charter schools. Perhaps change will "naturally" occur slowly, as charter schools overcome the inevitable complexities that come with starting any new enterprise. But more can be done than waiting out this maturation process.

First, at the state level, the policy community could enlarge and improve the incentives and rewards to encourage nontraditional providers to venture into education. While the notion of state laws requiring charter schools to partner with certain types of outside organizations is seen by some as anathema to the concept of autonomy, many of the current laws do impose limitations on autonomy by restricting certain types of involvement. Indeed, state charter school laws, while allowing new players to enter the field of education, are still very compliance oriented, in line with state education codes that dictate the behavior of district-run public schools. Charter school laws that purport to spur innovation by bringing in new players generally do little beyond stating the intention. Exceptions, such as a Massachusetts law that gives priority to petitions that show evidence of "broad community support" and Pennsylvania's provision giving enrollment preference to "a child of a parent who has actively participated in the development of the charter school" could serve as models for other states desiring to see more innovation on the ground.[50]

To push beyond incremental change, charter school authorizers could offer incentives and rewards parallel to and reinforcing state policies. With their authority and responsibility to fashion policies for initial petition approval as well as charter renewal, authorizers are in a pivotal position to contribute to system change at the local level in ways that complement state policies. Application preference could be given to charter schools that would be operated in partnership with local organizations, for example.

In addition to recommendations for expanding policies at the state and local levels to foster innovation, our findings suggest that people on the ground may need to be taught about the possibilities and opportunities that exist with partnering innovations. Indeed, innovation that does exist tends to be spotty and is rarely visible. One solution is to step up the emphasis on partnership innovations in training and technical assistance offered by various organizations that work with charter schools. Including the benefits and challenges of public-private partnerships as an integral part of charter launch programs makes good sense. Equally important are the governance implications of such partnerships. For example, should partners serve on the charter school governing board? How can partners collaborate in school decision making? What mechanisms will foster effective communication across partners?

Finally, more systematic and rigorous evaluation of the involvement of new players in charter schooling—in terms of implementation processes and their effects on key outcomes—is needed. More research is needed to better understand the conditions under which partnerships thrive and how these models can be adapted to local circumstances. The charter school community offers laboratories of innovation both for system change and for school improvement. While a "one best approach" is unlikely to present itself, the community—states, authorizers, and operators—can learn from the experience of others as they fine-tune their long-term efforts to provide meaningful learning opportunities for the students they serve.

CHAPTER 8

Hybridized, Franchised, Duplicated, and Replicated

Charter Schools and Management Organizations

Janelle T. Scott and Catherine C. DiMartino

THE EVOLUTION OF CHARTER SCHOOL MANAGEMENT AND GOVERNANCE

This is a pivotal era in charter school reform, where early visions of a movement characterized by community-centered and teacher-initiated schools are giving way to more market-driven and corporatized schools. Advocates and policy makers have been disappointed with mixed achievement data that indicate in the aggregate that charter schools have not outperformed traditional public schools. Moreover, they have been frustrated by the persistently small percentage of U.S. students enrolled in charter schools, despite the movement's expansion to forty-one states. For these reasons, advocates have begun to support charter school growth along more business-like models. Reflecting this shift, the theme of the 2008 National Charter Schools Conference, held in New Orleans, where the majority of charter schools are operated by management organizations, was "Still We Rise: Achieving Academic Excellence at Scale." With the encouragement and support of venture philanthropists, policy makers and, most recently, the federal government, schools started and managed by for-profit companies and nonprofit groups characterize the current wave of charter school reform.[1] In short, advocates are investing significant money, energy, and political capital into scaling up charter school models that they deem most effective at producing academic gains. The theme of the 2010 National Charter Schools Conference, held in Chicago, "Innovators in Education: Leading the Race to the Top," reflected the renewed national energy supporting charter schools under the Obama administration's Race to the Top program.

In this chapter, we organize the existing knowledge base on what is alternately referred to as the educational management organization, charter school management organization, or, simply, the management organization. The entities commonly labeled educational management organizations (EMOs) arrived almost simultaneously with the dawn of charter schools in 1992. In the intervening years, this private school-management sector has expanded and diversified. Policy researchers and advocates use various terms to refer to contemporary iterations of management organizations: The EMO usually oversees charter and noncharter schools. The charter school management organization (CMO) usually operates on a nonprofit basis and exclusively operates charter schools. The more general term, management organization (MO), is a catchall term for the entire sector.[2] Though not all schools run by MOs are charter schools, and neither are all charter schools run by MOs, a review of the development of the two sectors makes it clear that the growth of each has much to do with sustaining and expanding the other.[3] The relationship between charter schools and MOs has become especially symbiotic over the last decade, with philanthropists and policy makers lending their support to the development and expansion of MOs, hoping that their influence would help produce a more robust and better-quality charter school movement in light of mixed data on student achievement.[4]

ORGANIZATION OF THE CHAPTER

This chapter investigates the claims of charter school and MO advocates and critics through an analysis of the knowledge base on MOs. Our review comes in four sections. First, we consider the competing theories of change that have animated the charter school movement; we specifically discuss the competing visions of charter schools as market entities or tools for community empowerment. Second, we expand upon our initial description of MOs, noting that they have been in operation in several iterations since the early 1990s and have organizational antecedents dating back at least thirty years. In this section, we also describe the contemporary scope of MOs, finding that although they account for a small percentage of charter schools in the aggregate—9 to 12 percent, by some estimates—they appear to be concentrated in key urban districts, where they enjoy significant market share.[5] Third, we examine the empirical and advocacy-driven literature on MOs in terms of finance, equity, governance, and effectiveness. As we discuss, advocacy organizations and individual charter school boosters and critics produce much of the analysis on MOs, which can cloud empirical findings with political agendas. Despite these limitations, enough empirical study exists to point to key tensions in charter-school-MO relationships that require further examination. Finally, in the fourth section, we conclude by exploring the policy and normative implications of this chapter's findings for charter school research and practice, public education, and notions of democratic governance.

MARKET CONTROL OR DEMOCRATIC CONTROL? COMPETING VISIONS FOR CHARTER SCHOOL REFORM

From their origins, charter schools were animated by seemingly competing theories of school change. These theories are best described as *market control* models of school, which embrace private-sector practices and organizational arrangements, and *democratic* or *community control models*, which imagine schools as sites for local stakeholders to create spaces responsive to their particular and idiosyncratic educational and social needs. For market advocates, public schools had been too beholden to public-sector special interests, especially to teachers unions; these special-interest groups exerted undue influence over the way school systems operated. Market-control advocates believed that by restricting opportunities for the special-interest groups to exert their political will, schools would greatly improve. Specifically, market-based tools of competition, choice, and accountability would generate superior schools that were more efficient. This theory is most often attributed to John Chubb and Terry Moe, who wrote, "The nation is experiencing a crisis in public education not because these democratic institutions have functioned perversely or improperly or unwisely, but because they have functioned quite normally. Democratic control normally produces ineffective schools."[6] In short, not only is democratic participation not a priority under a market model for schools, but it is the prescription for school failure.

For charter school advocates also committed to democratic control of schools, the bureaucratic layers of school districts had rendered school administration too distant from the needs and concerns of local schools and communities. Adherents of democratic control consist of both supporters and opponents of charter school reform, but each tends to favor making schools and school systems more open to influence by marginalized communities so that they can be more responsive. Charter school reform, by giving control over governance, curriculum, personnel, and other key school functions to the people closest to them, would restore the democratic function of schools. Community control advocates, racial and ethnic centrists, and alternative curriculum supporters often articulate this progressive argument for charter schools.[7]

Some theorists argue that the democratic possibilities of choice reform become truncated under the influence of corporate and market reformers. The introduction of education management organizations into charter school reform complicates the potential of charter schools to realize their democratic potential and aligns them closer to market-controlled entities, argues Michael Engel:

> Charter schools are public-private hybrids that operate under the provisions of a contract negotiated between their organizers and a state or local public authority. Privatization, the last stop on the way to a free-market educational system, is contracting out writ large. It involves the transfer of control of school instructional services to managers who are neither elected nor on the public payroll and who are paid with public funds under contract with a governmental body.[8]

More recent scholarship has argued that the "market versus democratic control" theoretical frames fail to capture neoliberal policy activity.[9] In fact, as we will demonstrate in this chapter, it is often democratically elected public officials who have embraced private-sector actors in the form of MOs to run charter schools. This integration of market and democratic actors is especially poignant in charter school reform; within this terrain, they are not polar opposites, but rather partners. Under mayoral control, for example, it is democratically elected public officials who are most frequently ceding control of school management, data collection and analysis, testing and evaluation, school security, and food services to corporate entities.[10] Rather than being at tension, then, market and democratic forces become fused under contemporary school district governance and management.

MOs, Charters, and the Shift in Charter School Purpose

The trend in which private, for-profit, and nonprofit organizations run charter schools is a detour from an original, oft-cited intent of the charter school movement, which was to encourage educators, parents, and community members to create innovative and independent schools.[11] Charter advocates credit at least two men with the original charter school concept: former American Federation of Teachers president Al Shanker and University of Massachusetts education professor Ray Budde. Each man presented his theory of charter schools in articles written in 1988.[12] Shanker argued for allowing "any school or group of educators" to propose improved ways of educating their students, and being granted a "charter" to implement their plans.[13] Similarly, Budde imagined that a charter would be granted to someone with a vision or plan: "In a school district, the grantees would be teams of teachers with visions of how to construct and implement more relevant educational programs or how to revitalize programs that have endured the test of time. Note, that a charter was granted directly to the person or persons responsible for planning and carrying out the vision."[14] Shanker and Budde each proposed that school boards would review such charters, give these schools or programs greater autonomy that would allow teachers to use innovative tactics, and then be evaluated five to ten years after initiation. Both authors predicted that with school board resources and oversight, innovation and risk taking would flourish. Writing in the midst of the 1980s-era school district experiments with site-based management, both imagined that charter schooling would result in more locally created, educator-initiated schools that served as models of local control. These reformers' notions of the purposes of charter school reform seemed to align with early adopters. For example, the federal study of charter schools, conducted from 1997 to 2000, found that the primary reason charter school founders started schools was to realize a particular educational vision.[15]

Despite the dominance of these early reformers' visions, in reality, the charter school movement has always been composed of advocates who held diverse educational and social policy goals. As many researchers have noted, progressive activists, market adherents, ethnocentrists, conservatives, and educational traditionalists all join together under the charter school umbrella.[16] The idea that there was ever any singular vision for charter school reform is a fallacy. Yet what seems to be emerging, especially in key urban school districts, is a new policy consensus—driven by philanthropists, advocates, and policy makers—that MOs are the best way for the charter school movement to achieve competitive scale, academic quality, economic viability, and social equity by having an impact on the maximum number of students and their families.[17] These claims are contested by many critics, who argue that the increasing privatization of charter schools not only runs counter to their hopes for innovative, organizationally diverse, community-based schools, but also will result in more conformity, less accountability to local communities, and poorer quality.[18]

EDUCATION MANAGEMENT ORGANIZATIONS: AN HISTORICAL OVERVIEW AND A LOOK AT THE CONTEMPORARY LANDSCAPE

Contracting with the private sector to run schools or educational programs within schools is not a new phenomenon; nor is the privatization of public sector services, an observation noted by numerous researchers.[19] Still, contemporary discourse about policy too often ignores history, and although past experience does not necessarily predict the future, a historical context can help us evaluate the present effectiveness of EMOs. The current trend toward relying upon the private sector to deliver such services has many elements in common with earlier experiments in U.S. educational policy. While states and local educational authorities have also engaged in contracting and outsourcing, for the purpose of providing a broad policy history, we focus here primarily on federal efforts.

Initial Experiments with Privatization and Contracting: 1970s to the 1990s

An historical antecedent of MOs is the foray into contracting out for the operation of particular programs within high-poverty, high-minority schools. This practice had mixed results in terms of cost effectiveness, student outcomes, and public accountability.[20] Performance contracting, a federally funded program of the 1970s and early 1980s, involved over 150 school districts. It was launched to improve the academic performance of students of color in low-achieving schools in light of efforts to desegregate public education. The thinking was that African American and Latino children needed remediation before they could be put in schools with white children. A series of evaluations found that the contracts were difficult to enforce since achievement and performance benchmarks had been vague, curricula were narrow, and cost savings were minimal or nonexistent. Moreover, there was much instability in the pool of providers, with many going out of business or merging. Evaluators also found that public officials often lacked the capacity to hold contractors accountable to the terms of their contracts and that contractors taught to the tests to assure student performance on standardized assessments, shunned the teaching of subjects not tested, and often failed to adequately account for expenditures.[21]

A subsequent experiment with privatizing school restructuring took place under President George H. W. Bush and was launched in 1991 with the New American Schools Development Corporation, later called New American Schools.[22] This initiative resulted in the implementation of seven school restructuring models in several cities and states; the projects were funded with public and private funds. While several of the models proved to be promising, the ultimate test would be the ability to spread these models to public schools around the country after they had been successfully incubated. The goal was to scale up the implementation to other schools and districts—those that could purchase the model—once the restructuring was successfully adopted. Evaluators of the scale-up phase found that successful implementation was confounded by a lack of sufficient buy-in and fidelity to the reform models by schools that purchased the designs.[23]

In summary, research on nearly three decades of forays into contracting for private sector delivery of public education shows that policy claims of vast innovations, maximized efficiencies, and superior academic outcomes are often overstated and fail to account for issues of local context, which can be highly complex.[24] These claims also reveal a lack of understanding of the critical role of parents, community members, teachers, and school leaders in school reform. Research on the privatization of public services in other sectors also reflects the rhetoric-versus-reality mismatch upon implementation. This is not to say that such research cautions against contracting with the private sector altogether. Rather, researchers suggest that such engagement be carefully considered, regulated, and evaluated if it is to realize the desired benefits. The notion of engaging the private sector in education, never dormant, was revitalized with the 1991 passage of the first charter school legislation in Minnesota and with new scholarship that argued for the systemic use of contracting in public education. These developments were based largely on lessons learned from these earlier privatization experiments.[25] New privatization efforts were also informed by two other developments. First, a growing neoliberal and promarket ideology in public education was being advanced by think tanks funded by key philanthropies that supported school choice. Second, there were the real and legitimate frustrations of many low-income communities of color about the failure of public education in their locales. These movements led to coalitions in support of vouchers, private contracting, and expanded school choice and led to the growth of the MO sector as chronicled in the following section.[26]

The Rise of EMOs: 1992–1998

The middle 1990s marked EMOs' first experience in operating public schools and, in a few cases, whole districts. In 1992, Education Alternatives Incorporated (EAI) won contracts to manage nine schools in Baltimore and six in Hartford, and Edison Schools won contracts to operate four elementary schools: one each in Massachusetts, Michigan, Texas, and Kansas. While Edison continued to grow in the mid-1990s, EAI encountered trouble as schools under its management failed to show achievement gains. At a cost of 11 percent more per pupil than comparable schools in Baltimore and with no increase in test results, attendance, or other measures, the City of Baltimore, after three years, canceled its contract with EAI. Soon thereafter, Hartford terminated its contract as well. While this marked the gradual decline of EAI—encapsulated by its removal from NASDAQ in 2000—the EMO landscape was just beginning to heat up.

By 1998, new players had entered the for-profit education game and included Mosaica Education, Inc.; National Heritage Academies; and White Hat Management. Following the same business model that EAI and Edison employed, these for-profit EMOs aspired to deliver schools that were more efficient than traditional public schools, to scale up nationally, and to exploit economies of scale.[27] These new players fell into three categories: national firms, state-based firms, and virtual EMOs.[28] Both national and state-based firms offered management expertise in information management, payroll, and professional development and supplied their own curriculum and approaches to teaching and learning. The main difference between these two types was that national firms aimed to scale up nationally and operate schools across the United States. For example, Edison had schools in Michigan and Texas. In contrast, state-based firms developed a market in a single state. However, over time, many of the original state-based firms, such as National Heritage Academies, expanded and now work in multiple states. The third type, virtual EMOs, concentrated on distance learning, for example, K12 Inc. Overlap existed between the types, especially as EMOs tried to increase their market share. For example, White Hat Management offered a distance- and electronic-learning program called DELA. As the EMO sector gained momentum, proponents and critics turned to the achievement data to see if privately managed schools ran more efficiently, had more innovative approaches to teaching and learning, and infused competition into the public school system.

Diversification in the EMO Sector and the Growth of CMOs: 1999 to 2005

This period served as a reality check for advocates of the EMO movement. Evaluations and studies of EMO-managed charter schools revealed that achievement outcomes were mixed—in some cases were no better than district run schools—and that making a profit proved to be challenging. Additionally, mounting skepticism about the for-profit model raised questions about its impact. Specifically, the need to make a profit necessitated labor cost reduction by either hiring less experienced teachers or having larger class sizes; rapid expansion to create economies of scale; and fewer resources such as transportation and school lunch.[29] Since many of these policy decisions, especially larger class sizes and the lack of transportation, were unpopular with parents and concerned educators, policy makers and funders looked for other routes to expand the charter school movement.

As a result of mixed achievement results and increasing skepticism, for-profit EMOs, such as Edison and Mosaica Education, began to lose contracts. By 2001, EAI, which had changed its name to Tesseract, filed for bankruptcy, and by 2002, Edison's expansion had slowed down so much that its stock price dropped by 98 percent. Struggling to stay solvent and stave off over $60 million in defaulted loans, Edison's CEO, Chris Whittle, took the company private, ending its much-publicized run on the New York Stock Exchange.[30] A 2007 National Charter School Research Project report described this period as "the frontier 'land rush,' in which new operators were welcome even if they were undercapitalized, financially primitive, politically naïve, or educationally unprepared."[31] Widespread disillusionment with for-profit EMOs and the realization that more charter schools would be needed to transform the education sector required the emergence of a new type of charter school operator. This is when charter management organizations (CMOs) were developed.

Similar to EMOs, CMOs have an "identifiable instructional model—a curriculum and approach to instruction" and offer operational support to schools.[32] However, unlike EMOs, CMOs hailed from the nonprofit sector and were not subject to the pressures of turning a profit or the controversy of being a for-profit. CMOs also benefited from significant funding and support from foundations such as the Bill and Melinda Gates Foundation and venture capital organizations such as the NewSchools Venture Fund, which in 2002 gave $50 million "to help create dozens of new public charter schools and to develop organizations with the capacity to provide thousands of underserved students with an excellent education."[33] This funding supported a dozen CMOs and the management of over one hundred charter schools. CMOs supported by the NewSchools Venture Fund include Aspire Public Schools, Green Dot Public Schools, and Achievement First. Many CMOs, such as Green Dot Public Schools or Achievement First, started as successful charter schools and received funding to replicate their model and scale up nationally. As momentum congealed around CMOs, EMOs continued to struggle to prove their profitability and record of academic achievement. The passing of the No Child Left Behind Act of 2001 (NCLB) provided new hope for EMOs, opening up new educational markets for MOs and leading to diversification of the sector.

Stipulations in NCLB allowed for MOs to offer supplemental educational services and to ultimately run schools that fail to meet their annual yearly progress (AYP) indicators. Under NCLB, schools that fail to meet AYP three years in a row must offer supplemental educational services (SES) to students. Often, these services take the form of after-school programs or Saturday programs. Some EMOs, such as Edison Schools, provided SES to schools. In addition to SES, if a school fails to make AYP for five years in a row, it must be restructured. A school can be restructured by reopening it as a charter school or by contracting with an EMO, two solutions that help to enlarge the MO sector.

While CMOs remain focused on replicating charter school models nationally, EMOs, as illustrated by their role as SES providers, have been diversifying, branching out into assessment consulting and into creating customized achievement programs for schools to help them attain AYP.[34] True to the term *educational* in their name, EMOs seek to be generalists in their provision of services to schools and in their hope of being profitable. Alex Molnar and his colleagues described this situation: "Although our data suggests that the growth of for-profit EMOs has slowed, one should also be aware that some of the large and medium-size EMOs have been diversifying and expanding into new service areas such as the provision of supplemental education services . . . Thus a slowdown in EMO growth in schools under management may reflect a strategic change of direction for some EMOs."[35]As EMOs diversify to meet schools' needs—the needs of both traditional public and charter schools—CMOs continue to grow. By 2009, there were 103 CMOs in the United States, compared with 95 EMOs.[36]

Scale-Up of Charter Management Organizations and the Growth of School Development Organizations: 2006 to Present

The expansion of CMOs has led to variation within the management organization sector and has influenced the growth of school development organizations or intermediary organizations, which have been instrumental in starting new small schools across the nation. With over ninety firms in the sector—ranging from KIPP to High Tech High—CMOs have expanded in different ways. Some CMOs ascribe to a corporate style of growth, while others follow a franchising model.[37] Corporate-style growth emphasizes central management and gives CMOs more direct control over each school site, explains Julie Bennet: "The leaders of the corporate-model CMOs oversee the building and operation of each new school themselves. The trade-off for the slower growth is the assurance that each new school replicated the CMOs' standards for building design, staffing and programs."[38] Green Dot Schools and High Tech High are examples of corporate-style CMOs. In contrast, CMOs following the franchising model have a more decentralized structure, allowing for the organization to expand rapidly. Bennet explains: "While franchisees are building individual units, the central organization can spend its resources on promoting the brand and developing new products and services."[39] KIPP Schools and Uncommon Schools are examples of franchising CMOs. In terms of financial relationships, some CMOs, such as KIPP, require that schools provide a percentage of the revenue—usually 1 percent the first year. Other firms charge fees for specific services, while others, such as EdVisions, charge a flat start-up fee.[40] This rapid scale-up phase raises questions about quality. A recent Education Sector study raised questions about charter schools and the CMO's ability to scale up while still maintaining their quality.[41] The expense of educating high-needs students, the challenge and cost of ascertaining a physical space for the school, the churn and expense of high attrition rates for teachers and principals, and the heavy reliance on funding from philanthropies all make it difficult to bring high-quality, financially stable charter schools to scale.[42]

To ensure that their charters school models are being fully implemented, are of high quality and to address high attrition rates for principals and teachers, some CMOs have entered the field of principal and teacher preparation.[43] CMOs have been partnering with universities to offer certification for teachers and principals. For example, High Tech High has a partnership with the University of San Diego for a two-year certification program for its teachers. In 2008, three CMOs—KIPP, Uncommon Schools, and Achievement First—announced a partnership with the Hunter College School of Education, part of the City University of New York, to jointly create a new teacher preparation program. Courses in these programs will be cotaught by professors at Hunter College and practitioners from the CMOs. In terms of principal preparation, KIPP offers perspective school leaders either a one- or two-year-long, paid fellowship to prepare them to run a KIPP school.

While providing high-quality teacher and principal preparation programs represents one method of insuring quality, another means revolves around the termination of partnerships. CMOs function on the premise that if a school in a CMO's network does not meet its standards, the partnership will end. While the organization does not necessarily close the school, such schools face a daunting task in remaining open without the MO's institutional support. For example, in 2007, KIPP terminated its contract with the KIPP Sankofa Charter School in Buffalo. KIPP removed its name and official support because for over two years, the school had not been meeting KIPP standards. Specifically, students were not reaching their achievement markers.[44] As CMOs continue to scale up rapidly, it will be important for researchers and policy makers to monitor the frequency of broken contracts and the impact of termination on schools and the communities they serve.

Since 2003, CMOs have emerged as a lever for scaling up charter schools across the nation. Similarly, in the new small-schools movement, the emergence of nonprofit school development organizations, often referred to as *intermediaries*, has been pivotal in the rapid expansion of small schools. Similar to CMOs, many intermediary organizations—which also receive funding from the Bill and Melinda Gates Foundation—offer school design models and are involved in supporting the scale-up of new small schools. Examples of these organizations are Expeditionary Learning Outward Bound and Replications, Inc. While many of these intermediaries began in specific geographic regions, they are starting to expand nationally. For example, Replications began in New York City, but now has schools in Baltimore. Because overlap exists between the work of CMOs and intermediaries, it remains unclear if, over time, they will merge into a single type of organization or will remain distinct entities. As the MO field becomes more diverse, it will be important to become more precise and descriptive about the range of organizations involved in school management and restructuring. Table 8-1 depicts the current MO terrain.

The evolution of MOs in the United States has morphed from its beginning in the 1990s with a high concentration of for-profit EMOs to its current emphasis on nonprofit CMOs. Questions of profitability and achievement changed the sector, pushing it away from its for-profit status

TABLE 8-1   Institutional landscape of management organizations

Type of organization	Activities	Examples	Level of control
EMOs	Operate schools on a for-profit basis. Contracts with local charter school boards or school districts to operate schools.	Edison Schools, Charter Schools USA	Tight
CMOs	Operate schools on a nonprofit basis. Can hold the charter, or can contract with a charter school board to operate the school. Often run networks or franchises of schools.	Green Dot, Uncommon Schools, KIPP	Moderate to tight
Intermediaries	Work as liaisons between districts, school boards, and schools; provide start-up funding and sundry curricular and administrative support. Often have a network of affiliated schools.	The College Board, New Visions for Public Schools, Replications, Inc.	Moderate
Supplemental education service providers	Provide discrete services such as tutoring, professional development, data management, and analysis.	Sylvan Learning, Tungsten Learning Systems, Kaplan	Loose

Source: Adapted from Susan Colby, Kim Smith, and Jim Shelton, "Expanding the Supply of High-Quality Public Schools," September 12, 2005, Bridgespan Group, www.bridgespan.org.

and toward a nonprofit model, spurred on by federal policy that helped to diversify the work of EMOs and CMOs. Debates about policy are endemic as CMOs navigate rapid expansion while also trying to provide high-quality schools. A distinguishing feature is the level of control these organizations exert, which can range from loose to tight.[45] With similar organizational forms emerging in the current educational management landscape, such as intermediaries and partner support organizations in New York City's public schools, there remain questions about how the organizations will involve and potentially influence each other over time. Given the historical volatility of the MO sector, we predict that in the coming years, there will be more mergers, collaborations, and intersections between established MOs and MO-like organizations.

Contemporary Landscape of Management Organizations

The contemporary scale of MOs is difficult to determine with complete accuracy. Researchers following the development of MOs offer best estimates rather than exact numbers of organizations in operation. For example, the National Charter School Research Project (NCRP) estimates that MOs run just 9 percent of charter schools, while the Commercialism in Education Research Unit at Arizona State University estimates that EMOs operate 12 percent of charter schools.[46] Yet, these figures are potentially misleading for at least two reasons. First, given that few public agencies monitor the number of MOs in operation, it is likely that this sector is undercounted. Second, even if the NCRP estimate is accurate in the aggregate, it fails to recognize that in key urban school districts, MOs manage the majority, or a significant percentage of, charter schools.

New Orleans and Philadelphia are examples of this trend of MO concentration. Both cities are in the midst of district restructuring that has led to a large concentration of charter schools managed by MOs. Philadelphia's effort came in 2002 following a state takeover that initially recommended privatizing the entire school district. The New Orleans school district was reorganized after the tragic effects of Hurricane Katrina in 2005.

Key philanthropic and public policy support has facilitated these reforms, and while there has been community support for them, there has also been opposition. Teachers unions have been active in opposition movements (even as they have collaborated with MOs to start schools and functioned in MO-like roles to manage charter schools), but so have grassroots community members who have been displaced by how public officials have privatized the management of schools, sometimes with little community input. Critics have also objected when some MO leaders appeared to have utilized their connections with policy makers to secure school contracts.[47] In 2010, for example, the Los Angeles Board of Education rejected numerous applications from MOs and instead supported groups of district-employed teachers and administrator to run its underperforming schools. Notably, the Los Angeles Unified School District contains more charter schools than does any other district in the nation.[48]

In the face of evidence of academic struggles in urban school districts, as well as significant fiscal support for them, such opposition has, for the most part, been easily overcome. Table 8-2 shows the concentration of privatized charter schools in four urban school districts, as well as the similarity in funders and MOs across these districts. Although the example of the Los Angeles School Board hints at larger, community-based opposition to MO-oriented reforms, these district concentrations of MOs and charters demonstrates the significant presence of MOs in urban school reform.

MANAGEMENT ORGANIZATIONS: FINANCE, EQUITY, GOVERNANCE, AND EFFECTIVENESS

The current iteration of MOs is still in development, and empirical research is similarly in its early stages. Much of the literature is generated by the MOs themselves, by sympathetic think tanks or advocacy groups (see, for example, the Center on Reinventing Public Education at the University of Washington, or the National Alliance for Public Charter Schools), or by funders of MOs. Even if this literature comes from a supportive perspective, however, we find it helpful to utilize it in concert with existing empirical research to better establish the institutional terrain, policy tensions, and other issues to be explored in future research. Here we look at the literature on finance, equity, governance, and achievement.

Finance: Hybridized Funding of the MO Sector

Charter school finance is a complex issue. For a variety of reasons, charter schools are often ineligible for certain state funds, which, the charters argue, puts them at a disadvantage—especially in locales where real estate is expensive and scarce and they need to pay for capital expenses (see chapter 6 in this book). The passage of the American Recovery and Reinvestment Act of 2009, however, brings new resources for charter schools in this area in the form of real estate tax credits for charter schools as well as funding for charter school networks. Here we are less focused on this

TABLE 8-2 Defining the management sector in four urban school districts: type, size, and scope (academic year 2007–2008)

District	No. of schools	No. of charters	No. of charters managed by MOs (%)	MOs involved	Philanthropic support
New York City	1,466	61*	32 (52.5)	KIPP, Uncommon Schools, Achievement First, Beginning with Children, UFT, Victory Schools	Broad Foundation, Fisher Foundation, Bill and Melinda Gates Foundation
Los Angeles	714	139	63 (45)	Green Dot, KIPP, Inner City Education Foundation, Alliance of College Ready Public Schools, Aspire Public Schools, YPI, Bright Star, PUC, Celerity Education Group, Expectations Educational Excellence, Value Schools, Dialog Foundation	Broad Foundation, NewSchools Venture Fund, Fisher Foundation, Bill and Melinda Gates Foundation
New Orleans	5 (OPSB) 36 (RSD) (ACSA, no traditional public schools)	13 (OPSB) 21 (RSD) 9 (ACSA)	31 (72)	KIPP, SABIS, University of New Orleans, Pelican Education Foundation, Broadmoor Charter School Board, New Beginnings School Foundation, Choice Foundation, YMCA	Broad Foundation, Fisher Foundation, NewSchools Venture Fund
Philadelphia	270	63†	38 (55)	KIPP, Edison Schools, Mastery, Victory Schools, Chancellor Beacon Academies, Inc., Temple University, Foundations, Inc., Universal Companies, University of Pennsylvania, Alliance for Progress, Parents United for Better Schools	Broad Foundation, Fisher Foundation

* A recent increase to the state charter school cap will allow New York City charters to expand to 100 schools. Of these, 17 were to be managed by MOs.

† In 2008–2009, 15 new charter schools were scheduled to open in Los Angeles Unified School District. Of these, 14 were to be operated by MOs.

‡ In 2008–2009, 2 new charter schools were scheduled to open. In 2008, the School Reform Commission reclaimed the management of 6 schools previously managed by MOs.

Abbreviations: ACSA, Algiers Charter School Association; MOs, management organizations; OPSB, Orleans Parish School Board; PUC, Partnerships to Uplift Communities; RSD, Recovery School District; UFT, United Federation of Teachers; YPI, Youth Policy Institute.

broader financial picture for charter schools and instead interested in the prevailing fiscal incentives currently in place to increase the MO sector within the charter school movement.

In order to bring this movement to scale, several organizations have come to a policy consensus about the need to fund the growth of quality charter schools; the organizations concluded that the key to quality schools is through MOs that have a promising model. This more aggressive form of philanthropy is often referred to as *venture philanthropy* to capture its emphasis on the tangible return on investment and to contrast it with more traditional philanthropic forms.[49] The Philanthropy Roundtable, a group sympathetic to school choice, has published a guide for philanthropists interested in supporting school choice and recommends not only funding schools, but also funding research to demonstrate the effectiveness of school choice, as well as funding political candidates who are school choice supporters.[50] As table 8-2 demonstrates, key private donors are the backbone of this direction of charter school reform. These include several California-based philanthropies: the Broad Foundation, NewSchools Venture Fund, and the Fisher Foundation, for example, all of which have provided several millions of dollars to support charters and specific MOs.

These philanthropies are significant levers for the growth of particular MOs. In 2007, for example, KIPP was awarded $65 million from a group of philanthropic organizations to start forty-two charter schools in Houston. Since 2001, the Broad Foundation has distributed well over $60 million to help start charter schools in a number of cities—$56 million in Los Angeles—and has provided support for twelve charter school support organizations, ranging from MOs to advocacy groups to facility developers. Recently, the Broad Foundation awarded $23 million toward the creation of seventeen charter schools, funds that were allocated to KIPP, Aspire Public Schools (a CMO), and Pacific Charter School Development (a real estate development organization). The Donald and Doris Fisher Foundation is a key supporter of KIPP and Teach for America, many of whose alumni leave or graduate from the program to teach in KIPP and other CMO schools. Other foundations have long been supportive of school choice and continue to provide funding; these include the Thomas B. Fordham Foundation, the Lynde and Harry Bradley Foundation, the Olin Foundation, and the Walton Family Foundation. Of these, the Walton Family Foundation is the most active and generous funder of school choice. Together, these foundations in a given year provide over $100 million to school choice efforts, not only helping to support MOs and other school choice providers, but also providing a solid financial foundation for the broader school choice movement.[51] A recent Education Sector report found that "funding from foundations is so important to the rise of charter school management organizations that executives like Marco Petruzzi of Green Dot say flatly that the CMO movement 'would stop in its tracks' without philanthropic support."[52]

Public funds also support MOs and the broader school choice expansion effort. The federal government has increased its allocations to charter schools and, by extension, to MOs. Under NCLB's choice provisions, charter schools are prominent alternatives. Since 2006, the U.S. Department of Education's Office of Innovation and Improvement has provided over $278 million annually to charter school reform, an amount more than double the allocations to magnet schools and not inclusive of funds that have gone to support choice and charter advocacy organizations.[53]

The 2010 budget continues this trend by increasing funding to the Federal Charter Schools Program by $52 million and by making—for the first time—charter school networks eligible for funding. Additionally, Congress and the Obama administration have shown their support for charter schools and MOs through the American Recovery and Reinvestment Act (AARA) of 2009. This legislation leverages billions of dollars in federal funding to foster the development of charter schools and MOs through four initiatives: Race to the Top (RTTT), Investing in Innovation Fund (i3), Title 1 school improvement grants, and real estate tax credits. Each of these initiatives favors charter school development and MOs. For example, in the RTTT competition, priority is given to states that have created environments friendly to charter schools. States that lift caps on the number of charter schools and support charter school networks are viewed as being more likely to win a part of the $4.35 billion initiative. Similarly, the i3 Fund, which has over $750 million ($650 million from AARA and $100 million from the 2010 budget) to support new educational ventures, allows charter schools and CMOs to compete for grants because they are deemed to be local school systems.[54] Both the RTTT and the i3 are administered by former employees of the NewSchools Venture Fund. Jim Shelton, who currently administers i3, exemplifies this connection. Before joining the Department of Education, Shelton developed and ran his own for-profit EMO until he sold it to Edison Schools, where he worked as a division president. The use of charter schools and MOs also features prominently in Title 1 school improvement grants. This $3.5 billion effort champions four models, including a "restart model," which closes underperforming schools and replaces them with charter schools or places underperforming schools under MOs.[55] Finally, the AARA legislation opened up over $25 billion in real estate tax credits to charter schools and MOs to acquire new properties for school construction. Since most states require charter schools to find their own space, this legislation marks a significant shift in favor of charter schools and MOs. The trifecta of new funding mechanisms, new charter-friendly policies, and new MO-oriented administrators in the Department of Education creates a fertile environment for the expansion of charter schools and MOs. These groups have also enjoyed significant support from the private sector, especially from venture philanthropies. Thus, while charter advocates may have a legitimate claim to the state funds they feel they are shortchanged, they also enjoy considerable private and federal support that is unavailable to noncharter and nonchoice schools.

While robust policy debates are in progress about the normative aspects of private funding, our goal is not to draw such conclusions here. Rather, we will briefly establish the private-funding landscape and explore some of the policy debates it raises. The private support does come with expectations for fairly rapid achievement outcomes, lest CMOs and charters lose their philanthropic support, and so in addition to the accountability demands of public agencies, the schools and their leaders are also accountable to the venture philanthropies. A relationship with a private donor can help MOs and charter schools and motivate them to perform better, even as it has the potential to cause some schools to cede over issues of curriculum or personnel in order to placate donors, or overpromise what their academic impact will be in order to secure and sustain funding.

Governance and MOs

A related source of tension in the MO and charter school sector occurs around the policy of school governance. In theory, many charter school founders seek to realize an alternative educational vision while MOs increasingly look to maximize standardization and effectiveness according to their educational and fiscal models. We are interested in how governance unfolds when actors with various visions for the schools come together (by *actors*, we mean leaders, teachers, parents, students, funders, school district officials, state officials, and board members). Research on governance in charter schools managed by MOs, which we define as the interaction between power, values, and decision making, while not as prevalent as research into other charter school policy issues, reveals that despite original intentions for value alignment, there are often significant disagreements at the school level about the mission and operation of the such schools. The questions of how such issues are negotiated and who or which parties prevail in the midst of such disagreements are important to explore.

A few studies have explored these issues. A team of researchers examined the relationship between MO-like organizations (which they termed "institutional partners") and the charter schools the organizations supported.[56] The researchers found that in four of the ten schools they examined, the partners exerted significant control over decision making. Since the partners had given money and other support to the school, they felt a sense of ownership over school operations and felt entitled to have ultimate authority over them. Institutional partners had more control in these schools, said the researchers, because they comprised a majority on the schools' boards of directors:

> The chair or president of the boards of trustees in three of the four charter schools with institutional partners was a key official in that organization; in the fourth school, the institutional partner approved the chair. In all four schools, institutional partners' representatives or appointees comprised at least thirty percent of the boards of trustees. Moreover, since the institutional partner filled additional slots with acquaintances or professional colleagues with compatible interests, boards tended to support the partner organization's objectives in major policy decisions.[57]

The study found that in three of these schools, the boards of trustees did not include the school administrators. "Furthermore, two institutional partners were clear that executive sessions of their boards would be held in the administrator's absence, and that decisions about budgeting, capital funding, and facilities construction were outside the purview of the school administrator."[58] Finally, teachers in these schools reported being unsure about who had authority in the school; they felt pulled between the school leader's preferences and those of the institutional partners.

Other studies of the negotiation of power between public school stakeholders and their MOs, intermediaries, or institutional partners have revealed similar issues in a variety of geographic and state policy contexts. The studies suggested that the power of local actors within such schools to influence school policy is limited since MOs often have specific models they plan to implement, and since the MOs often hold greater fiscal and political power.[59] This research has found that many times, schools, parents, and teachers exit partnerships as the only route available to exercise their own voice.[60]

These governance issues matter from the perspective of democratic governance, a construct that the current direction of charter school reform challenges and an issue that has always been in contention, even under traditional school district governance models.[61] In fact, most MO leaders and their supporters argue that for their models to be successfully implemented, local stakeholders must buy into them and implement them with fidelity, leaving little room for local voice.[62] Indeed, their theory of action holds that increased student achievement comes from solid school design, and so the most powerful indicator of their success becomes student performance on standardized assessments. And given the academic struggles of many communities that MOs target, the laserlike focus on achievement is in many ways laudable. In this new policy arena, however, there is still much work for researchers to do in further examining governance issues among the variety of actors involved in starting and sustaining particular MOs.

Equity, Achievement, and MOs

Perhaps no two issues surrounding charter schools and MOs are as contentious and confounding as those of equity and student achievement. Since one of the key policy claims supporting the development of charter schools was that student achievement would flourish when schools were freed from school district bureaucracies, and since charters are theoretically supposed to be held to accountability goals they set in their applications to their authorizers, or risk being dechartered, all policy eyes are on student achievement. Thus far, the empirical research on charter school student achievement has been confounded by a number of methodological issues that researchers are trying to reconcile. Most researchers recognize the difficulty in drawing conclusions about the achievement of charter schools using aggregated data, given the tremendous organizational and pedagogical diversity of the movement, though ironically, many researchers see little problem with reaching conclusions about aggregated data from traditional public schools that are equally diverse.

Recent analyses of charter school and traditional school student performance on the National Assessment of Educational Progress indicate that charter school students perform at lesser levels in some grades and slightly higher levels in others when compared with traditional public schools.[63] Another controversial analysis conducted by researchers affiliated with the American Federation of Teachers found that charter schools underperformed compared with traditional public schools, despite enrolling fewer poor students.[64] While the methodology of this study has been widely criticized, many of its key findings were echoed by a federal government analysis.[65] Some of the problems associated with these aggregate analyses have to do with the difficulty of controlling for local school policies that shape and structure student enrollment in charter schools, thereby making comparisons with other public schools without such admissions and other controls exceedingly difficult.[66] Still, meta-analyses of charter school achievement have produced similar conclusions about the relatively flat performance of charter school students on standardized assessments (see chapter 4 in this book).

Within schools managed by MOs, these same issues prevail, and in some ways, they are magnified. An unresolved policy tension related to student outcomes in MO-run schools is the relationship between at least three dynamics: the need to show rapid and consistent results according to prevailing accountability systems; the use of selective or screened admissions, or both, and other school-level policies to control and structure enrollment; and the need to prove that an MO is demonstrating results for underserved populations. Some data suggest that particular MOs have student bodies with fewer poor, minority, and special-education students; fewer English language learners; and proportionally more girls, even as other data indicate that MOs serve predominantly poor children (as indicated by eligibility for the federal free-lunch program), the majority of whom are students of color.[67] Given these demographic trends, parsing through the data on MOs and their effects on student achievement is difficult. For even if some MOs show positive student outcomes, any policy conclusions drawn from these data, if responsible, should consider the impact that parent and student contracts, longer school days and years, significant private funding, and school demographics have on those outcomes. As efforts increase to scale up MO-run charter schools, these broader contextual issues help to raise important questions about sustainability, the ability to replicate and duplicate models across diverse social contexts, and the effects on surrounding schools that do not require applications or behavior codes and enroll more special-education students or more English language learners.

If MOs' ability to increase student learning were not convincing, it is unlikely that they would have attracted such significant financial and political support. And some promising data indicate that many MOs are succeeding on several academic benchmarks: high graduation rates; high performance on state standardized assessments, especially in comparison with traditional public schools in their host districts; and students' acceptance into four-year colleges or elite private high schools.[68] Recent analyses of standardized assessments in New York showed that New York City charter schools' performance outperformed statewide averages, though there were also problematic data on the relative under enrollment of special education students in charter schools.[69] In the context of a national conversation about the racial achievement gap, this array of research serves as evidence to reformers that MOs can help to ameliorate it.

Other research presents a more complex picture of achievement in MO-run schools. Specifically, the data indicate that there is variability in achievement within the MO sector, but also within particular MO networks. Some schools perform well and some do not, even when run according to the same educational model. One statewide study used longitudinal data for Arizona students in grades 2–8 between 2001 and 2003.[70] The researchers examined students who attended schools in the same sector for all three years—charter, traditional, and EMO. They found that charters and EMO schools overenrolled white students. EMO students were far less likely to be classified as English language learners (1.2 percent, versus 14 percent in traditional public schools). The researchers also found higher achievement in basic skills but lower achievement in complex-thinking skills. They suggest that the emphasis on cost savings, prepackaged curricula, and less experienced young teachers may be the reason for these results. Researchers have also examined student performance in Edison Schools and concluded that while there had been positive student achievement gains in some of the company's schools, others have lost ground, and the company often overstated overall achievement gains in its marketing.[71]

Studies on the performance of students in Philadelphia under the diverse-provider model are contradictory, yet indicate that such schools are not outperforming district-run schools.[72] In 2002, following a state takeover, Philadelphia undertook a diverse-provider model for school management in which forty-five schools were turned over to nonprofit and for-profit MOs to run. A collaborative study conducted by RAND Education and the Philadelphia-based Research for Action (RFA) found that student gains in proficiency in the district rose in the years after the state takeover, but that scores in privately managed schools did not keep pace with schools that were restructured, supported with additional resources, and kept under the purview of the school district.[73] In contrast, Paul Peterson looked at public test scores for fifth-graders between 2002 and 2006.[74] He found that private companies were very effective at raising test scores of students at or above the basic level. In 2008, the Philadelphia school district leadership, citing poor performance, announced that it was revoking the contracts for the management of six schools that had failed to perform, and would be monitoring some twenty others for one year. The remainder were given new three-year contracts.[75] Peterson argues that the MOs were disadvantaged from the beginning since they were given the lowest-performing schools to manage and since there was very high teacher turnover in these schools.[76] This contention has some merit in that in state and school district policy, academic failure is the reason policy makers use to adopt private management strategies.[77] Thus, to prove their efficacy, MOs must serve academically struggling populations, which are often students of color whose families live in poverty, at least in urban contexts. In some respects, then, MOs can perpetuate long-standing patterns of racial and socioeconomic segregation in public education and potentially can exacerbate them, since as we have discussed, the MO sector is growing rapidly.[78] In short, the data on achievement and equity in the MO realm are complex, and much more study is needed to determine why such variability exists not only in the MO sector as a whole, but also within particular MO networks, such as KIPP or Uncommon Schools.

CONCLUSION: POLITICAL, NORMATIVE, AND DEMOCRATIC IMPLICATIONS OF MANAGEMENT ORGANIZATIONS

The question of how to evaluate the work of MOs remains unanswered by research and public debate. Given the Obama administration's commitment to developing "effective" charter schools, and given the substantial philanthropic support for MO-operated charter schools in selected urban school districts, the tensions around control, achievement, and MOs' and charter schools' roles in public education are likely to persist and grow. In a post-NCLB policy environment, student performance on standardized tests, and schools' progress in making AYP generally trumps other measures of effectiveness. And as the research has shown, thus far the MO sector has mixed results in this area. There are other standards, however, by which we might judge the value of MOs and their management of charter schools, even if these are muted by the high-stakes accountability rhetoric in the national and state capitols. These would include more normative considerations of how Americans would like their public institutions to be governed; how to consider levels of parent and student satisfaction; how to evaluate the impact of the MO sector on the professional life of teachers, students, and school leaders; the role of privatization of public services; and the relationship between the MO sector and racial segregation.

For example, in the area of governance, we argue that more attention is needed regarding the shifts in control over school policy and decision making that MOs seem to be heralding, issues over which there have long been struggles in American education. In 1990, John Chubb and Terry Moe argued in their influential critique of American public education that the problem plaguing schools was not that there was insufficient democracy governing them, but rather that there was too much; competing goals for schooling and the ensuing struggles over realizing them prevented schools from meeting anyone's preferences. In many ways, their vision for a marketized system of schooling has been realized through the intersection of charter schools and MOs in several urban districts. These trends have been coupled with mayoral control of school districts, in which corporate and market reforms often arrive in tandem.[79] And philanthropists are exerting unprecedented influence over the direction of reforms in many urban school districts.[80]

How democratic governance has fared under new institutional and managerial arrangements is unclear, but given the emphasis on scaling up and replicating particular school models, the space left for local decision making—for the teacher who has doubts that an instructional program is meeting her students' needs, for a parent who is unhappy with some aspect of school policy—appears diminished. Market advocates like Chubb and Moe might argue that teachers and parents expressed their democratic rights by choosing to work in the school or enroll their child there, but they are not to expect the school to conform to their whims. In the context of the growing numbers of MOs, the place and meaning of democratic governance of schools is clearly in flux.

Progressive policy analysts such as Paul Bauman have argued that "the central question in governance reform is interpreting the meaning of the word 'public' in public education. The public purposes of schooling require a democratic system of decision-making both as a means of school control and a demonstration of political values," but this iteration of school choice challenges this vision, long held by community-control advocates.[81] Future research will need to consider the following: Will the expansion and franchising of MOs create a new educational bureaucracy, supplanting the much-critiqued public one with a less transparent private one? Will market theory prove successful, and will low-performing schools be closed because of low consumer demand?

Other topics that warrant future research are the assumptions driving the expansion of the MO sector, that is, the arguments that it is possible and desirable to scale up and replicate or duplicate seemingly successful schools. While highly functioning public schools are certainly desired by most observers of U.S. public education, the definition of what constitutes a good school has always been contested across schools and school systems in America.[82] Ultimately, if the history of educational politics offers any lessons, while elites might primarily shape the broader policy context for charter schools and MOs, it will ultimately be parents, teachers, administrators, and local communities who will shape, implement, perhaps subvert, and determine the sustainability of the MO sector's involvement in public school reform.

CHAPTER 9

Information Use and Epidemics in Charter School Policy

Christopher A. Lubienski and Peter C. Weitzel

On June 4, 2009, Representative George Miller, Democrat from California's Seventh Congressional District and chairman of the House Education and Labor Committee convened a hearing titled "Building on What Works at Charter Schools." Noting that many of these schools are "laboratories of innovation," he lauded the movement for using "data-driven research and focusing relentlessly on results . . . These are models we can learn from to boost student achievement and improve accountability on a larger scale."[1] Addressing the audience of liberal charter school reformers, he went on to conclude:

> I think in fact the charter school movement . . . is rolling out as we had hoped it might. And that is that it would be on the cutting edge, that it would provide innovation, that it would give us an alternative model to look at, and hopefully it would give us the results that would encourage us to move in that direction in the district schools . . . [W]e ought to use this as a beacon and a lantern to show us the way on what we ought to expect and have a right to expect and what parents more importantly have a right to expect. These parents may be poor, but the waiting list suggests they're not stupid. They know what they want. They have the same instincts for their children as anybody, whether they live in the Palisades or East LA. The fact of the matter is that's what they want for their kids. They're lining up in the District of Columbia, they're lining all

over the country to ask for a better educational opportunity. I think the trick is to integrate this into the models in the district schools . . . to try to achieve the best outcomes for those children.[2]

But less than two weeks later, researchers just down the road from Miller's district, at Stanford University, released a multistate report on charter school achievement, finding that charter schools students are generally performing at a level similar to or significantly worse than if they had attended their local public school.[3] According to the researchers, almost half of the charter school students showed no difference in math, while 37 percent had lower gains than comparable students in public schools.

Representative Miller's comments suggest some disconnect between policy makers' beliefs about charter schools and the data on the schools' performance to date. Perhaps these differing conclusions would make sense if the Stanford report's findings represented a dramatically new understanding about the record of charter schools. But in fact, the Stanford study was just another in an extended series of research reports that have questioned the highly publicized potential of charter schools to reach the goals set out for them.

Like many advocates of expanded choice, Miller frames charter schools as successful experiments from which the broader educational system can learn. The long waiting lists for charter schools are cited as indications that charters are providing superior alternatives to local public schools. But is Miller wrong about the level of innovation and performance produced by charter schools? Are researchers failing to capture crucial attributes that make charter schools popular? Or are the policy makers and the parents who, as Miller notes, add their children to charter school waiting lists simply misinformed?

In this chapter, we examine the availability and use of information by parents and policy makers in the selection and regulation of charter schools. While expectations for charter schools often revolve around important issues such as student achievement, integration, and resources, the underlying presupposition that ties together such objectives for charter schools is the availability and use of information. Informational flows are crucial to charter school policy for two major reasons. First, inasmuch as charter schools are public policy experiments, policy makers need reliable information on performance to determine if the experiment should be expanded, ended, or altered and if lessons from it can be incorporated more broadly in existing public services. Second, many of the benefits of charter schools are expected to emerge from informed consumption in educational markets. More specifically, informed parents are thought to select higher-performing schools for their children, creating pressure on lower-performing schools to improve. (The competitive response of lower-performing schools also hinges on awareness of students' departure and their reasons for it—another informational issue.) At both the macro level of state and federal policy making and the microeconomic level of educational consumption, the idea of charter schools presumes the availability and use of quality information. And yet surprisingly little attention has been paid to how that information is produced and made available, and serious questions emerge as to whether such quality information is even used effectively.

So, quality information is crucial both (1) to ensure the smooth operation of markets and (2) to profit from the lessons of policy experiments. In markets for complex goods and services, producers often enjoy considerable informational advantages over consumers. Product information in many such markets is often regulated by public overseers to protect the interests of consumers. Since information on the quality and nature of educational services is both complex and relatively loosely regulated, it is important to determine what types of information are available to educational consumers and how they evaluate and act on it. On the issue of informed policy making, public policies that are fashioned without reference to data and past experience run the serious risk of reinventing the wheel or repeating the same mistakes as before. Public policy makers focused on education and interested in the efficient use of public resources presumably would refer to evidence on the effects of charter schools in advancing these programs. However, in this chapter, we show that information is not being produced and used as expected or needed for the optimal operation of charter markets and policy experiments. Indeed, we argue that informational problems are inherent in the market model for charters, and unfortunately, these pathologies are reflected in the policy movement advocating charters.

In fact, the reasons for the disuse and misuse of information in educational markets and educational policy making are both structural and political. In light of the initial expectations of charter advocates, this chapter describes the structural impediments to the effective production and distribution of information—impediments that are inherent in educational markets. Furthermore, we demonstrate that policy claims about the effectiveness of charter schools, which were used to advance these programs, are questionable at best when viewed from a research perspective. Instead of evidence-based policies, charters were championed by policy entrepreneurs and state and federal policy makers largely on assumptions about how these schools should work toward goals such as innovation, consumer satisfaction, and achievement. These assumptions were in large part drawn from other models and sectors. Efforts to tinker with regulations on information in education markets ignore some of the fundamental characteristics of such markets. Moreover, these efforts must attempt to straddle a basic tension between school autonomy for charters and mandated information requirements. On the whole, the idea of charter schools as a data-driven reform movement fueled by parental demand for higher-quality educational options is hard to sustain.

In the following section, we examine the purposes that were set out for the charter school movement by advocates and embraced and echoed by policy makers. These goals relied on assumptions about how market-style mechanisms would work in education. The predicted benefits of competition depended on the rational production and consumption of information by parents, practitioners, and policy makers. We then turn to the question of what information is actually known on charter schools, both in the popular perceptions of these schools and in the evidence available in research on these schools. We consider how both parents and policy makers actually use such information. In the concluding discussion, we examine the patterns of, and impediments to, the use of information on charter schools, noting the difficulties these obstacles may present to the movement. In particular, we highlight the viral nature of charter school expansion. The idea of rational consumers collecting and weighing evidence—on either school or policy options—appears to offer a very limited and somewhat flawed basis for charter school reforms, but that serious shortcoming has not preempted the rapid proliferation of this movement.

THE ENDS AND MEANS OF CHARTER SCHOOLS

Although charter school policies vary considerably between states, there is actually a notable consensus on the central goals for these schools. As the movement expanded, policy makers in different states embraced goals from legislative templates that reflect the early purposes set out for charter schools. For instance, in his widely cited primer on charter schools, early advocate Joe Nathan offered a model of charter school legislation that specified the following goals:

1. Improve student learning.
2. Encourage the use of different and innovative learning and teaching methods.
3. Increase choice of learning opportunities for pupils.
4. Establish a new form of accountability for public schools.
5. Require the measurement of learning and create more effective, innovative measurement/assessment tools.
6. Make the school the unit for improvement.
7. Create new professional opportunities for teachers, including the opportunity to own the learning program at the school site. [4]

Nathan also notes that these goals are not just aimed at charter schools, but are instead intended to drive "systemic change—about the state creating the dynamics that will make the system a self-improving system." These purposes for schools were also adopted by the American Legislative Exchange Council in its template for charter school legislation.[5] They also appear in the authorizing legislation of most states, as well as in the advocacy materials for national charter school groups.[6]

A closer look at these goals indicates that information is a core consideration for charter school policy to be successful. Questions of student learning, school improvement, measurement and assessment are all based in the assumption that data will be produced and utilized. Likewise, goals such as innovation and choice require information for individuals considering different alternatives. Most notably, charter schools create "a new form of accountability for public schools," which thereby necessitates two distinct paths for information production and consumption. First, like other public schools, charter schools are accountable to a public entity such as a district or another authorizing body. However, that form of governmental accountability is transformed by the charter, which can be renewed or revoked, depending on how well a charter school is performing—a question that presumes that accurate information will be produced for the governing body. Indeed, it is not only the authorizer, but also policy makers themselves who expressed interest in such data; some states established small charter schools programs specifically as pilot programs, and often included evaluation components for the programs in their state to examine evidence of their effectiveness.[7] Second, as schools of choice, charters are responsible to their choosers, creating a consumer-centered form of accountability that is also evident in other markets that depend on the availability of information to prospective consumers.

The expanded use of quality information has generally not been explicitly stated as a core goal of the charter school movement. Rather, rational information use is a necessary precondition for achieving the more publicized goals such as greater innovation and achievement. For instance, consider the latter of these two goals. Raising student achievement is often seen as an ultimate goal for charter schools, as outlined both in individual charters and in the movement as a whole.[8] In contrast to traditional public schools that can rely on residence-based attendance zones, charters, as schools of choice, must strive to attract and satisfy families. The primary means for appealing to parents was to be through offering a more effective academic experience than the assigned public school.[9] Therefore, an essential element of this equation is information on school effectiveness, or at least relative performance, not to mention information on curriculum and instruction for parents looking to find a match between school programs and their child's learning style.

Mechanisms of Parental Choice

While we discuss here the mechanisms by which this information would be produced and distributed, it is important to emphasize that a dearth of solid information on schools would cripple a system that relies on rational choices to drive organizational improvement. Actionable information put in the hands of consumers can encourage them to consider the exit option and can thereby induce schools to improve. In fact, consumer preferences for higher-quality schools not only are intended to cause charter schools to offer superior academic programs, but—as Nathan noted—were expected to drive public schools to improve as well.

Expectations for improved achievement in both charter schools and traditional public schools through competition for students places even greater demands on the flow and consumption of information. In these models, public school improvements in achievement will emerge from a cascade of events linked by rational responses to information. First, parents must select higher-achieving schools when they exit public schools. Then, public schools must be aware of the departure of students to these schools and the reasons for it. Feeling pressure to stem the loss of students or risk closure by superiors, the public schools will improve their performance, convincing families to remain in their school or perhaps even return to it. This chain of events depends not just on the availability of good information but also on the consumption and strategic use of it by the parties involved. If families lack information on the availability of quality school programs, schools then would lose the incentive to support such programs, especially if other methods are more readily available for attracting students.

In fact, early supporters of charter schools apparently were quite convinced that parents would use such information in choosing charter schools (or others) for their children. Drawing on a *rational-choice model* from economics, advocates argued that "improved student achievement is one of the major reasons the charter movement continues to grow," since, without evidence of superior academic growth, parents would choose other alternatives to a failing charter school.[10] This would presumably then lead to expansions in enrollment, as the Little Hoover Commission predicted: "Charter schools may grow rapidly as word-of-mouth information spreads and more students enroll."[11] The *New York Times* summarized the logic:

> For the supporters of charter schools, the issues are choice and competition. Consumers—parents with school-age children—will enjoy the freedom to choose between charter and public schools, and any choice, it is reasoned, is better than no choice. And letting charter schools compete with public schools will presumably cause public schools to work harder; in districts with low-performing public schools, charter schools will either displace them or force genuine improvement. Implicit in this assumption is a classic free-market notion: that perfect consumers having perfect information will abandon failing public schools for promising charter schools.[12]

So this expectation was often framed in contrast to the situation in public education in general. In a public school monopoly, a lack of choice meant there were no incentives for schools to provide information on their effectiveness, nor for families to gather information on schools—a problem noted by a number of charter school advocates who saw lack of information as an obstacle to the growth of the movement.[13] Moreover, a few noted that the information that was available tended to be inequitably distributed among families.[14]

But even as charter school advocates criticized the lack of information to support choice in the public sector, they were not always terribly specific about how such information would be generated in the emerging charter sector. Most advocates evidently assumed that market mechanisms that underlie the charter sector would also serve to address any informational issues around charter schools—as Paul Hill wrote, "After a few years, private information providers will probably fill the need."[15] Only a few choice proponents have explicitly considered this challenge. Theorists such as Herbert Walberg and Joseph Bast concur on the role of independent organizations (such as Consumer Reports) in generating information, but also point to the importance of earned trust, advertising, and experience.[16] In fact, many advocates and policy makers have argued that charters would inject competition into the public sector, and presumably this would include competitive strategies around information.[17] Most importantly, advocates assume that market incentives would encourage consumers to act on their self-interest to seek out information on different school options, even as producers would have the competitive incentive to produce information on their effectiveness or be punished by consumers. Even when many families fail to actively search for schools on the basis of evidence of their academic effectiveness, economic theory holds that a critical mass of engaged consumers who seek out information on school quality may be enough to drive quality improvements for all.[18]

Information and Policy Making

The idea of using data to improve policy making is perhaps even less articulated around charter schools, but at least as important as the goal of generating information for parents choosing schools. In fact, the logic of utilizing data on the effects of charter schools is integral to the charter school idea, which has always been intended both as an experimental element within the public school sector and a policy alternative to traditional district-run schools. Indeed, the policy goals for charters in this respect have gone through three stages, all of which are premised on the availability of information on charter school effects. In all three cases, data on individual and aggregate school performance, innovations, and other outcomes are necessary to understand how these schools work relative to other policy alternatives. Again, as with parent choices, a lack of information can severely hinder effective policy making.

The conception of charter schools as an experimental unit within the larger public schools sector first goes back to the earliest iterations of the idea. Education leaders and reformers such as Ray Budde and Al Shanker advanced the notion of charter schools as small-scale innovations in governance where groups of teachers could contract with a district for the opportunity to try something new or different and then be evaluated on the results.[19] Thus, rather than assessing the movement as a whole, the main focus was on evaluating the specific program that had received the charter.

But this conception changed dramatically as the charter movement was scaled up. Advocates highlighted in particular the potential for the charter school sector to serve as research and development (R&D) centers for the whole of public education. According to Bruno Manno and his colleagues, then notable champions of charter schools at the Hudson Institute, a "major purpose of the charter movement, we believe, is to inspire the development of innovative and effective approaches to education throughout the public school . . . This R & D potential is an important part of any policy-oriented appraisal of the charter phenomenon."[20] In the logic characterizing this second phase, charter school educators would have the opportunity to try "different and innovative" approaches because the schools were not impeded by the regulations believed to stifle innovation. Other schools would then be able to adopt the innovative practices that charters developed. This model, including the diffusion of new practices among schools, depends on the availability of information on the effects of charter schools in areas such as innovation, organizational practices, and achievement. Charter advocates such as the Center for Education Reform's Jeanne Allen continue to promote the notion that policy makers will draw on such data.[21]

More recently, especially during the Bush and Obama administrations, charter schools have been singled out as part of a federal policy package emphasizing "what works" in education. While the Clinton administration strongly supported charter schools, it was Bush's No Child Left Behind (NCLB) legislation that first treated charter school organizations as an effective remedy to ailing public schools. The law mandates "scientifically based" interventions for chronic educational failure and establishes conversion to charter status as one of the corrective measures for schools that fall short of improvement goals. NCLB certainly creates a data-rich environment, but the point is not simply that parents have more information on school options, including charter schools, or that policy makers use the law to create systems to gather data—although that is true, too. Instead, it is also important to emphasize that policy makers essentially equated charter schools with policies that have a scientific- or evidence-based grounding. The Obama administration has embraced this view, although there is some inconsistency in whether it supports all charter schools, or only so-called successful charter schools, as an effective intervention—a distinction that again requires that good information be made available for policy makers.[22]

WHAT DO WE KNOW ABOUT CHARTER SCHOOLS?

Given these stated and unstated assumptions about how charter schools would be situated in, and nurtured by, information-rich environments and how these data would in turn be utilized by parents and policy makers, then what is actually known about charter schools in this respect? In addressing this question, we must distinguish between conventional wisdom in popular discussions, as with popular and advocacy media, and research evidence.[23] As we indicate later, the disconnect between the two discourses is quite illuminating.

Common Wisdom

In the popular discourse, as well as in much of the advocacy literature, the rapid expansion of charter schools and their attractiveness for parents is ample evidence of their effectiveness. Although there is still much widespread confusion as to what charter schools are, many commentators point to lengthy waiting lists of students seeking admission to charter schools as an indication that people with the most intimate knowledge of schools reveal a preference for charters.[24] But for better or for worse—and perhaps contributing to their attractiveness—charters are also widely (and erroneously) believed to be exclusive private schools than can select students and charge tuition.[25] Many of these views appear to be supported by statements in the popular media from charter advocates.[26] In that way, many public figures often implicitly endorse themes about the academic superiority of charter schools, which may consequently buttress popular, if mistaken, impressions.

Likewise, policy makers from across the political spectrum have strongly embraced the expectations for improved competition, achievement, and innovation in charter schools. For instance, President Obama pointed to charter schools in arguing that "it's important to foster competition inside the public schools."[27] Pointing to the notable growth in charter schools' market share and the effects of competition on public schools, many policy makers have called for lifting state-level caps on charters.[28] In doing so, they affirm the rational-choice assumption that parents have the best information on educational options for their children.[29] In this regard, state limits on charter schools are seen as an unwarranted imposition by policy makers, with inherently imperfect information, over the preferences of informed consumers. According to this logic, informed parents can more effectively force schools to improve than can expertise-driven policy making. As Bush's secretary of education argued, "parents armed with information and options are the most powerful advocates for quality education."[30]

However, the commonly cited wisdom about charter schools differs in some significant ways from the research findings. These findings offer some interesting contrasts in the areas of information availability and use for parents and policy makers.

Research Evidence on Parents and Information

For education markets to function effectively, there must be useful sources of information available to parents, who act as proxy consumers on behalf of their children.[31] Although most choosers believe they have sufficient information to make good choices, even some charter advocates are now observing that the charter sector is not generating the consumer information necessary for the smooth operation of an education market.[32]

A small but growing body of research has examined how parents use available information to make school choices. This work tends to challenge the most idealized concepts of the rational chooser, although there are some indications that lowering information costs can lead to increased emphasis on school effectiveness.[33] On one hand, surveys consistently find that academic quality is by far the highest stated priority for parents who are selecting schools.[34] Charter parents also pursue more sources of information and place greater importance on academic concerns, particularly when exiting charter schools.[35] Eric Hanushek and colleagues also find, however, that school-quality issues were more important to higher-income families in charter schools.[36] Charter school parents were also somewhat more likely to speak to administrators, emphasize written materials, attend school fairs, and believe that their children have important or unique personal characteristics that should influence school selection.[37] However, parents' actual decisions may rely heavily on other factors, including those that parents may not wish to state openly.

The emerging field of behavioral law and economics (BLE) critiques the rational-choice model in school selection.[38] BLE has identified numerous shortcuts, heuristics, and biases in the real-world decision making of consumers. These information imperfections, which can include biases in favor of privately acquired information and shortcuts based on seemingly representative characteristics, often increase the role of social capital and socioeconomic status in decision making. Numerous studies have found that race—rather than simply academic effectiveness—appears to influence parents' selection of schools or their development of short lists of realistic options.[39] Although parents rarely acknowledge that race is an important factor, their revealed preferences in seeking information on Web sites suggests otherwise.[40] In fact, parents who were more educated were actually more likely to look at demographics, and there was no evidence that school performance shaped the narrowing of parents' searches. A school's racial composition seems to be a factor that parents deem to be reflective of school quality. For white parents, schools with high minority populations are regarded as academically inferior, even when achievement data refute such conclusions.[41] Race is also a key factor for minority parents. In general, parents tend to prefer schools where their children will be in the racial majority.[42] Studies of school enrollment shifts in Arizona and North Carolina, although not directly examining parental decision making, likewise suggest that families are seeking schools where they will be in the racial majority, sometimes at the expense of school effectiveness.[43]

Biases in favor of information that is readily available or personally acquired play considerable roles in parents' school selection. Word of mouth and common knowledge is consistently cited as one of the common and trusted sources of information for choosers.[44] Although written materials are often consulted, parents tend to place greater value on the soft information they get from peers and from direct contact with teachers and school leaders.[45] Although all racial groups depend heavily on this soft information, white parents often trust information from their personal networks more, while minority parents often place greater trust in school officials. Parents rely heavily on their social networks to identify short lists of schools and make choices. Since social networks tend to be racially and socioeconomically segregated and families that are more affluent have greater social capital, these information biases can limit the overlap in schools that are realistically considered among different types of parents. Choice sets, which are usually limited to two or three schools, tend to be heavily influenced by geographic, racial, and socioeconomic factors.[46] White parents and more educated parents tend to consult wider social networks and are less likely to choose primarily on the basis of location. Choosers of higher socioeconomic status are also more likely to find "market mavens" who often possess detailed knowledge of local options.[47]

Based on Web site usage, parents do examine school achievement data, but not at rates that would be predicted by survey results on parental priorities.[48] Also, low-income parents tend to place less weight on academic issues in school selection, and there are some indications that parents have difficulty obtaining or interpreting achievement data.[49] Justine Hastings and Jeffrey Weinstein conducted an experiment in the Charlotte education market in which lower-income families were provided with direct, simplified achievement information.[50] Charlotte parents, who can select three school preferences for their kids, normally had to search district Web sites to obtain achievement information, and school comparisons had to be done manually. The district later sent test information directly to parents with students at NCLB-sanctioned schools, and researchers also sent simplified achievement data to parents with children in randomly selected schools. Both of these forms of information increased the proportion of parents who selected higher-scoring schools for their kids. Geographic proximity to high-scoring schools nonetheless remained an important predictor of selecting alternative schools. It seems that reducing the search costs for obtaining achievement data can help facilitate better decision making by parents, but mere knowledge of school achievement alone will not trump geographic constraints and other preferences.

Also important, the achievement data available in the vast majority of cases are measures of proficiency, rather than student growth. Thus, even if parents have ready access to achievement information and use it in their school selection, they are not necessarily selecting more effective schools or generating positive competitive pressure for school improvement. As of the 2007–2008 school year, eleven states had received approval from the U.S. Department of Education to implement pilot growth models for school accountability. Although some states have had longitudinal data for multiple years, school achievement reports from states, districts, and independent information providers like Greatschools.org still primarily present proficiency rates. Some commentators have expressed concern that longitudinal data, even when available, will be difficult to understand for many parents.[51]

New York City public schools have implemented a sophisticated longitudinal assessment system that examines student gains, attendance, and parental satisfaction and compares a school with other schools with similar demographics. This approach produces an A through F rating that should be understandable for virtually any parent, but this simplicity has not prevented and may even exacerbate controversy over the ratings, particularly when they fly in the face of more popular sentiment. Many times, well-reputed schools that have been attracting middle-class families received low ratings due to poor student growth, befuddling parents.[52] Often, parents and school leaders have responded by asserting the importance of softer indicators of school success like parent satisfaction and school environment. There are also major discrepancies with other school ratings. Schools deemed "failing" according to proficiency rates or listed as "dangerous" due to violence reports have nonetheless received As for achievement growth.[53] These discrepancies and the relative volatility of school ratings from year to year may be eroding confidence in the rating system among both parents and school leaders.

Overall, the evidence on parents' use of information calls into question the idealized rational-choice model of the education consumer. Although information on school quality is intended to drive parent choices and school improvement, problems with the production, availability, and consumption of information, as well as biases and what rational choice theorists would see as irrational behavior on the part of parents, seriously compromises that model. Although advocates have explored some mechanisms that can nudge consumers into focusing on the information that advocates have deemed necessary to promote charter school and system-wide improvements, major obstacles still hinder parents' effective use of information in school selection.

Research Evidence and Charter School Policy Making

The questions raised by research on parents' access to and use of information on school options are not necessarily evident in the advocacy discourse; nor are they obvious if one examines recent education policy making in these areas. Indeed, there are several areas where charter school policy making, often bipartisan, appears to be at odds with the information available from research. In fact, the record of charter schools around three key goals to the movement—effectiveness, innovation, and equitable access—would appear to conflict with policy-making trends around charter schools and challenges assumptions about how policy makers obtain and use information on charter schools. This raises questions about the relationship of policy making and research evidence on charters, the production and availability of information for policy makers, and how policy makers use research evidence.

Of course, there has been much theorizing and modeling on how policy is made.[54] Because of the varied and often opaque nature of state-level policy making on this question, few researchers have delved deeply into how policy making around charter schools has used data. We look here at the available research information on the policies that are produced at a given point in time.

In fact, charter schools expanded very rapidly starting in the early to mid-1990s as more states adopted charter school legislation. Although there are significant differences between the laws in some states, there are also remarkable similarities in some areas, such as the purposes legislators assigned to charters.[55] As noted above, many of the purposes reflect the list set out in the original Minnesota law, which was then promulgated in the model legislation in Joe Nathan's book.[56] The list was also adopted by the American Legislative Exchange Council in its legislative template for lawmakers working on education issues.[57]

In view of this consensus among policy makers on the purpose of charter schools, the rapid expansion of this policy approach would likely indicate compelling information on its success on the goals that they set out. Particularly in an era where policy makers call for "scientifically based" or "data-driven" decisions, one might expect that lawmakers in different states embraced charter schools after seeing evidence of their success on these key goals. In fact, the expansion of charter schools largely predated any research evidence—positive or negative—on their effectiveness, and as the research record did accumulate, it hardly provided the strong, empirical basis one might expect for a policy approach so popular with lawmakers.

Figure 9-1 is a timeline of the expansion of charter schools. It shows, by year, the number of states with laws authorizing charter schools, along with the total number of charters that started during the period when laws were spreading across states. Table 9-1 summarizes the main findings of reports on charter school achievement during that time. Note that although there have been many reports over time—and lest we be accused of cherry-picking certain studies—we summarize here only the research identified by leading charter school advocacy groups as rigorous or useful for examining the performance of charter schools.[58]

Well over half the states adopting charter laws did so even before any real research was available on the record of these schools regarding achievement. And when such research became available, as charter laws continued to spread across the states, the bulk of those studies found mixed, minimal, or even negative academic outcomes for charter schools. As charters expanded, the vast majority of the studies available found those schools performing at a level equal to or lower than other (often demographically comparable) public schools in terms of academic outcomes. Although a few studies find that charter schools may be making up ground over time, about the same number of studies find that gains in charters are statistically equal to or lower than those in other public schools.

FIGURE 9-1   Number of charter schools and states with charter school laws by year

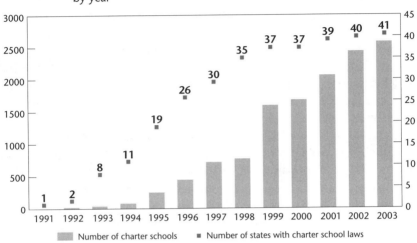

Year	Report and observations*
1998	**TX Center for Ed. Research:** 40% of TX charters scored at acceptable or higher, compared with 91% of publics. **MA Dept. of Ed.:** MA charter students equal to or beneath public students, although some potential for gains. **WI Leg. Audit Bureau:** mixed results, but early data are incomplete. **WestED:** Charter academic growth in Los Angeles is similar to publics. **Clayton Foundation:** CO charters participating in the study outscored state average in 4th grade writing.
1999	**MA Charter School Resource Center:** Initial performance of MA charter about average or slightly better. **Mulholland:** AZ charter gains are similar to publics, but better data needed. **Public Sector Consultants:** MI charters perform at level lower than public schools, but some are gaining ground. **Clayton Foundation:** CO charters participating in the study outscored host districts and state in Grades 3, 4, and 7.
2000	**Miron & Nelson:** PA charter scored significantly lower than public schools in host districts and state. **Horn & Miron:** MI charters clearly underperform relative to host district. **Whitt:** Disadvantaged students in TX charters more likely to fail. **Clayton Foundation:** CO charter participating in the study outscored host district and state in grades 3, 4, and 7.

Year	Report and observations
2000	**Miron & Nelson:** PA charter scored significantly lower than public schools in host districts and state.
	Horn & Miron: MI charters clearly underperform relative to host district.
	Whitt: Disadvantaged students in TX charters more likely to fail.
	CO State DOE: CO charter participating in the study outscored host district and state in grades 3, 4, and 7.
2001	**Gronberg & Jansen:** Negative effect of TX charters on academic achievement except for at-risk students
	Noblit & Dickson: Students in NC charters less likely to be proficient, and more likely to make similar gains.
	Henig et al.: DC students in charters much more likely to be behind, less likely to see gains.
2002	**Hanushek, Kain, & Rivkin:** TX charter gains are lower or not significantly different.
	Miron & Horn: CT charters score lower at first, but surpass districts scores after 4-5 years.
	Miron & Nelson: Fewer MI charter students reaching proficiency compared with public school students.
	Miron et al.: PA charter students score beneath other students although gains may be greater.
	Eberts & Hollenbeck: MI charter students score significantly behind.
	Miron & Nelson: IL charters slightly beneath similar publics.
2003	**Greene et al.:** "General population" charters have slightly higher performance than nearby publics (*although many data are inexplicably missing*).
	Loveless: Charters have lower achievement, but may make greater gains.
	NY State: NY charter students behind, but often had greater gains.
	Raymond: CA charters behind publics, gains similar.
	Rogosa: CA charters behind publics, gains similar.
	Slovacek et al.: Slightly faster growth in CA charters.
	Zimmer et al.: No statistical difference between gains in CA charters and publics.
	CO State DoE: CO charters outperformed publics in early grades, but fell behind in later grades.
	OH leg.: OH charters performing beneath publics.

*Sources for this table are located in the notes section of this book.

Of course, in using this representation we had to be overly general in summarizing what are sometime sophisticated studies with complex findings in different contexts—studies that include caveats, have weaknesses, and are open to methodological challenges. For example, early studies often focused on one of only a handful of states—several were on Colorado—and they used methodological approaches so primitive as to tell us virtually nothing.[59] There are also a number of early studies that were essentially descriptive, with no analysis of charter school outcomes, and thus they are not included here, although those studies often documented the popularity of the schools with parents, reformers, and policy makers.[60]

Still, despite the limitations of these generalizations, this summary of studies that were highlighted by charter advocacy organizations offers a sense of the research consensus, as it were, when state lawmakers proposed and adopted charter schools. Most laws were implemented even before the first studies became available, and the record over the first decade was less than compelling. Yet, even as news reports at the time noted the disappointing research findings on the mediocre achievement record of charter schools, policy publications often still emphasized the potential benefits of charters.[61] When such advocates did pay attention to the research, it was often as apologists: to argue that comparisons with public schools are inaccurate, since the schools serve different populations; that older charter schools may be more effective; or that charter schools may show greater gains (of course, one would expect greater gains in lower-performing schools). Some valid points in these concerns reflect the youthful state of research around charter schools in the first decade of the movement (for both positive and negative findings). Nevertheless, several more sophisticated, comprehensive, and rigorous peer-reviewed studies examining national and state-level data have since demonstrated that charters are often underperforming relative to public schools, even when differences in student populations are considered.[62]

And while student achievement is often the most evident goal for charter schools, research on other key purposes set out for these schools also raises questions about how intensively policy makers considered empirical information in embracing this movement. For instance, charter schools were intended to create innovations throughout education, not only in governance—indeed, charter schools are themselves a policy innovation—but also in learning and teaching methods in the classroom. Although various studies have noted the remarkable record of charters in introducing organizational innovations such as marketing and employment arrangements, an established consensus in the research contends that charter schools are no more innovative (and at times less so) than other public schools in terms of changing classroom practice—even as policy makers continue to hold up these "innovative schools."[63] Another widely understood goal for charters was to open up choice of learning opportunities for different students, especially disadvantaged students trapped by the boundaries of failing schools and districts. Yet the question has always lingered as to whether unleashing market-style choice would lead to greater integration or segregation.[64] As is now readily apparent from high-quality research studies (see chapters 2 and 3 in this book), the actual evidence from charter schools is less than encouraging.

CAN INFORMATION DRIVE EFFECTIVE CHARTER SCHOOL GROWTH?

All of this is not to say that charter schools in general are failing or that we see little potential for this prolific reform. But policy making around charters appears to have failed to consider the important differences between theoretical assumptions about how markets in education should work and actual evidence about how they do work. Indeed, research highlights the disjuncture between evidence and policy making in this area. The idea of stakeholders making policy based on evidence of program effectiveness seems to have little support in this case, as does the idea of charters as a policy experiment—where policy makers sought and even required data collection on charter school outcomes.[65]

In fact, the contrast between the optimism and enthusiastic rhetoric of charter advocates and evidence on the actual behavior of information consumers is quite apparent. Charter advocacy advanced from a strong and compelling theory about how individuals and organizations would respond to competitive incentives by producing or collecting information. Yet serious problems appear to exist around these theoretical assumptions. Early charter advocates assumed that parents would seek out the best education for their children using empirical measures of school quality. While that happens to some extent, even charter advocates are now acknowledging the problems with that assumption in view of considerable evidence that many parents make choices that would not be predicted by rational-choice assumptions regarding their behavior. For instance, the assumption that parents would leave demonstrably failing schools (charter or public schools) for better options and that the failing schools would then "go out of business" due to market discipline has just not materialized. Too often, there are waiting lists for bad schools.[66] Although parents may pursue considerations other than academic quality, the failure to punish schools for poor academic effectiveness threatens the very idea of charters as a force to drive systemic change throughout the public school sector. Thus, some charter advocates and others have lamented that parents are simply misinformed."[67]

But the remedies for this situation are not obvious, since informational asymmetries—advantages in knowledge about products and services for service providers—are built into charter markets. School productive processes are inherently difficult to observe, so consumers must rely instead on proxy data on school inputs and outcomes.[68] These imperfections in information give producers an advantage over consumers, so consumers get information largely from sources such as marketing produced by schools or virally through word of mouth in social networks with other consumers. These sources are problematic, though—often unreliable and unequally distributed. This does not necessarily mean that the rational-choice model is useless. Since information on school effectiveness is opaque, but peer effects may have a strong influence on a child's performance and later earnings, it may be a rational decision for parents to shop for peers for their children. Thus, unfortunately, parents may choose schools not because of school effects but on the basis of obvious information like the social characteristics of other choosers, leading to student sorting (see chapter 3, this volume).

Reformers seek to address these concerns through information centers or by requiring certain data from schools. This approach produces a basic tension in the charter model between encouraging school autonomy and generating useful information from consumers. Charter schools have an incentive to hoard information—not only data that might cast them in a less favorable light, but also information on new innovations they develop (but which, policy makers then assumed, the schools would share with their competitors). Even when information is legally mandated from producers to address inadequate sharing of information, there is no guarantee that consumers will understand or use it, as the recent subprime mortgage mess demonstrates.

If parents often get information on schools virally through social networks, the same may be even more true for policy makers, as indicated by the spread of charter school legislation before any empirical evidence of charter effectiveness (or ineffectiveness) was ever available. Indeed, without making any judgments on the merits of charter schools, a simple examination of the pace and extent to which charter authorizing laws were adopted in the United States is reminiscent of how viruses spread exponentially across a population. Policy makers appear to have embraced charters for their theoretical potential—an attractive and compelling idea that led to replication across states. And this viral policy thrived in a fertile policy environment that nurtured neoliberal ideas about rolling back the state, contracting with private providers, and moving power to service users. Yet actual evidence of charter schools' effectiveness was and is lagging. Indeed, advocacy for charter expansion continues and is sustained by advocacy networks in states where charters are demonstrably inferior to other schools.[69] Therefore, instead of drawing on hard data from rigorous research, policy makers may turn instead to reports from advocacy organizations such as the Center for Education Reform and the National Alliance for Public Charter Schools. Yet, as agenda-driven organizations, the reports that these types of groups offer should be very suspect. Indeed, even though it is often presented as research, it is often seriously flawed in how the information is collected, analyzed, and presented.

In summary, there is a marked contrast between the assumptions and optimism around the notion of charters as an empirically based reform mechanism fueling competitive incentives and the actual evidence on information production, distribution, and consumption at both the user and the policy levels. This is not to say that charters shouldn't expand or that there is no evidence of their benefits. Our analysis should not be read as a critique of charter schools themselves—we agree that the charter idea holds much potential. Instead, this chapter describes problems with the policy conceptualization of charter schools as market entities whose improvement is driven by consumer-style information use. Even as this idea for charters spread in an epidemic-like manner in the last two decades, policy makers have largely failed to address serious pathologies built into the movement as a reform model, which may seriously hinder the ability of charters to drive wider systemic reform.

Assessing the Charter School Experiment

Peter C. Weitzel and Christopher A. Lubienski

The last two presidential administrations have placed a strong rhetorical emphasis on examining "what works" in evaluating and promoting policies. At the same time, both Barack Obama and George W. Bush—as well as Bill Clinton before them—have actively advanced charter schools through federal funding initiatives, as well as through requiring conversion to charter status for failing schools under No Child Left Behind (NCLB) and Race to the Top programs. This makes sense, since charter schools represent an exciting and perhaps seminal development on the American educational landscape as the country increasingly turns away from older models of educational organization. They have proliferated rapidly across the United States, are popular with parents, and are enjoying a uniquely bipartisan following in an era of bitter ideological rancor. Simply in the light of those facts, one might assume that charter schools work. But the evidence indicates that the question is considerably more complex than this simplistic standard would suggest.

This volume was motivated by the need to focus the best thinking in this area for understanding what is and what is not working as we enter the third decade of charter schools. Some of the best-established and rising new researchers in the country were asked to synthesize the existing knowledge around key aspects of these schools, looking specifically at the expectations for charter schools on various dimensions, how they are addressing those objectives, and their potential to fulfill their promise on values central to American public education. Yet Americans' tendency to hold multiple and sometimes conflicting goals for their schools presents some quandaries in determining "what works, since policy makers often fail to identify the specific ends they seek for reforms such as this.[1] Are charter schools simply intended to expand the range of choices available to parents? Or are we hoping to create incentives that raise the overall quality of educational options for children? Do charter schools represent an attempt to bring greater efficiencies to public education? Or do the increasing demands for funding parity with other public schools reflect a shift in goals toward equitable inputs, if not outcomes? Are charter schools meeting the expectation for innovation through their phenomenal record in creating new partnerships and governance arrangements? Or should we expect to see dramatic developments in classroom practice as well?

While the answers to many of these questions are still disputed, as the contributions to this volume demonstrate, there is indeed now an established empirical record with which to assess what works and what is not working, and why. Although there are still disputes about interpreting particular studies and trends, the overall picture is pretty clear that charter schools are no panacea for the ills that afflict the larger public education enterprise. Although we have seen some bright spots and some stellar schools in the charter movement, after two decades, the movement as a whole has so far failed to live up to the early expectations that drove its expansion, especially on the central issues that we noted in the beginning of this volume (and discuss further below).[2]

But aside from supporting evidence from the research, charter schools still represent a powerful idea, both for policy makers and for parents. The rapid spread of charter schools across the country, and the many waiting lists of families hoping to enroll their children in these schools, stand as testaments to the compelling nature of the idea, even if the evidence of the schools' effectiveness is less than compelling. Parents want educational alternatives, especially to low-performing public schools. And policy makers have been actively pursuing alternatives to district-administered educational schemes in a number of nations for some time now. The charter school movement is perhaps the most successful example of this policy strategy. Despite any apparent shortcomings, we have no doubt that charter schools will be a prominent fixture on the educational landscape for some time to come.

Still, the gap between the expectations and the evidence, between the remarkable growth and the research record on charter schools, raises some intriguing questions about the role of research and program popularity in policy making. Here we briefly summarize the central goals set out for charter schools and highlight the main findings from the research, as noted in this book. Then, we offer some concluding comments that may be of useful for researchers and policy makers working on this topic.

ACCESS, INNOVATION, AND COMPETITION

Discussions about whether charter schools work typically revolve around the most obvious academic outcomes such as test scores, graduation rates, or college attendance. However, the nuanced and retrospective examination presented in this volume notes that the original goals set out for charter schools focused not only on these most apparent concerns, but also on other, more subtle questions of internal processes such as innovation, secondary effects such as the competitive impacts on neighboring public schools, and institutional relationships such as partnerships with new stakeholders. In looking over the outcomes anticipated for charter schools noted at the beginning of this book, we discerned three main areas of expectations for charter schools: equity of access, competition, and innovation—criteria by which the successes and shortcomings of charter schools could be measured.

While there is a constant refrain of researchers reporting mixed results when studying a policy intervention—particularly a social policy—in some ways, that conclusion is quite useful when applied to charter schools. In fact, in terms of the goals originally set out for charter schools, the evidence indicates that these schools have still largely failed to reach the optimistic objectives set out by reformers.

In innovation, charter schools have largely failed to meet the sky-high expectations, at least in the ways initially set out for them by many advocates. Instead, they appear to have made advances in innovation in other ways, suggesting that the goals may be shifting. Of the three major goals for charters discussed here, research on this topic has perhaps reached more definitive conclusions than have the examinations of competitive effects and equity of access. While there is a consensus that the track record of charter schools developing classroom innovations is far from the original expectations of advocates, charter schools have produced some remarkable organizational innovations in areas such as partnerships and governance arrangements.

The literature on competitive effects suggests that charter schools may not be the high-performing catalysts for system-wide improvements that some proponents expected. The record on achievement is mixed, with most of the best evidence showing results similar to or somewhat below those of other public schools. And even the most favorable studies tend to show modest results that fall far short of the optimistic predictions of early advocates. After almost two decades of the charter school experiment, it is still far from clear that these schools are "doing more with less." However, some commentators argue that the jury is still out, because large-scale benefits from competition will only emerge when a large proportion of parents in a particular market are actively choosing schools. In this view, it is impossible to fully assess the potential of competition for students, since the vast majority of local education markets have not reached a point where active school selection is the norm rather than the exception.

The argument that charter schools will create greater equity of educational access is perhaps the most difficult to assess. From one perspective, any expansion of schooling options for families could be seen as an end in itself. In this sense, the removal of many enrollment regulations through charter schools has allowed many families greater freedom to pursue their private interests. On the other hand, the mere existence of expanded schooling options in a metropolitan area does not mean they are readily accessible for the most disadvantaged families. School location, marketing strategies, unequal access to information by parents, and demands on parental involvement can often make charter schools more accessible to middle-class families. While there has not been the massive white flight to charter schools that some skeptics predicted, evidence on student enrollment patterns animates continued concerns about charter schools' potential to further segregate American society.

Despite this mixed and perhaps disappointing assessment, charter schools are enjoying considerable successes in other areas. Their obvious popularity with parents and policy makers speaks to the demand for alternatives to assigned public schools and tuition-charging private schools in many areas of the country. And the high profile they enjoy in policy circles highlights the effectiveness of charter proponents in advancing efforts to remake public education. In fact, rather than measuring their success in terms of the original goals set out for them, proponents appear to be pleased simply by gauging the annual growth in the number of charter schools in the United States, increases in the number of students enrolled in charters, or the level of satisfaction reported by parents with children still in these schools. While these are all laudable objectives, they are not necessarily the ultimate goals laid out for the charter school movement. And policy makers have to consider whether enlarging the movement and pleasing a group of stakeholders, rather than creating innovative approaches and mechanisms to generate system-wide improvements, is a sufficient goal.

Although charter schools as a movement have still not met many of their original objectives after almost two decades of operation, the shift of charter school objectives strongly suggests that the movement has staying power and is likely to become a permanent fixture on the American educational landscape. A shift in goals indicates a flexible movement with some degree of political acumen. Moreover, the charter school movement exhibits many of the characteristics associated with sustainable reforms that have successfully survived an education system famously resistant to change.[3] For instance, charter schools have developed their own constituency of parents, policy makers, and other stakeholders. These groups push for continued and expanded support and are unlikely to stand by and watch the movement shrink or disappear. Moreover, charter schools may enhance, rather than replace, existing educational governance structures. That is, they may challenge district monopolies, but the actual integrity of district governance appears to be intact, with charters acting as new forms of districts without geographical boundaries. As groups of charters become more institutionalized and emulate traditional district forms and functions, this raises intriguing questions about the usefulness of setting up parallel bureaucratic structures to compete with each other. Also, charter schools advance from promises that can be monitored. Even though those objectives may have changed in recent years, metrics such as the number of students or schools or states are visible. Finally, charter schools fit well with some of the dominant trends in federal and state policy. Charter school governance embodies the dual-accountability model of NCLB— the idea that schools should be accountable for their performance to both state government and individual consumers.

LOOKING TO THE FUTURE

With the likely longevity of the charter school movement in mind, we conclude by offering a brief summary on crucial aspects of charter schools that deserve further attention not only from policy makers, but also in research and media circles, where many of the debates around charters are played out.

Better Schools or Better Students?

Charter schools do not escape the fundamental truism in American education that family background factors are still a primary predictor of student achievement. Although a handful of charter schools appear to be effective at working with the disadvantaged populations that have been chronically underserved in American education, many of the "successful" charter schools held up by advocates or in the media are simply reflecting more advantaged student enrollment. Researchers have grappled with these effects of selection bias for some time, usually in appropriate and fair-minded ways. However, the influence of student background and selection bias on outcomes is less understood by the general population, and problems emerge when the apparent successes or failure of charter schools are discussed in the popular press without considering the demographic factors that heavily influence school performance.

Even randomized approaches that claim to make the "unobservable" factors of student initiative or parent motivation meaningless can suffer from this problem. By comparing achievement gains for students randomly selected from an applicant pool to attend charters from those randomly denied entry, some researchers argue that unobservable factors are held constant and thus do not conflate achievement measures. However, students do not go to school in a vacuum. Instead, their achievement is shaped not only by instruction and family background factors, but also by the achievement, attitudes, and aspirations of their schoolmates.[4] This well-known peer effect is important to consider here because randomized studies that fail to account for demographic differences when comparing students in different schools are attributing gains in charter schools to more effective educational processes when those differences may instead simply reflect a richer social mix at a chosen school. While charter schools overall do serve a fair number of disadvantaged students, the question is really one of student mix at individual schools and classrooms.

It is wise to keep this crucial issue in mind in further considerations of charter schools. Like any school, charter schools can boost student outcomes through more effective educational practices. But as schools of choice, charter schools also have the ability to capitalize on accumulated student advantages, as do private schools and public schools in affluent districts. Given the achievement pressures they face from day one, charter schools have a built-in incentive to attract groups of more advantaged—or even just less disadvantaged—students, whose aggregated social advantages can have a significant impact on outcomes for students at a school. Likewise, for better or worse, parents then have a rational justification to shop not just for a better school, but for "better" classmates for their children. State-collected student enrollment data offers only a very limited portrait of how charter school and traditional public school students may be different. A better understanding of these differences is necessary for a more accurate sense of what charter schools add to students rather than just what students bring to charter schools.

Implementation Research and Shifts in Political Power

Much of charter school research treats the individual consumer or school provider as the primary economic actor or unit of analysis. Political analyses have often looked at large-scale coalitional politics or at the political activities of individual actors. Compared with other areas of education research, charter school research is somewhat lacking in meso-level research that examines how policies are interpreted and implemented at district levels. Paul Teske, Mark Schneider, and E. Cassese note: "The practice of creating, overseeing, and renewing or closing charter schools is evolving in a typically complicated American policy environment about which much is speculated and little is really known."[5]

A handful of studies have examined charter school authorizing boards, considering the types of charters they approve and how they hold charter schools accountable. These studies have found that authorizers often use a "negotiated" rather than "enforced" approach to compliance, and that local school boards sometimes lack the capacity to sufficiently oversee charters.[6] Bruce Fuller suggests that some local school boards actively block charter schools because they fear the competition and worry about offending local interests.[7] Others have expressed concern that local school boards will block charters or approve mostly those serving hard-to-educate populations.[8] Teske, Schneider, and Cassese found that political concerns often shape the actions of charter authorizers, particularly authorizers that are local school boards.[9] Heath Brown, Thomas Holyoke, and Jeffrey Henig have demonstrated that charter schools are indeed very politically active, both as individual organizations and as members of coalitions.[10] It seems quite likely that the implementation of charter school policy through authorizing boards is having a substantial effect on school outcomes, though this issue has not been studied directly.

Many questions remain about charter school implementation. Beyond the formal rules laid out in legislation, how are new charter schools proposed, and how do school branding, leaders' networks, and political access influence the types of schools proposed? What determines which proposals are blocked or supported by district officials, political elites, or other types of coalitions? How do district leaders, private funders, management organizations, and local networks influence where schools are located, and what populations are targeted in their marketing? How are new schools bolstered or steered by private funds, and does private funding influence the likelihood of charter school approval or renewal? This governance reform provides both public and private actors with new ways to attempt to meet the needs of local families, yet we know relatively little about how leaders understand this opportunity or shape the changes in the provision of education that may occur through it.

Charter School Accountability

The most significant and unique contribution charter schools make to American education is in introducing new forms of accountability to educational governance. But this may also be an area where the impact is more abstract—in terms of changing the thinking—than in substance. Charter schools were advanced largely under the banner of "autonomy in exchange for accountability." The thinking was that these schools would be given greater freedom from school codes and would then have to demonstrate results that would justify that flexibility. As opposed to traditional public schools that were under the direct authority of a centralized district bureaucracy, charter schools would be responsible to a more hands-off chartering agency that authorized the school for the outcomes specified in the charter. But, in addition to this form of governance accountability in which authorities had been shifted, charters also are directly responsible to consumers. That is, charter schools blur the boundaries between public and private institutions, bringing a form of market accountability into public education.

Empowering both charter authorizers and parents to judge the quality of schools is an innovative effort at decentralizing school governance. But even as charter schools introduced these new, mixed mechanisms of accountability, it appears that at least part of the effort has failed. Newly established governance authorities are thought to possess or be capable of developing the expertise necessary to make sound judgments on charter school performance. However, it is much less clear that parents, as a group, have exercised similar acumen in identifying the attributes of quality schools. Schools of demonstrably inferior quality are still often popular with parents, even when better schooling options are available. Parents generally seem more interested in enjoying alternatives than in investigating different schools for evidence of effectiveness. But this means the critical element of market incentives for school improvement is missing, corrupted, or broken.

Of course, as we noted before, we still see the charter school movement continuing well into the future. But this accountability problem suggests that one of the two main structures for charter school quality is tenuous, at best. This observation then raises questions as to whether policy makers are prepared or equipped to create resources and policies that "nudge" parents into making the choices desired by the rational-choice reformers advocating for charter schools. Or will the burden of school oversight fall mostly on authorizing entities, and if so, to what extent will they simply replicate the functions of existing districts? (After all, one of the attributes of long-lasting reforms is that they are co-opted into the larger system.) Or is charter schooling just about deregulation, with no real concern for developing the mechanisms that will improve schools?

Do the Rules Matter?

An inherent tension between the state and the market is playing out at the core of the charter school idea. On the one hand, charter schools are public schools—publicly funded, chartered by public authorities, and serving the public. On the other hand, charters elevate private consumer choice, market competition, and the profit motive into prominent positions within the publicly funded system. In fact, market mechanisms were embraced specifically to counter the apparent forces of stagnation and inertia associated with state monopolies in education. While early debates about privatization around charter schools have receded for now, with some notable exceptions, both skeptics and advocates alike have expressed concerns about embracing too much of a free market for education through charter schools.[11]

In fact, a popular claim around charter schools and other forms of school choice is that "the rules matter" in restraining some of the more egregious problems associated with markets.[12] Children are a particularly vulnerable population, and schools (as producers) may hold a disproportionate degree of power in the consumer-provider relationship in this case. For this reason, both charter school advocates and critics have generally agreed that some regulation of market mechanisms is essential either to limit their potentially harmful nature or to at least make markets for education function more effectively. Still hotly debated, however, is the extent of regulation needed.

However, after almost two decades of wide-scale charter and choice programs in the United States, questions still remain about the usefulness of state restraints placed on market forces in education. Should the state limit which groups can authorize or open a charter? Should government experts conduct inspections of these facilities (as they do in other countries) to ensure that minimum standards of quality are being met and that children are not harmed in these programs? Or is the government inherently incapable of performing such duties effectively, as some have argued? In that situation, should we look to the market to regulate itself, as consumers should gradually leave poorer services, and competition should drive quality improvements? Or should we look to extra-market but nongovernment actors such as accrediting or rating agencies to provide the expertise and insights consumers can use?

Or have we opened a Pandora's box of self-interest that can never be contained once unleashed in a field that is built on cooperative action, pooled resources, professional values, and a sense of the common good? While rules might be implemented, elevating self-interested behavior for individuals and organizations through competitive incentives very well might make the rules more or less meaningless. Parents have reason to get their child into their preferred school, regardless of state constraints on racial concentrations, just as some parents violate residency rules to get their children into neighborhood public schools outside the district in which they live. Charter schools might be required to provide certain services to students, but a new emphasis on competition may mean that charters avoid such risks and costs as students who are more expensive and harder to educate are slighted, just as they have been in the past in public schools. We do not pretend to have the answer to these questions, but only point out that this concern continues, and charter schools represent an intriguing experiment around these issues.

THE END OF "CHARTER SCHOOLS"

While we have been discussing charter schools in more general terms, in many respects it may no longer make sense to talk about these schools as one model. Of course, all charter schools do share some fundamental commonalities: they are schools of choice; they are publicly funded (for the most part); they are authorized by public entities; and they are open to the public—again, for the most part. But, as is evident in this volume, once we begin to look at the range of charter schools across the nation, any monolithic sense of charters quickly falls apart.

There is nearly as much variety in charter school policy as there is in charter school operations. Besides teacher-run co-ops, corporate-run charters, core knowledge programs, environmental programs, Reggio Emilia schools, schools using Saxon math, schools for college prep, and those for at-risk students (the latter two schools sometimes as one program), there are also substantive variations in what is meant by "charter schooling" across states. Thus, charter schools in Arizona are quite different from what we see in Connecticut, and charter schools in Colorado are different from the "public school academies" in Michigan or the "community schools" in Ohio. Charters are tightly regulated and serve a small proportion of the students in places like Iowa, while cities such as Washington, D.C., are seeing a substantial proportion of their students attending these open-access institutions, and post-Katrina New Orleans, with the largest market share for charters, is leading the way in allowing some of these schools to use academic admissions criteria.

This variety is in line with some of the original thinking on charter schools: "To let a thousand flowers bloom"—even if the hope that the market would weed out the bad ones has fallen far short. Yet the across-state variation in charter schools is not in itself the desired outcome. Reformers rightfully sought a greater diversity of options for families within local communities. The grand narratives on charter schools in America and even in individual states do little to tell us if or how those options are increasing, how they might be meeting specific needs of families, or how they might be driving improvements in academic quality. Instead, researchers need to refocus their efforts on charter school effects in local contexts.

A focus on local contexts is particularly important because charter schools are designed to create more and better options largely through competitive incentives generated in local education markets, or LEMs.[13] Yet researchers and policy makers know very little about how market mechanisms actually operate in LEMs, how LEMs function, or even how competition may or may not emerge (or be measured) in LEMs. Moreover, LEMs vary considerably by their contextual elements, including policy, demographic, institutional, and geographic factors. Although researchers are now beginning to develop the capabilities to investigate how these environmental factors can shape different types of schooling experiences, some important contextual factors must be considered if we are to understand how different types of charter schools work. That is, researchers desperately need to gain insights into the "black box." Much attention has been focused on charter schools as opaque production units—looking at inputs into charter schools, such as demographics or external incentives, and the consequent outcomes, such as student achievement, with little attention devoted to understanding the internal mechanisms in different types of schools, so that policies and practices associated with successful schools can be considered for replication in other schools where possible. But, inasmuch as school successes appear to be informed by contextual factors, those black-box questions become even more difficult to explore in any meaningful manner, since what works in one school may not work in similar schools in different contexts.

In the next twenty years, these questions and many others will shape the research on charter schools and other forms of school choice. Though many important and fundamental questions remain, educational researchers in the last twenty years have made great progress in understanding how this popular policy innovation may alter the provision and consumption of publicly funded education in the United States in coming years. However, it is not at all clear that policy makers are considering the evidence on what is working, and what is not, as they expand charter schools.

We agree with the current policy making emphases on *what works*, and hope that such a standard eventually assumes more than just a rhetorical significance in this rapidly evolving area of policy and research. Our desire is that this volume will shed some light on the key policy questions concerning charter schools and will help inform the next wave of research and policy making on these new institutions on the educational landscape.

Notes

Foreword

1. J. L. Pressman and A. Wildavsky, *Implementation: How Great Expectations in Washington Are Dashed in Oakland; or, Why It's Amazing That Federal Programs Work at All* (Los Angeles: University of California Press, 1984).
2. S. Mettler and J. Soss, "The Consequences of Public Policy for Democratic Citizenship: Bridging Policy Studies and Mass Politics," *Perspectives on Politics* 2 (2004): 55–73.
3. Jeffrey R. Henig, *Spin Cycle: How Research Is Used in Policy Debates: The Case of Charter Schools* (New York: Russell Sage Foundation, 2008).
4. Kurt Vonnegut, *Cat's Cradle* (New York: Holt, Rinehart and Winston, 1963).

Introduction

1. Kolderie, Ted. 2002. *Origins of the Charter Idea.* St. Paul, MN: Education Evolving, Center for Policy Studies, Hamline University.
2. Garn, Gregg A. 1999. Solving the Policy Implementation Problem: The Case of Arizona Charter Schools. *Education Policy Analysis Archives* 7 (26).
3. Nathan, Joe. 1996. *Charter Schools: Creating Hope and Opportunity for American Education.* San Francisco, CA: Jossey-Bass.
4. National Commission on Excellence in Education. 1983. *A Nation At Risk: The Imperative for Educational Reform.* Washington, DC: U.S. Government Printing Office.
5. Chubb, John E., and Terry M. Moe. 1990. *Politics, Markets, and America's Schools.* Washington, DC: Brookings Institution.
6. Kirst, Michael W. 2007. Politics of Charter Schools: Competing National Advocacy Coalitions Meet Local Politics. *Peabody Journal of Education* 82 (2-3):184-203.
7. Hess, Frederick M., Robert Maranto, and Scott Milliman. 1999. Coping with competition: How school systems respond to school choice. Cambridge, MA: Harvard Program on Education Policy and Governance; Ladd, Helen F., and Edward B. Fiske. 2003. Does Competition Improve Teaching and Learning? Evidence from New Zealand. *Educational Evaluation and Policy Analysis* 25 (1):97-112. Lubienski, Christopher, Charisse Gulosino, and Peter Weitzel. 2009. School Choice and Competitive Incentives: Mapping the Distribution of Educational Opportunities across Local Education Markets. *American Journal of Education* 115 (4):601-647.
8. Lubienski, Christopher, and Jack Dougherty. 2009. Mapping Educational Opportunity: Spatial Analysis and School Choices. *American Journal of Education* 115 (4):485-492.
9. See, for example, Teske, Paul, Jody Fitzpatrick, and Gabriel Kaplan. 2007. Opening Doors: How Low-Income Parents Search for the Right School.

Seattle, WA: Center on Reinventing Public Education.

Chapter 1

1. P. Rooney, W. Hussar, and M. Planty, "The Condition of Education 2006," paper, U.S. Department of Education, Washington, DC, 2007.
2. Peter Frumkin, *On Being Nonprofit: A Conceptual and Policy Primer* (Cambridge, MA: Harvard University Press, 2002).
3. John E. Brandl, "Governance and Educational Quality," in *Learning from School Choice*, ed. P. E. Peterson and Bryan C. Hassel (Washington, DC: Brookings Institution, 1998).
4. T. Besley and M. Ghatak, "Competition and Incentives with Motivated Agents," *American Economic Review* 95 (2005): 616–636.
5. See, for example, Courtney A. Bell, "Geography in Parental Choice," *American Journal of Education* 115 (2009): 493–522; Justine S. Hastings and Jeffrey M. Weinstein, "Information, School Choice, and Academic Achievement: Evidence from Two Experiments," *Quarterly Journal of Economics* 123 (2008): 1373–1414.
6. See, for example, Lois Andre-Bechely, "Finding Space and Managing Distance: Public School Choice in an Urban California District," *Urban Studies* 44 (2007): 1355–1376.
7. Bell, "Geography in Parental Choice"; Jennifer Jellison Holme, "Buying Homes, Buying Schools: School Choice and the Social Construction of School Quality," *Harvard Educational Review* 72 (2002): 177–205; Paul Teske, Mark Schneider, and E. Cassese, "Local School Boards As Authorizers of Charter Schools," in *Besieged: School Boards and the Future of Education Politics*, ed. W. G. Howell (Washington, DC: Brookings Institution, 2006); John B. Diamond and Kimberley Gomez, "African American Parents' Educational Orientations: The Importance of Social Class and Parents' Perceptions of Schools," *Education and Urban Society* 36, no. 4 (2004): 383–427.
8. Gary Orfield, *Reviving the Goal of an Integrated Society: A 21st Century Challenge* (Los Angeles: Civil Rights Project, 2009).
9. *Parents Involved in Community Schools v. Seattle School District No. 1*, 127 S. Ct. 2738 (2007).
10. Peter Weitzel, "Who Chooses? Evidence on Choosy Parents from the Early Childhood Longitudinal Study," paper presented at the 2010 annual conference of the American Educational Research Association, Denver.
11. See, for example, Joe Nathan, *Charter Schools: Creating Hope and Opportunity for American Education* (San Francisco: Jossey-Bass, 1996).
12. Jeffrey R. Henig, *Spin Cycle: How Research Is Used in Policy Debates; The Case of Charter Schools* (New York: Russell Sage Foundation, 2007).
13. Sol Stern, "School Choice Isn't Enough," *City Journal* (winter 2008), www.city-journal.org/2008/18_1_instructional_reform.html.
14. Jay P. Greene et al., "Is School Choice Enough?" *City Journal*, January 24, 2008, www.city-journal.org/2008/forum0124.html.
15. Caroline M. Hoxby, "School Choice and School Productivity: Could School Choice Be a Tide That Lifts All Boats?" in *The Economics of School Choice*, ed. Caroline M. Hoxby (Chicago: University of Chicago Press, 2003).

16. See, for example, David N. Figlio and Cecilia Elena Rouse, *Do Accountability and Voucher Threats Improve Low-Performing Schools?* (Cambridge, MA: National Bureau of Economic Research, 2004).
17. Caroline M. Hoxby, "Does Competition Among Public Schools Benefit Students and Taxpayers?" *American Economic Review* 90 (2000): 1209–1238.
18. Jesse Rothstein, "'Does Competition Among Public Schools Benefit Students and Taxpayers?' A Comment on Hoxby (2000)," *American Economic Review* 97 (2007): 2026–2037.
19. Hoxby, "School Choice and School Productivity."
20. Russell W. Rumberger et al., "The Educational Consequences of Mobility for California Students and Schools," paper, Policy Analysis for California Education, University of California, Berkeley, 1999.
21. Katherine K. Merseth, *Inside Urban Charter Schools: Promising Practices and Strategies in Five High-Performing Schools* (Cambridge, MA: Harvard Education Press, 2009).
22. John E. Chubb and Terry M. Moe, *Politics, Markets, and America's Schools* (Washington, DC: Brookings Institution, 1990).
23. Christopher Lubienski, "Charter School Innovations in Theory and Practice: Autonomy, R&D, and Curricular Conformity," in *Taking Account of Charter Schools: What's Happened and What's Next?* ed. Katrina E. Bulkley and Priscilla Wohlstetter (New York: Teachers College Press, 2004).
24. Christopher Lubienski, "Innovation in Education Markets: Theory and Evidence on the Impact of Competition and Choice in Charter Schools," *American Educational Research Journal* 40 (2003): 395–443; Merseth, *Inside Urban Charter Schools.*
25. Thomas L. Good, Jennifer S. Braden, and Darrel W. Drury, *Charting a New Course: Fact and Fiction About Charter Schools* (Alexandria, VA: National School Boards Association, 2000); Lubienski, "Innovation in Education Markets"; Christopher Lubienski, "Educational Innovation and Diversification in School Choice Plans," paper, Education Policy Research Unit, Arizona State University, Tempe, and Education and the Public Interest Center, University of Colorado, Boulder, 2008; Robin J. Lake, "In the Eye of the Beholder: Charter Schools and Innovation," *Journal of School Choice* 2 (2008): 115–127.
26. E. Unseem, J. B. Christman, and W. L. Boyd, "The Role of District Leadership in Radical Reform: Philadelphia's Experience under the State Takeover 2001–2006," paper for Research for Action, Philadelphia, 2006.
27. Chester E. Finn Jr., "Lessons Learned," *Education Week*, February 27, 2008, www.edweek.org; Caroline M. Hoxby, "School Choice and School Productivity (Or Could School Choice Be a Ride That Lifts All Boats?)," paper, National Bureau of Economic Research, Cambridge, MA, 2002; Matthew Ladner and Matthew J. Brouillette, "The Impact of Limited School Choice On Public School Districts," Mackinac Center for Public Policy, Midland, MI, 2000; Alexis Moore, "Teaching Public Schools a Thing?" *Philadelphia Inquirer*, January 2, 2000, www.phillynews.com/inquirer/00/Jan/02/city/PROFIT02.htm.
28. Courtney A. Bell, "All Choices Created Equal? The Role of Choice Sets in

the Selection of Schools," *Peabody Journal of Education* 84 (2009): 191–208; S. DeJarnatt, "School Choice and the (Ir)rational Parent," *Georgetown Journal on Poverty Law and Policy* 15 (2008), http://papers.ssrn.com/sol3/papers.cfm?abstract_id=1014047; Paul Teske, Jody Fitzpatrick, and Gabriel Kaplan, "Opening Doors: How Low-Income Parents Search for the Right School," paper, Center on Reinventing Public Education, Seattle, 2007.

29. Jeffrey R. Henig, "Choice in Public Schools: An Analysis of Transfer Requests Among Magnet Schools," *Social Science Quarterly* 71 (1990): 69–82; Salvatore Saporito and Annette Lareau, "School Selection As a process: The Multiple Dimensions of Race in Framing Educational Choice," *Social Problems* 46 (1999): 418–439; Mark Schneider and Jack Buckley, "What Do Parents Want From Schools? Evidence From the Internet," *Educational Evaluation and Policy Analysis* 24 (2002): 133–144; Jeffrey R. Henig, "Race and Choice in Montgomery County, Maryland, Magnet Schools," *Teachers College Record* 96 (1995): 729–734; DeJarnatt, "School Choice and the (Ir)rational Parent."

30. David R. Garcia, "Academic and Racial Segregation in Charter Schools: Do Parents Sort Students into Specialized Charter Schools?" *Education and Urban Society* 40 (2008): 590–612.

31. Justine S. Hastings and Jeffrey M. Weinstein, "Information, School Choice, and Academic Achievement: Evidence from Two Experiments," *Quarterly Journal of Economics* 123 (2008): 1373–1414.

32. Chubb and Moe, *Politics, Markets, and America's Schools.*

33. Ted Kolderie, "Beyond Choice to New Public Schools: Withdrawing the Exclusive Franchise in Public Education," paper, Progressive Policy Institute, Washington, DC, 1990; Ted Kolderie, "The States Begin to Withdraw the 'Exclusive,'" *Changing Schools* (November 1993): 1–8.

34. Ted Kolderie, "The Charter Idea: Update and Prospects, Fall 95," in *Public Services Redesign Project* (Washington, DC: Center for Education Reform, 1995).

35. Joe Nathan, "Progressives Should Support Charter Public Schools," *Rethinking Schools* (winter 1996): 20–21.

36. Danny K. Weil, *Charter School Movement: History, Politics, Policies, Economics and Effectiveness* (Amenia, NY: Grey House Publishing, 2009).

37. Mitch Price, "Still Negotiating: What Do Unions Mean for Charter Schools?" in *Hopes, Fears & Reality: A Balanced Look at American Charter Schools in 2009,* ed. Robin J. Lake (Bothell, WA: National Charter School Research Project, Center on Reinventing Public Education, University of Washington, 2010), 40.

38. Katrina E. Bulkley, "Bringing the Private into the Public: Changing the Rules of the Game and New Regime Politics in Philadelphia Public Education," *Educational Policy* 21 (2007): 155–184.

39. P. Lipman and N. Haines, "From Accountability to Privatization and African American Exclusion: Chicago's 'Renaissance 2010,'" *Educational Policy* 21 (2007): 471–502.

Chapter 2

1. See, for example, Jeffrey R. Henig, *Spin Cycle: How Research Is Used in Policy Debate; The Case of Charter Schools* (New York: Russell Sage Foundation, 2008);

Martin Carnoy et al., *The Charter School Dust-Up: Examining the Evidence on Enrollment and Achievement* (New York: Teachers College Press, 2005).

2. See, for example, Eric Rofes and Lisa M. Stulberg, eds., *The Emancipatory Promise of Charter Schools: Towards a Progressive Politics of School Choice* (Albany: SUNY, 2004); Stacy Smith, "The Democratic Potential of Charter Schools," in *Counterpoints: Studies in the Postmodern Theory of Education,* vol. 136, ed. J. L. Kincheloe and S. R. Steinberg (New York: Peter Lang, 2001); and K. B. Smith and K. J. Meir, *The Case Against School Choice: Politics, Markets and Fools* (Armonk, NY: M. E. Sharpe, 1995).

3. William W. Wayson, "Charter Schools: Franchise for Creativity or License for Fractionation?" *Education and Urban Society* 31, no. 4 (1999): 446–464; Seymour B. Sarason, *Charter Schools: Another Flawed Educational Reform?* (New York: Teachers College Press, 1998).

4. Patrick J. McEwan, "The Potential Impact of Large-Scale Voucher Programs," *Review of Educational Research* 70, no. 2 (2000): 103–149.

5. Amy Stuart Wells et al., "Underlying Policy Assumptions of Charter School Reform: The Multiple Meanings of a Movement," *Teachers College Record* 100, no. 3 (1999): 513–535; Bryan C. Hassel, *The Charter School Challenge* (Washington, DC: Brookings Institution, 1999).

6. Martin Carnoy, "School Choice? Or Is It Privatization?" *Educational Researcher* 29, no. 7 (2000): 15.

7. Elaine L. Halchin, "And This Parent Went to Market: Education As Public Versus Private Good," in *School Choice in the Real World: Lessons from Arizona Charter Schools,* ed. Robert Maranto et al. (Boulder: Westview Press, 1999), 24.

8. Kenneth R. Howe, Margaret Eisenhart, and Damian Betebenner, "The Price of Public School Choice," *Educational Leadership* 59, no. 7 (2002): 20–24; Alex Molnar, "Charter Schools: The Smiling Face of Disinvestment," *Educational Leadership* 54, no. 2 (1996): 9–15.

9. Frederick M. Hess and David L. Leal, "Quality, Race, and the Urban Education Marketplace," *Urban Affairs Review* 37, no. 2 (2001): 249–266.

10. Casey D. Cobb and Gene V. Glass, "Ethnic Segregation in Arizona Charter Schools," *Education Policy Analysis Archives* 7, no. 1 (1999), http://epaa.asu.edu/ojs/article/view/536; see especially Discussion, paragraph 6.

11. Kim K. Metcalf, Neil D. Theobald, and Gerardo Gonzalez, "State University Roles in the Charter School Movement," *Phi Delta Kappan* 84, no. 7 (2003): 543.

12. Sandra Vergari, "Federalism and Market-Based Education Policy: The Supplemental Educational Services Mandate," *American Journal of Education* 113 (2007): 311–339.

13. Gary Orfield, "Schools More Separate: Consequences of a Decade of Resegregation," paper, the Civil Rights Project, Cambridge, MA, 2001.

14. Paul T. Hill and Kacey Guin, "Baselines for Assessment of Choice Programs," in *Choice with Equity,* ed. Paul T. Hill (Stanford, CA: Stanford University, 2002).

15. Chester E. Finn Jr., Bruno V. Manno, and Gregg Vanourek, *Charter Schools in Action: Renewing Public Education* (Princeton, NJ: Princeton University Press, 2000).

16. Bruno V. Manno, Gregg Vanourek, and Chester E. Finn Jr., "Charter Schools: Serving Disadvantaged Youth," *Education and Urban Society* 31, no.

4 (1999): 429–445; Joe Nathan, *Charter Schools: Creating Hope and Opportunity for American Education* (San Francisco: Jossey-Bass, 1996).

17. Mark Schneider et al., "School Choice and the Culture Wars in the Classroom: What Different Parents Seek from Education," *Social Science Quarterly* 79, no. 3 (1998): 489–501.

18. Manno et al., "Charter Schools: Serving Disadvantaged Youth."

19. Ibid., 440.

20. RPP International, "The State of Charter Schools 2000: Fourth-Year Report," in *The State of Charter Schools*, ed. U.S. Department of Education: U.S. Department of Education (Washington, DC, 2000).

21. Ibid.

22. Amy Stuart Wells et al., "Charter Schools and Racial and Social Class Segregation: Yet Another Sorting Machine?" in *A Notion at Risk: Preserving Public Education As an Engine for Social Mobility*, ed. Richard D. Kahlenberg (New York: Century Foundation/Twentieth Century Fund Inc., 2000).

23. National Assessment of Educational Progress, "The Nation's Report Card, America's Charter Schools: Results from the NAEP 2003 Pilot Study," paper, National Center for Education Statistics, Washington, DC, 2003.

24. Carnoy et al., *The Charter School Dust-Up.*

25. Erica Frankenberg and Chungmei Lee, "Charter Schools and Race: A Lost Opportunity for Integrated Education," *Education Policy Analysis Archives* 11, no. 32 (2003), http://epaa.asu.edu/ojs/article/view/260.

26. Erica Frankenberg, Genevieve Siegel-Hawley, and Jia Wang, "Choice Without Equity: Charter School Segregation and the Need for Civil Rights Standards," paper, Civil Rights Project/Proyecto Derechos Civiles, University of California at Los Angeles, 2010, www.civilrightsproject.ucla.edu.

27. Bettie Landauer-Menchik, "How Segregated Are Michigan's Schools? Changes in Enrollment from 1992–93 to 2004–05," paper, Education Policy Center, Michigan State University, East Lansing, 2006.

28. Jeffrey R. Henig and Stephen D. Sugarman, "The Nature and Extent of School Choice," in *School Choice and Social Controversy: Politics, Policy and Law*, ed. Stephen D. Sugarman and Frank R. Kemerer (Washington, DC: Brookings Institution, 1999); Mary Gifford, Melinda Ogle, and Lewis C. Solomon, "Who Is Choosing Charter Schools? A Snapshot of Geography and Ethnicity of Charter Schools Students," in *Arizona Issue Analysis* (Phoenix: Center for Market-Based Education, 1998). See also Gary Miron and Jerry Horn, "Evaluation of Connecticut Charter Schools and the Charter School Initiative," in *1-150* (Kalamazoo, MI: Evaluation Center, Western Michigan University, 2002). On the other hand, Steven M. Glazerman, "School Quality and Social Stratification: The Determinants and Consequences of School Choice," paper presented at American Education Research Association, San Diego, April 13–17, 1997, found that parents were more likely to choose schools relatively close to home.

29. Casey D. Cobb, Gene V. Glass, and Carol Crockett, "The U.S. Charter School Movement and Ethnic Segregation," paper presented at American Educational Research Association, New Orleans, April 24–28, 2000.

30. Cobb and Glass, "Ethnic Segregation in Arizona Charter Schools."

31. As in all studies that group charter and district schools according to geographic proximity, the accuracy of school comparisons using geographic tools is predicated on the assumption that charter schools enroll their students from "nearby" neighborhood schools. To the extent that students chose to attend charter schools that were located far from their neighborhood school, district boundary and geographic mapping created less accurate comparison groups.

32. Brian P. Gill et al., *Rhetoric Versus Reality: What We Know and What We Need to Know About Vouchers and Charter Schools* (Santa Monica, CA: RAND, 2001).

33. Gregory R. Weiher and Kent L. Tedin, "Does Choice Lead to Racially Distinctive Schools? Charter Schools and Household Preferences," *Journal of Policy Analysis and Management* 21, no. 7 (2002): 79–92. Hispanic parents rated test scores as the fourth-highest priority (of six options) in their school choice decision.

34. David R. Garcia, "The Impact of School Choice on Racial Segregation in Charter Schools," *Educational Policy* 22, no. 6 (2008): 805–829.

35. Ibid. The large number of Arizona charter high schools serving at-risk students is a possible explanation for the increased exposure of white and minority students in charter elementary high schools. In 2000, 53 percent of Arizona charter high schools served at-risk students, and at-risk charter high schools enrolled nearly 62 percent of the total charter high school student population (David R. Garcia, "Academic and Racial Segregation in Charter Schools: Do Parents Sort Students into Specialized Charter Schools?" *Education and Urban Society* 40, no. 5 [2008]: 590–612).

36. Robert Bifulco and Helen F. Ladd, "School Choice, Racial Segregation, and Test-Score Gaps: Evidence from North Carolina's Charter School Program," *Journal of Policy Analysis and Management* 26, no. 1 (2006): 31–56.

37. Richard Buddin and Ron Zimmer, "Student Achievement in Charter Schools: A Complex Picture," *Journal of Policy Analysis and Management* 24, no. 2 (2005): 351–371.

38. Kevin Booker, Ron Zimmer, and Richard Buddin, "The Effects of Charter Schools on School Peer Composition," Santa Monica, CA: RAND Corporation, working paper no. WR-306-EDU, 2005.

39. Gary Orfield, foreword in *Choice Without Equity: Charter School Segregation and the Need for Civil Rights Standards,* by Erica Frankenberg, Genevieve Siegel-Hawley, and Jia Wang (Los Angeles: Civil Rights Project/Proyecto Derechos Civiles, University of California at Los Angeles, 2010).

40. See, for example, Tim R. Sass, "Charter Schools and Student Achievement in Florida," *Education Finance and Policy* 1, no. 1 (2006): 91–122; Robert Bifulco and Helen F. Ladd, "The Impacts of Charter Schools on Student Achievement: Evidence from North Carolina," *Education Finance and Policy* 1, no. 1 (2004): 50–90; Eric A. Hanushek, John F. Kain, and Steven Rivkin, *The Impact of Charter Schools on Academic Achievement* (Stanford, CA: Stanford University, 2002).

41. Marc F. Bernstein, "Why I'm Wary of Charter Schools," *School Administrator* 56, no. 7 (1999): 24–28.

42. Christopher Lubienski, "Marketing Schools: Consumer Goods and

Competitive Incentives for Consumer Information," *Education and Urban Society* 40, no. 1 (2007): 118–141.

43. Thomas B. Fordham Institute, *Charter School Funding: Inequity's Next Frontier* (Washington, DC, 2005): Thomas B. Fordham Institute.

44. Alex Molnar et al., "Profiles of for-Profit Education Management Organizations, Ninth Annual Report, 2006–2007," paper, Commercialism in Education Research Unit, Arizona State University, Tempe, 2007.

45. Janelle T. Scott and Adriana Villavicencio, "School Context and Charter School Achievement: A Frame Work for Understanding the Performance 'Black Box,'" *Peabody Journal of Education* 84 (2009): 227–243.

46. Natalie Lacireno-Paquet et al., "Creaming Versus Cropping: Charter School Enrollment Practices in Response to Market Incentives," *Educational Evaluation and Policy Analysis* 24, no. 2 (2002): 145–158.

47. Ibid., 155.

48. Garcia, "Impact of School Choice on Racial Segregation."

49. White students were compared with Hispanic students because the latter is Arizona's largest minority group. Hispanic students constitute 40 percent of all Arizona public school students (Arizona Department of Education, "Annual Report of the Arizona Superintendent of Public Instruction: Fiscal Year 2006–2007," http://ade.az.gov/AnnualReport/annualreport2007/Vol1.pdf).

50. David R. Garcia, Lee McIlroy, and Rebecca T. Barber, "Starting Behind: A Comparative Analysis of the Academic Standing of Students Entering Charter Schools," *Social Science Quarterly* 89, no. 1 (2008): 199–216.

51. Bruce Fuller et al., "Localized Ideas of Fairness: Inequality Among Charter Schools," in *Taking Account of Charter Schools: What's Happened and What's Next?* ed. Katrina E. Bulkley and Priscilla Wohlstetter (New York: Teachers College Press, 2003).

52. Garcia, "Do Parents Sort Students into Specialized Charter Schools?"

53. Amy Stuart Wells et al., "Charter Schools As Postmodern Paradox: Rethinking Social Stratification in an Age of Deregulated School Choice," *Harvard Educational Review* 69, no. 2 (1999): 172–204.

54. Ibid., 201.

55. Amy Stuart Wells et al., "Underlying Policy Assumptions of Charter School Reform: The Multiple Meanings of a Movement," *Teachers College Record* 100, no. 3 (1999): 513–535.

56. Lacireno-Paquet et al., "Creaming Versus Cropping."

57. Leigh Dingerson et al., eds., *Keeping the Promise: The Debate over Charter Schools* (Williston, VT: Rethinking Schools Ltd, 2008).

58. Brian P. Gill, "School Choice and Integration," in *Getting Choice Right: Ensuring Equity and Efficiency in Education Policy*, ed. J. R. Betts and T. Loveless (Washington, DC: Brookings Institution, 2005).

59. Frankenberg and Lee, "Charter Schools and Race."

60. James E. Ryan and Michael Heise, "The Political Economy of School Choice," *Yale Law Journal* 111, no. 8 (2002): 2043–2136.

61. Wendy Parker, "The Color of Choice: Race and Charter Schools," *Tulane Law Review* 75, no. 3 (2001): 563–630.

62. *Nev. Rev. Stat. Ann.* § 386.580[1] (2000).

63. *N.C. Code Ann.* § 115C-238.29F[5] (2005).

64. Amy Stuart Wells, "Charter School Reform in California: Does It Meet Expectations?" *Phi Delta Kappan* 80, no. 4 (1998): 305–312.

65. Parker, "The Color of Choice."

66. Nathalis G. Wamba and Carol Ascher, "An Examination of Charter School Equity," *Education and Urban Society* 35, no. 4 (2003): 462–476.

67. Linda A. Renzulli, "District Segregation, Race Legislation, and Black Enrollment in Charter Schools," *Social Science Quarterly* 87, no. 3 (2006): 618–637.

68. Kelly E. Rapp and Suzanne E. Eckes, "Dispelling the Myth of 'White Flight': An Examination of Minority Enrollment in Charter Schools," *Educational Policy* 21, no. 4 (2007): 615–661.

69. Education Commission of the States, "ECS State Policies for Charter School Database," www.ecs.org/html/educationIssues/CharterSchools/CHDB_intro.asp.

70. Robert E. Crew Jr. and Mary Ruggiero Anderson, "Accountability and Performance in Charter Schools in Florida: A Theory-Based Evaluation," *American Journal of Evaluation* 24, no. 2 (2003): 189–212, put forth the hypothesis that Florida charter schools will not differ significantly from regular public schools in student composition. The researchers remained "skeptical" in accepting the hypothesis because Florida charter schools were specialized and did not serve the "average" child. This hypothesis, however, appears contradictory to the objective of Florida's charter school law, which provides the means for such schools to tailor themselves to serve specific students. Also, the racial segregation data should be interpreted with caution because less than one-half of the charter schools in operation during the school year 1999–2000 reported data in their annual reports about the demographic characteristics of their students.

71. Natalie Lacireno-Paquet, "Charter School Enrollments in Context: An Exploration of Organization and Policy Influences," *Peabody Journal of Education* 81, no. 1 (2006): 79–102.

72. Natalie Lacireno-Paquet, "Do EMO-Operated Charter Schools Serve Disadvantaged Students? The Influence of State Policies," *Education Policy Analysis Archives* 12, no. 26 (2004), http://epaa.asu.edu/ojs/article/view/181.

73. Gary Orfield, foreword in "Charter Schools and Race: A Lost Opportunity for Integrated Education," by Erica Frankenberg and Chungmei Lee, *Education Policy Analysis Archives* 11, no. 23 (2003), http://epaa.asu.edu/ojs/article/view/251.

74. Ibid., paragraph 9.

75. Terry M. Moe, "The Structure of School Choice," in *Choice with Equity,* ed. Paul T. Hill (Stanford, CA: Hoover Institution, 2002), 180.

76. Wendy C. Chi and Kevin G. Welner, "Charter Ranking Roulette: An Analysis of Reports That Grade States' Charter School Laws," *American Journal of Education* 114, no. 2 (2008): 273–298.

77. Amy Stambach and Natalie Crow Becker, "Finding the Old in the New: On Race and Class in US Charter School Debates," *Race Ethnicity and Education* 9, no. 2 (2006): 159–182; Suzanne E. Eckes, "Barriers to Integration in the Mississippi Delta: Could Charter Schools Be the New Vehicle for Desegrega-

tion?" *Analyses of Social Issues and Public Policy* 6, no. 1 (2006): 15–30.

78. Henig, *Spin Cycle.*

Chapter 3

1. Center for Education Reform, "Ed Reform FAQs: Just the FAQs—Charter Schools," November 1, 2009, www.edreform.com/Fast_Facts/ Ed_Reform_ FAQs/?Just_the_FAQs_Charter_Schools.

2. Ibid.

3. U.S. Charter Schools, "Charter Laws," [no date], www.uscharterschools.org/ pub/uscs_docs/o/charterlaws.htm.

4. Jay P. Heubert, "Schools Without Rules? Charter Schools, Federal Disability Law, and the Paradoxes of Deregulation," *Harvard Civil Rights-Civil Liberties Law Review* 32, no. 2 (1997): 301–354.

5. Rebekah Gleason, "Looking Back and Moving Forward: New Approaches to Legal Advocacy in the 21st Century; Charter Schools and Special Education—Part of the Solution or Part of the Problem?" *University of the District of Columbia Law Review* 9, no. 1 (2007): 145–172; Joseph Oluwole and Preston C. Green, "Charter Schools: Racial-Balancing Provisions and Parents Involved," *Arkansas Law Review* 61, no. 1 (2008): 1–52.

6. Michael W. Kirst, "Politics of Charter Schools: Competing National Advocacy Coalitions Meet Local Politics," *Peabody Journal of Education* 82, no. 2–3 (2007): 184–203.

7. Suzanne Eckes and Anne E. Trotter, "Are Charter Schools Using Recruitment Strategies to Increase Student Body Diversity?" *Education and Urban Society* 40, no. 1 (2007): 62–90; Roslyn A. Mickelson, Martha Bottia, and Stephanie Southworth, "School Choice and Segregation by Race, Class, and Achievement," paper, Education Policy Research Unit, Arizona State University, Tempe, 2008, http://epsl.asu.edu/epru/documents/EPSL-0803-260-EPRU.pdf.

8. Eckes and Trotter, "Recruitment Strategies to Increase Student Body Diversity?"

9. David R. Garcia, "Charter Schools Challenge Notions of Segregation Under School Choice Policies" (unpublished manuscript, 2008) .

10. Suhrid S. Gajendragadkar, "The Constitutionality of Racial Balancing in Charter Schools," *Columbia Law Review* 106, no. 1 (2006): 144–181.

11. Mickelson, Bottia, and Southworth, "School Choice and Segregation."

12. Julie F. Mead, "How Legislation and Litigation Shape School Choice," paper, Education Policy Research Unit, Arizona State University, Tempe, 2008, http://epsl.asu.edu/epru/documents/EPSL-0803-254-EPRU.pdf.

13. *McFarland v. Jefferson County Public Schools*, 330 F.Supp.2d 834 (W.D. Ky 2004), 836.

14. *Parents Involved in Community Schools v. Seattle School District No. 1*, 426 F.3d 1162 (11th Cir. 2005).

15. Casey D. Cobb and Gene V. Glass, "Ethnic Segregation in Arizona Charter Schools," *Education Policy Analysis Archives,* 7, no. 1 (1999), http://epaa.asu. edu/epaa/v7n1/; Jennifer L. Hocschild and Nathan Scovronick, *The American Dream and the Public Schools* (New York: Oxford University Press, 2003); Jenny Horn and Gary Miron, "An Evaluation of Michigan's Charter School

Initiative: Performance, Accountability, and Impact," paper, Evaluation Center, Western Michigan University, Kalamazoo, 2000; Kenneth R. Howe, Margaret Eisenhart, and Damien W. Betebenner, "School Choice Crucible: A Case Study of Boulder Valley," *Phi Delta Kappan* 83, no. 2 (2001): 137–146; Natalie Lacireno-Paquet et al., "Creaming Versus Cropping: Charter School Enrollment Practices in Response to Market Incentives," *Educational Evaluation and Policy Analysis* 24, no. 2 (2002): 145–158; Kelly E. Rapp and Suzanne Eckes, "Dispelling the Myth of 'White Flight': An Examination of Minority Enrollment in Charter Schools," *Educational Policy* 21, no. 4 (2007): 615–661; Amy Stuart Wells et al., "Charter Schools and Racial and Social Class Segregation: Yet Another Sorting Machine?" in *A Nation at Risk: Preserving Education As an Engine for Social Mobility*, ed. Richard D. Kahlenberg (New York: Century Foundation Press, 2000), 169–222.

16. Richard F. Elmore, *Choice in Public Education* (Santa Monica, CA: RAND, 1986); Joy Fitzgerald et al., "1997 Colorado Charter Schools Evaluation Study: The Characteristics, Status and Student Achievement Data of Colorado Charter Schools," paper, Clayton Foundation, Denver, 1998; Preston C. Green III, "Racial Balancing Provisions and Charter Schools: Are Charter Schools Out on a Constitutional Limb?" *Brigham Young University Education and Law Journal* (2001): 65–84.

17. Institute of Race and Poverty, "Failed Promises: Assessing Charter Schools in the Twin Cities," November 2008, www.irpumn.org/uls/resources/projects/2_Charter_Report_Final.pdf.

18. Erica Frankenberg and Chungmei Lee, "Charter Schools and Race: A Lost Opportunity for Integrated Education," paper, the Civil Rights Project, Harvard University, Cambridge, MA, 2003, www.civilrightsproject.harvard.edu/research/deseg/Charter_Schools03.pdf; Gary Miron et al., "Schools Without Diversity: Education Management Organizations, Charter Schools and the Demographic Stratification of the American School System," paper, Education and the Public Interest Center, Education Policy Research Unit, Arizona State University, Tempe, 2010, http://epicpolicy.org/publication/schools-without-diversity; National Center for Education Statistics, "The Condition of Education 2002," NCES 2002-025, Washington, DC, U.S. Government Printing Office; Rapp and Eckes, "Dispelling the Myth of 'White Flight.'"

19. Center for Education Reform, "Charter Schools Today: Changing the Face of American Education, Part I: Annual Survey of America's Charter Schools, 2005 Data," http://edreform.com/_upload/cer_charter_survey.pdf.

20. Rapp and Eckes, "Dispelling the Myth of 'White Flight.'"

21. Cobb and Glass, "Ethnic Segregation in Arizona Charter Schools."

22. Frankenberg and Lee, "Charter Schools and Race."

23. Robert Bifulco and Helen F. Ladd, "School Choice, Racial Segregation, and Test-Score Gaps: Evidence from North Carolina's Charter School Program," *Journal of Policy Analysis and Management* 26, no. 1 (2006): 31–56; David R. Garcia, "The Impact of School Choice on Racial Segregation in Charter Schools," *Educational Policy* 22, no. 6 (2007): 805–829; Caroline M. Hoxby, Sonali Murarka, and Jenny Kang, "How New York City's Charter Schools

Affect Achievement," paper, New York City Charter Schools Evaluation Project, Cambridge, MA, 2009.

24. Suhrid S. Gajendragadkar, "The Constitutionality of Racial Balancing in Charter Schools," *Columbia Law Review* 106, no. 1 (2006): 144–181.

25. Frankenberg and Lee, "Charter Schools and Race."

26. Robert J. Martin, "Charting the Court Challenges to Charter Schools," *Penn State Law Review* 109, no. 1 (2004): 43–103.

27. Oluwole and Green, "Racial-Balancing Provisions and Parents Involved."

28. Robert J. Martin, "Court Challenges to Charter Schools."

29. *North Carolina General Statute* § 115C-238.29F(g)(5) (2007).

30. *New Jersey Statute Annotated*, § 18A:36A-8(e) (2008).

31. *Minnesota Statute* § 124D.10(9)(1)-(3) (2007).

32. *South Carolina Code Annotated* § 59–40-60(F)(8), (2007); amended by 2002 S.C. Acts 341.

33. Ibid.

34. *Nevada Revised Statutes Annotated* § 386.580(1) (2007).

35. *Parents Involved in Community Schools v. Seattle School District No. 1.*, 127 S. Ct. 2738 (2007).

36. Jonathan Dolle and Anne Newman, "Luck of the Draw? On the Fairness of Charter School Admissions Policies," unpublished manuscript, 2008; U.S. Department of Education, "Title V, Part B: Non-Regulatory Guidance," Charter Schools Program, Washington, DC, 2004, www.ed.gov/policy/elsec/guid/cspguidance03.doc; Suzanne Eckes and Anne E. Trotter, "Are Charter Schools Using Recruitment Strategies to Increase Student Body Diversity?" *Education and Urban Society* 40, no. 1 (2007): 62–90; Suzanne E. Eckes, "Barriers to Integration in the Mississippi Delta: Could Charter Schools Be the New Vehicle for Desegregation?" *Analyses of Social Issues and Public Policy* 6, no. 1 (2006): 15–30.

37. U.S. Office of Management and Budget, "Expect More: Detailed Information on the Charter Schools Grant Assessment," Washington, DC: U.S. Government Printing Office, 2005, www.whitehouse.gov/OMB/expectmore/detail/10003302.2005.

38. U.S. Department of Education, "Title V, Part B: Non-Regulatory Guidance."

39. Ibid., 5.

40. Suzanne Eckes, "Desegregation Decrees Versus the NCLB Choice Provision: Implications for Resegregated Schools," *Journal of School Choice* 1, no. 3 (2006): 63–76.

41. Dolle and Newman, "Luck of the Draw?"

42. Rapp and Eckes, "Dispelling the Myth of 'White Flight.'"

43. Ibid.

44. *Missouri Revised Statute* § 160.400(2) (2007).

45. Bifulco and Ladd, "North Carolina's Charter School Program."

46. Ibid.

47. Ibid.

48. Robin C. Miller, "Validity, Construction, and Application of Statute or Regulation Governing Charter Schools," *American Law Reporter* 78 (2008): 533–585.

49. S.C. Code Annotated (1997).

50. *Beaufort County Board of Education v. Lighthouse Charter School Committee,* 516 S.E.2d 655 (S.C. 1999).
51. Ibid.; *Beaufort County Board of Education v. Lighthouse Charter School Committee,* No. 97-CP-7-794 (S.C. Ct. Com. Pleas May 8, 2000); *Beaufort County Board of Education v. Lighthouse Charter School Committee,* 576 S.E.2d 180, 182 (S.C. 2003).
52. Maurice R. Dyson, "Putting Quality Back into Equality: Rethinking the Constitutionality of Charter School Enabling Legislation and Centric School Choice in a Post-Grutter Era," *Rutgers Law Journal* 36, no. 1 (2004): 1–52.
53. *Beaufort County Board of Education v. Lighthouse Charter School Committee,* No. 97-CP-7-794 (S.C. Ct. Com. Pleas May 8, 2000), 238.
54. *Beaufort County Board of Education v. Lighthouse Charter School Committee,* 576 S.E.2d 180, 182 (S.C. 2003), 181.
55. Ibid., 182.
56. *Save Our Schools v. Board of Education,* 2006 U.S. Dist. LEXIS 45081 (D.D.C. 2006).
57. Suzanne Eckes, Robert Fox, and Nina Buchanan, "Legal and Policy Issues Regarding Niche Charter Schools: Race, Religion, Culture and the Law," unpublished manuscript, written for the Hawaii International Conference on Education, Honolulu, HI, 2010.
58. *D.C. Code* § 2–1402.41 (2008).
59. Eckes, Fox, and Buchanan, "Niche Charter Schools."
60. *McFarland v. Jefferson County Public Schools,* 330 F.Supp.2d 834 (W.D. Ky 2004), 842.
61. Suzanne Eckes, "Public School Integration and the 'Cruel Irony' of the Decision in *Parents Involved in Community Schools v. Seattle School District No. 1,*" *Education Law Reporter* 228, no. 3 (2008): 1–18.
62. Ibid., 836.
63. Eckes, "Public School Integration and the 'Cruel Irony' of the Decision."
64. Ibid.
65. Ibid.
66. *Comfort v. Lynn School Committee,* 418 F.3d 1 (1st Cir. 2005); *Tuttle v. Arlington County School Board,* 195 F.3d 698 (4th Cir. 1999).
67. A compelling state interest is an extremely high legal standard to meet. In essence, in order for the government (e.g., a K–12 public school) to treat students differently on the basis of race, it must demonstrate a compelling reason for doing so (as opposed to a good or rational reason).
68. Eckes, "The 'Cruel Irony'"; *Parents Involved in Community Schools v. Seattle School District No. 1,* 127 S. Ct. 2738 (2007).
69. Eckes, "Public School Integration and the 'Cruel Irony' of the Decision."
70. *Parents Involved in Community Schools v. Seattle School District No. 1,* 127 S. Ct. 2797 (2007).
71. Eckes, "The 'Cruel Irony.'"
72. Frankenberg and Lee, "Charter Schools and Race."
73. Suzanne Eckes and Anne E. Trotter, "Are Charter Schools Using Recruitment Strategies to Increase Student Body Diversity?" *Education and Urban Society* 40, no. 1 (2007): 62–90; Frankenberg and Lee, "Charter Schools and

Race"; Rapp and Eckes, "Dispelling the Myth of 'White Flight.'"

74. Civil Rights Project, "Joint Statement of Nine University-Based Civil Rights Centers," June 28, 2007, www.civilrightsproject.ucla.edu/policy/court/voltint_joint_full_statement.php; Eckes, "The 'Cruel Irony.'"

75. U.S. Government Accountability Office, "No Child Left Behind Act: Education Needs to Provide Additional Technical Assistance and Conduct Implementation Studies for School Choice Provision," U.S. GAO, Washington, DC, 2004, www.gao.gov/new.items/d057.pdf.

76. Eckes and Trotter, "Recruitment Strategies to Increase Student Body Diversity?"

77. Nina K. Buchanan and Robert A. Fox, "Back to the Future: Ethnocentric Charter Schools in Hawaii," in *The Emancipatory Promise of Charter Schools: Toward a Progressive Politics of School Choice*, ed. Eric Rofes and Lisa M. Stullberg (Albany: SUNY Press, 2004), 80.

78. Ibid., 82.

79. Leonard L. Sykes Jr., "In Seeking Best Education, Some Choose Segregation," *Milwaukee Journal Sentinel*, March 14, 2004, A1.

80. Elissa Gootman, "Regents Consider New Hebrew Charter School in Brooklyn," *New York Times*, January 12, 2009, 1.

81. Wendy Parker, "The Color of Choice: Race and Charter Schools," *Tulane Law Review* 75, no. 3 (2001): 563–630.

82. Ibid.

83. Jon Schroeder, "Charter Schooling in Minnesota, the Nation's First Charter School State," Progressive Policy Institute, Washington, DC, 2004, www.ppionline.org/documents/MN_Charters_0504.pdf.

84. Buchanan and Fox, "Back to the Future."

85. Parker, "The Color of Choice."

86. Joanne Jacobs, "Immigrants Choose Ethnocentric Charters," Salon, January 13, 2009, http://open.salon.com/blog/joanne_jacobs; David Sikkink and Michael O. Emerson, "School Choice and Racial Segregation in U.S. Schools: The Role of Parents' Education," *Ethnic and Racial Studies* 31, no. 2 (2008): 267–293.

87. Sikkink and Emerson, "The Role of Parents' Education."

88. Mickelson, Bottia, and Southworth, "School Choice and Segregation."

89. Richard D. Kahlenberg, "High-Poverty Schooling in America: Lessons in Second-Class Citizenship: Reflections: Socioeconomic School Integration," *North Carolina Law Review* 85, no. 2 (2007): 1545–1594.

90. Richard D. Kahlenberg, *A New Way on School Integration* (New York: The Century Foundation, 2006), www.tcf.org/publications/education/schoolintegration.pdf; Kahlenberg, "High-Poverty Schooling in America."

91. Alan Finder, "As Test Scores Jump Raleigh Credits Integration by Income," *New York Times*, September 25, 2005, A1.

92. Eckes, "The 'Cruel Irony.'"

93. *Rhode Island Statute* § 16–77–4(b)(10) (2007).

94. *Villanueva v. Carere*, 85 F.3d 481 (10th Cir. 1996).

95. Ibid., 488.

96. Mickelson, Bottia, and Southworth, "School Choice and Segregation."

97. Denise M. Kazlauskas, "Education: Elementary and Secondary Education:

Provide for Charter School Status," *Georgia State University* 15, no. 1 (1998): 101–114.

98. Mickelson, Bottia, and Southworth, "School Choice and Segregation."

99. Garcia, "Impact of School Choice on Racial Segregation."

100. Frankenberg and Lee, "Charter Schools and Race."

101. Mitchell L. Yell, *The Law and Special Education* (Upper Saddle River, NJ: Pearson, 2006).

102. Kim K. Metcalf, Neil D. Theobald, and Gerardo Gonzalez, "State University Roles in the Charter School Movement," *Phi Delta Kappan* 84, no. 7 (2003): 542–545.

103. *North Carolina Statute* § 115C-238.29F(g)(5) (2007).

104. Bruce Fuller et al., "Charter Schools and Inequality: National Disparities in Funding, Teacher Quality and Student Support," working paper 03-2, Policy Analysis for California Education, University of California at Berkeley, Berkeley, 2003; Gleason, "Looking Back and Moving Forward"; Gary Miron, Christopher Nelson, and John Risley, "Strengthening Pennsylvania's Charter School Reform: Findings from the Statewide Evaluation and Discussion or Relevant Policy Issues," paper, Evaluation Center, Western Michigan University, Kalamazoo, 2002; Kevin Welner and Kenneth R. Howe, "Steering Toward Separation: The Evidence and Implications of Special Education Students' Exclusion from Choice Schools," in *School Choice and Diversity*, ed. Janelle Scott (New York: Teachers College Press, 2005), 93–111.

105. Thomas A. Fiore et al., *Charter Schools and Students with Disabilities: A National Study* (Washington, DC: Office of Educational Research and Improvement, U.S. Department of Education, 2000).

106. Mary B. Estes, "Choice for All? Charter Schools and Students with Special Needs," *Journal of Special Education* 37, no. 4 (2004): 257–267.

107. Mary B. Estes, "Charting the Course of Special Education in Texas' Charter Schools," *Education and Treatment of Children* 26, no. 4 (2003): 452–466; Mark D. Evans, "An End to Federal Funding of For-Profit Charter Schools?" *University of Colorado Law Review* 79, no. 2 (2008): 617–650; Kevin Welner and Kenneth R. Howe, "Steering Toward Separation: The Evidence and Implications of Special Education Students' Exclusion from Choice Schools," in *School Choice and Diversity: What the Evidence Says*, ed. Janelle Scott (New York: Teachers College Press, 2005), 93–111.

108. Fiore et al., *Charter Schools and Students with Disabilities.*

109. Julie F. Mead, "Charter Schools Designed for Children with Disabilities: An Initial Examination of Issues and Questions Raised," Primers on Special Education in Charter Schools, U.S. Department of Education, Washington, DC, 2008, www.uscharterschools.org/specialedprimers/download/special_report_mead.pdf.

110. Mickelson, Bottia, and Southworth, "School Choice and Segregation."

111. Mary B. Estes, "Charter Schools and Students with Disabilities," *Remedial and Special Education* 30, no. 4 (2008): 216–224.

112. Lauren M. Rhim et al., "Project Intersect: Studying Special Education in Charter Schools," paper, Project Intersect, University of Maryland, College Park, 2006.

113. Estes, "Charter Schools and Students with Disabilities."

114. Mead, "Charter Schools Designed for Children with Disabilities."

115. Ibid.

116. Ibid.

117. *Ohio Revised Code Annotated* §3314.06(D)(1)(b).

118. Mead, "Charter Schools Designed for Children with Disabilities."

119. *Florida Statute* § 1002.335(4)(b)(13)(b).

120. Mead, "Charter Schools Designed for Children with Disabilities."

121. Margaret Weertz, "The Benefits of Theme Schools," *Educational Leadership* 59, no. 7 (2002): 68–71.

122. Sherry Saavedra, "Gifted Curriculum Charter School Gets Encinitas OK," *San Diego Union Tribune*, May 2, 2006, www.signonsandiego.com/news/education/20060502-9999-1m2gifted.html.

123. Mickelson, Bottia, and Southworth, "School Choice and Segregation."

124. Kerry J. Gruber et al., *Schools and Staffing Survey, 1999–2000: Overview of the Data for Public, Private, Public Charter, and Bureau of Indian Affairs Elementary and Secondary Schools* (Washington, DC: National Center for Educational Statistics, 2002).

125. Daniel J. Losen and Kevin G. Welner, "Disabling Discrimination in Our Public Schools: Comprehensive Legal Challenges to Inappropriate and Inadequate Special Education Services for Minority Children," *Harvard Civil Rights–Civil Liberties Review* 36, no. 2 (2001): 407–460.

126. Suzanne Eckes, "Barriers to Integration in the Mississippi Delta: Could Charter Schools Be the New Vehicle For Desegregation?" *Analysis of Social Issues & Public Policy* 6, no. 1 (2006): 15–31.

127. Michael W. Kirst, "Politics of Charter Schools: Competing National Advocacy Coalitions Meet Local Politics," *Peabody Journal of Education* 82, no. 2–3 (2007): 184–203.

Chapter 4

1. Levin has developed a comprehensive framework for evaluating the diverse and sometimes contrasting outcomes of school choice reforms, which considers such criteria as freedom of choice, productive efficiency, equity, and social cohesion (H. M. Levin, "A Comprehensive Framework for Evaluating Educational Vouchers," *Educational Evaluation and Policy Analysis* 24, no. 3 [2002]: 159–174).

2. Gary Miron and Christopher Nelson, "Student Academic Achievement in Charter Schools: What We Know and Why We Know So Little," occasional paper no. 41, National Center for the Study of Privatization in Education, Teachers College, Columbia University, New York, 2001, http://ncspe.org/keepout/papers/00041/590_OP41.pdf.

3. In 2001, 77 percent of the state charter school laws only required a criterion-referenced test, and 6.5 percent of the states only required a norm-referenced test. Sixteen percent of the states required both criterion-referenced and norm-referenced tests. Interestingly, only a few charter school laws actually require an independent evaluation (ibid.).

4. Some states, such as Ohio, wait until a school's third year before publicly

reporting data. Most states also do not post data for subgroups when there are too few test takers, typically ten to fifteen students.

5. For California, see SRI International, "Evaluation of Charter School Effectiveness," December 11, 1997, www.lao.ca.gov/1997/121197_charter_schools/ sri_charter_schools_1297-part1.html. For the District of Columbia, see Jeffrey R. Henig et al., "Making a Choice, Making a Difference? An Evaluation of Charter Schools in the District of Columbia," paper, Center for Washington Area Studies, George Washington University, Washington, DC, 1998. For Michigan, see Eric P. Bettinger, "The Effect of Charter Schools on Charter Students and Public Schools," occasional paper no. 4, National Center for the Study of Privatization in Education, Teachers College, Columbia University, New York, 1999; Jerry Horn and Gary Miron, "Evaluation of Michigan Public School Academy Initiative," Evaluation Center, Western Michigan University, Kalamazoo, 1999.

6. For the 2001 study, see Miron and Nelson, "Student Academic Achievement." For the 2008 study, see Gary Miron, S. Evergreen, and J. Urschel, "The Impact of School Choice Reforms on Student Achievement," Education and the Public Interest Center Education Policy Research Unit, Arizona State University, Tempe, 2008, http://epicpolicy.org/files/EPSL-0706-236-EPRU. pdfhttp://epicpolicy.org/files/CHOICE-10-Miron-FINAL-withapp22.pdf. In more recent years, a number of reviews and Web-based systems have facilitated the tracking of charter school research. Most noteworthy is an online searchable database of studies maintained by the National Charter School Research Project at the University of Washington. This useful database now contains seventy-seven studies that consider charter school student achievement, although many of these studies lacked the technical reports or comparison groups required for this synthesis (see Center on Reinventing Public Education, National Charter School Research Project Web page, www.ncsrp. org/cs/csr/print/csr_docs/pubs/achieve_wp.htm). Bryan C. Hassel et al., "Charter School Achievement: What We Know," National Alliance for Public Charter Schools, Washington, DC, 2007, www.publiccharters.org/content/ publication/detail/2974/, also identified seventy charter school studies, although the particular methodology allowed for some studies to be counted two or three times, and the paper included studies that did not have technical reports. Diverse studies and publications on charter schools are also available from the searchable database on the U.S. Charter Schools Web site, http:// www.uscharterschools.org, which is maintained by various charter supporters.

7. In close to 40 percent of the states, the state board of education or the state department of education is expected to submit an annual descriptive report to the state's legislature regarding the status of the charter schools. Such reports are completed only irregularly. Most descriptive reports prepared by state education agencies contain only brief profiles of the schools, with little or no reference to the academic progress of students.

8. F. H. Nelson, B. Rosenberg, and N. Van Meter, "Charter School Achievement on the 2003 National Assessment of Educational Progress," paper, American Federation of Teachers, Washington, DC, 2004.

9. D. J. Schemo, "Charter Schools Trail in Results, U.S. Data Reveal," *New York Times*, August 17, 2004, A1.

10. Caroline M. Hoxby, "A Straightforward Comparison of Charter Schools and Regular Public Schools in the United States," paper, Department of Economics, Harvard University, Cambridge, MA, 2004.

11. The widespread controversy and public debate sparked by these studies was unexpected. Martin Carnoy et al., *The Charter School Dust-Up: Examining the Evidence on Enrollment and Achievement* (New York and Washington, DC: Teachers College Press and Economic Policy Institute, 2005); Jeffrey R. Henig, *Spin Cycle: How Research Is Used in Policy Debates; The Case of Charter Schools* (New York: Russell Sage Foundation, 2008), examine these studies and the controversy surrounding them. J. Roy and L. Mishel, "Advantage None: Re-Examining Hoxby's Finding of Charter School Benefits," briefing paper no. 158, Economic Policy Institute, Washington, DC, 2005, reviews the key flaws and unreported limitations of the Hoxby analyses.

12. Henry Braun, Frank Jenkins, and Wendy Grigg, *A Closer Look at Charter Schools Using Hierarchical Linear Modeling*, NCES 2006-460 (Washington, DC: U.S. Department of Education, 2006); S. T. Lubienski and Christopher Lubienski, "School Sector and Academic Achievement: A Multilevel Analysis of NAEP Mathematics Data," *American Educational Research Journal* 43, no. 4 (2006): 651–698.

13. This Lubienski and Lubienski study also included the performance of diverse types of private schools, which is not discussed here.

14. T. Loveless, "The 2003 Brown Center Report on American Education: Charter schools: Achievement, Accountability, and the Role of Expertise," paper, Brookings Institution, Washington, DC, 2003.

15. Gary Miron, Christopher Nelson, and J. Risley, *Strengthening Pennsylvania's Charter School Reform: Findings from the Statewide Evaluation and Discussion of Relevant Policy Issues* (Harrisburg: Pennsylvania Department of Education, 2002); G. Miron and B. Applegate, "An Evaluation of Student Achievement in Edison Schools Opened in 1995 and 1996," Evaluation Center, Western Michigan University, Kalamazoo, 2000, www.wmich.edu/evalctr/edison/edison.html.

16. Gary Miron, C. Coryn, and D. Mackety, "Evaluating the Impact of Charter Schools on Student Achievement: A Longitudinal Look at the Great Lakes States," Education and the Public Interest Center, Education Policy Research Unit, Arizona State University, Tempe, 2007, http://epicpolicy.org/files/EPSL-0706-236-EPRU.pdf.

17. L. Solmon, K. Paark, and David R. Garcia, "Does Charter School Attendance Improve Test Scores?" paper, Goldwater Institute's Center for Market-Based Education, Phoenix, 2001.

18. Ron Zimmer et al., *Charter School Operation and Performance: Evidence from California* (Santa Monica, CA: RAND, 2003); Gary Miron, Anne Cullen, Brooks Applegate, and Patricia Farrell, *"Evaluation of the Delaware Charter School Reform: Final Report.* (Dover, DE., Delaware State Board of Education, 2007).; Robert Bifulco and Helen F. Ladd, "School Choice, Racial Segregation and Test-Score Gaps: Evidence from North Carolina's Charter School

Program," *Journal of Policy Analysis and Management* 25, no. 1 (2006): 31–56; T. Gronberg and D. W. Jansen, "Texas Charter Schools: An Assessment in 2005," paper, Texas Public Policy Foundation, Austin, 2005.

19. Caroline M. Hoxby and J. E. Rockoff, "The Impact of Charter Schools on Student Achievement: A Study of Students Who Attend Schools Chartered by the Chicago Charter School Foundation," paper, Department of Economics, Harvard University, Cambridge, MA, 2004.

20. Caroline M. Hoxby and Sonali Murarka, "Charter Schools in New York City: Who Enrolls and How They Affect Their Students' Achievement," paper, National Bureau of Economic Research, Cambridge, MA, 2007; Atila Abdulkadiroglu et al., "Informing the Debate: Comparing Boston's Charter, Pilot and Traditional Schools," paper, Boston Foundation, Boston, 2008.

21. See, for example, Cecilia Elena Rouse, "Private School Vouchers and Student Achievement: An Evaluation of the Milwaukee Parental Choice Program," NBER working paper no. 5964, National Bureau of Economic Research, Cambridge, MA, 1997.

22. Gene V. Glass, "Primary, Secondary, and Meta-Analysis of Research," *Educational Researcher* 5, no. 10 (1976): 3–8; R. E. Slavin, "Best-Evidence Synthesis: An Alternative to Meta-Analytic and Traditional Reviews," *Educational Researcher* 15, no. 9 (1986): 5–11.

23. J. Betts and Y. E. Tang, "Value-Added and Experimental Studies of the Effect of Charter Schools on Student Achievement: A Literature Review," paper, National Charter School Research Project, University of Washington, Seattle, 2008.

24. A common rule of thumb is that effect sizes of 0.80 or higher are thought to represent large differences, and an effect sizes of 0.02 is deemed small (J. Cohen, *Statistical Power for the Behavioral Sciences* [Hillsdale, NJ: Erlbaum, 1988]).

25. Miron and Nelson, "Why We Know So Little"; Gary Miron and Christopher Nelson, "Student Achievement in Charter Schools," in *Taking Account of Charter Schools*, ed. Katrina E. Bulkley and Priscilla Wohlstetter (New York: Teachers College Press, 2004), 161–175. There have been a few other attempts to synthesize the research on student achievement. Back in 2001, Brian P. Gill et al., *Rhetoric Versus Reality: What We Know and What We Need to Know About Vouchers and Charter Schools* (Santa Monica, CA: RAND, 2001), summarized the research on student achievement in charter schools. Because the researchers set the bar so high for the studies to be included, only three studies were actually considered and summarized. More recent summaries have been prepared by Bryan C. Hassel et al., "Charter School Achievement: What We Know," paper, National Alliance for Public Charter Schools, Washington, DC, 2007; Carnoy et al., *The Charter School Dust-Up*; and P. Hill, "Assessing Achievement in Charter Schools," in *Hopes, Fears, and Reality: A Balanced Look at American Charter Schools in 2005*, ed. Robin J. Lake (Seattle: National Charter School Research Project, University of Washington, 2005). The later three examples have grouped the studies according to whether they were positive or negative, and in some cases they are grouped by design type, although no effort has been made to weigh and synthesize the results across studies.

26. Miron, Evergreen, and Urschel, "Impact of School Choice Reforms."

27. This study was repeated by other independent researchers as well as by the U.S. Department of Education. These studies used more rigorous controls but still came to the same conclusion as the AFT study.
28. Miron and Applegate, "Student Achievement in Edison Schools"; M. A. Mac Iver and D. J. Mac Iver, "Privatizing Education in Philadelphia: Are Educational Management Organizations Improving Student Achievement?" occasional paper no. 141, National Center for the Study of Privatization in Education, New York, 2007, www.ncspe.org/publications_files/OP141.pdf.
29. Miron and Applegate, "Student Achievement in Edison Schools"; D. A. Stuit and T. M. Smith, "Teacher Turnover in Charter Schools," paper presented at the American Educational Research Association annual meeting, San Diego, April 12–18, 2009.
30. Miron and Nelson, "Why We Know So Little."
31. Note that I have written or otherwise contributed to nine of the studies mentioned in this overview. These include two that found that charter schools were outperforming traditional public schools and two with mixed results. The remaining four studies concluded that charter schools were not performing as well as comparable traditional public schools.

Chapter 5

1. Our use of the designation *traditional public schools* (TPSs) refers only to the governance and not the instructional practices of these public schools. This is important to clarify in light of early predictions, now largely diminished, that charter schools would be distinguished by high levels of innovation (Christopher Lubienski, "Innovation in Education Markets: Theory and Evidence on the Impact of Competition and Choice in Charter Schools," *American Educational Research Journal* 40, no. 2 [2003]: 394–443). For the purposes of this chapter, one could substitute the phrase *district-run schools* for traditional public schools without any change in intended meaning.
2. In fact, available empirical evidence on the direct effect of charter schools on student performance is very mixed and has yet to clearly establish the benefits for active choosers (Gary Miron, S. Evergreen, and J. Urschel, "The Impact of School Choice Reforms on Student Achievement," paper no. EPSL-0803-262-EPRU, Education and the Public Interest Center, Education Policy Research Unit, Arizona State University, Tempe, 2008.
3. We do not pursue the impact of charter competition on other charter schools and private schools, both very interesting and important issues, because of the lack of rigorous quantitative evidence so far comparable to the competitive-effects research on TPSs.
4. See, for example, Caroline M. Hoxby, "School Choice and School Productivity: Could School Choice Be a Tide That Lifts All Boats?" in *The Economics of School Choice*, ed. Caroline M. Hoxby (Chicago: University of Chicago Press, 2003).
5. Natalie Lacireno-Paquet and C. Brantley, "Who Chooses Schools, and Why?" paper no. EPSL-0801-247-EPRU, Education and the Public Interest Center, Education Policy Research Unit, Arizona State University, Tempe, 2008.

6. Paul Teske et al., "Can Charter Schools Change Traditional Public Schools?" in *Charters, Vouchers & Public Education*, ed. P. E. Peterson and D. Campbell (Washington, DC: Brookings Institution, 2001).

7. Frederick M. Hess, *Revolution at the Margins: The Impact of Competition on Urban School Systems* (Washington, DC: Brookings Institution, 2002).

8. David Arsen, David Plank, and Gary Sykes, "School Choice Policies in Michigan: The Rules Matter," paper, Michigan State University, East Lansing 1999; J. Ericson and D. Silverman, "Challenge and Opportunity: The Impact of Charter Schools on School Districts," paper, U.S. Department of Education, Washington, DC, 2001; Frederick M. Hess, Robert Maranto, and Scott Milliman, "Responding to Competition: School Leaders and School Culture," in *Charters, Vouchers & Public Education*, ed. P. E. Peterson and D. Campbell (Washington, DC: Brookings Institution, 2001); Frederick M. Hess, Robert Maranto, and Scott Milliman, "Small Districts in Big Trouble: How Four Arizona School Systems Responded to Charter Competition" *Teachers College Record* 103, no. 6 (2001): 1102–1124; Eric Rofes, "How Are School Districts Responding to Charter Laws and Charter Schools? A Study of Eight States and the District of Columbia," paper, Policy Analysis for California Education, Berkeley, 1998.

9. Bryan C. Hassel, *The Charter School Challenge: Avoiding the Pitfalls, Fulfilling the Promise* (Washington, DC: Brookings Institution, 1999); Hess, Maranto, and Milliman, "Responding to Competition"; Hess, Maranto, and Milliman, "Small Districts in Big Trouble."

10. Arsen, Plank, and Sykes, "School Choice Policies in Michigan"; Katrina E. Bulkley and J. Fisler, "A Decade of Charter Schools: From Theory to Practice," *Educational Policy* 17, no. 3 (2003): 317–342; Hess, *Revolution at the Margins*.

11. Hoxby, "School Choice and School Productivity."

12. J. Merrifield, *The School Choice Wars* (Lanham, MD: Scarecrow Press, 2001), for example, dismisses existing empirical evidence of competitive effects in education, because none of the actual school choice reforms has established an entirely private, market-based system in which inter alia there would be no significant barriers to schools entering the publicly funded system and they could compete freely on price (tuition).

13. D. Goldhaber et al., "How School Choice Affects Students Who Do Not Choose," in *Getting Choice Right: Ensuring Equity and Efficiency in Education Policy*, ed. J. R. Betts and T. Loveless (Washington, DC: Brookings Institution, 2005).

14. If this is the case, random-trends modeling, in which each school is allowed to have its own development trend, can be used. As long as charter location is correlated with linear time-invariant development trends but uncorrelated with nonlinear or temporary trends, this will eliminate the bias associated with charter location. When charter location responds to nonlinear changes in schools, even random-trends modeling will not remove all bias.

15. A limitation with the IV method is that there is usually no statistical way to test the second condition. Rather, it has to be tested through common sense and economic theory. In practice, truly external IVs are very hard to

find in charter school research. Using weak IVs that do not satisfy the two conditions tends to inflate the bias. More often than not, a slight correlation between the IVs and the variables that they are instrumented for could cause larger bias than estimators using no IVs (J. M. Wooldridge, *Econometric Analysis of Cross Section and Panel Data* [Cambridge, MA: MIT Press, 2002]).

16. H. Lankford and J. Wyckoff, "Why Are Schools Racially Segregated? Implications for School Choice Policy," in *School Choice and Diversity: What the Evidence Says*, ed. Janelle Scott (New York: Teachers College Press, 2005); Mark Schneider and Jack Buckley, "What Do Parents Want From Schools? Evidence from the Internet," *Educational Evaluation and Policy Analysis* 24, no. 2 (2002): 133–144.

17. If TPS parents observe their schools making positive responses to charter competition, they may decide to keep their kids in the TPS. Alternatively, the perception of negative effects could prompt parents to move their children to a different school. In either case, the estimated competitive effect will be exaggerated and biased away from zero.

18. For example, a strategy of simply dividing schools into different groups according to characteristics of interest and then comparing their outcomes would suffer from the regression-to-mean problem. Quantile regression methods that have been applied in some areas of economics and educational research may hold promise for studying patterns of competitive effects across public schools.

19. K. Booker et al., "The Effect of Charter Schools on Traditional Public School Students in Texas: Are Children Who Stay Behind Left Behind?" paper no. 104, National Center for the Study for the Privatization in Education, New York, 2005.

20. Yongmei Ni, "Do Traditional Public Schools Benefit from Charter School Competition? Evidence from Michigan," *Economics of Education Review* 28, no. 5 (2009): 571–584.

21. Hoxby, "School Choice and School Productivity."

22. Eric P. Bettinger, "The Effect of Charter Schools on Charter Students and Public Schools," *Economics of Education Review* 24, no. 2 (2005): 133–147.

23. Ni, "Evidence from Michigan."

24. G. M. Holmes, J. DeSimone, and N. Rupp, "Does School Choice Increase School Quality?" working paper no. W9683, National Bureau of Economic Research, Cambridge, MA, 2003.

25. Robert Bifulco and Helen F. Ladd, "The Impacts of Charter Schools on Student Achievement: Evidence from North Carolina," *Education Finance and Policy* 1, no. 1 (2006): 50–89.

26. J. Bohte, "Examining the Impact of Charter Schools on Performance in Traditional Public Schools," *Policy Studies Journal* 32, no. 4 (2004): 501–520.

27. Booker et al., "Are Children Who Stay Behind Left Behind?"

28. A provision in the Texas charter school legislation permits an unlimited number of schools that commit to enrolling at least 75 percent at-risk students.

29. Tim R. Sass, "Charter Schools and Student Achievement in Florida," *Education Finance and Policy* 1, no. 1 (2006): 91–122.

30. Richard Buddin and Ron Zimmer, "Is Charter School Competition in California Improving the Performance of Traditional Public Schools?" paper no. WR-297-EDU, RAND Corporation, Santa Monica, CA, 2005.
31. M. Carr and G. Ritter, "Measuring the Competitive Effect of Charter Schools on Student Achievement in Ohio's Traditional Public Schools," paper no. 146, National Center for the Study of Privatization in Education, New York, 2007.
32. S. A. Imberman, "The Effect of Charter Schools on Non-Charter Students: An Instrumental Variables Approach," paper no. 149, National Center for the Study of Privatization in Education, New York, 2008.
33. Patrick J. McEwan, "The Potential Impact of Large-Scale Voucher Programs," *Review of Educational Research* 70, no. 2 (2000): 103–149.
34. Goldhaber et al., "How School Choice Affects Students Who Do Not Choose."
35. Researchers consistently find that students with disabilities constitute a lower share of charter school than district school enrollment. David Arsen and Lisa Ray, "When Do Charter Schools Enroll Students with Disabilities?" *Journal of Special Education Leadership* 17, no. 2 (2004): 71–81, note that over a third of the charter schools in Michigan have no students with individualized educational programs (IEPs), which are required for students with disabilities under the Individuals with Disabilities Education Act.
36. Arsen, Plank, and Sykes, "School Choice Policies in Michigan."
37. Justine S. Hastings and Jeffrey M. Weinstein, "Information, School Choice, and Academic Achievement: Evidence from Two Experiments," *Quarterly Journal of Economics* 123 (2008): 1373–1414.
38. Hess, *Revolution at the Margins*, 238.
39. Ibid., 38.
40. Frederick Hess, *Education Unbound: The Promise and Practice of Greenfield Schooling* (Alexandria, VA: ASCD, 2010).

Chapter 6

1. Carol Ascher et al., "The Finance Gap: Charter Schools and Their Facilities," Institute for Education and Social Policy, New York University, New York, 2004, http://steinhardt.nyu.edu/iesp/publications/pubs/The%20Finance%20Gap.pdf; Bruce Fuller et al., "Localized Ideas of Fairness: Inequality Among Charter Schools," in *Taking Account of Charter Schools: What's Happened and What's Next*, ed. Katrina E. Bulkley and Priscilla Wohlstetter (New York: Teachers College Press, 2004), 93–120; Jeffrey Henig et al., "Growing Pains: An Evaluation of Charter Schools in the District of Columbia, 1999–2000," paper, Center for Washington Area Studies, George Washington University, Washington, DC, 2001; Howard F. Nelson, Edward Muir, and Rachel Drown, *Venturesome Capital: State Charter School Finance Systems* (Washington, DC: U.S. Department of Education, 2000); Howard F. Nelson, Edward Muir, and Rachel Drown, *Paying for the Vision: Charter School Revenue and Expenditures* (Washington, DC: U.S. Department of Education, 2003); Eric Osberg, "Charter School Funding," in *Charter Schools Against the Odds: An Assessment of the Koret Task Force on K–12*, ed. P. Hill

(Stanford, CA: Hoover Institution, 2006), 45–69; Chester E. Finn Jr., Bryan C. Hassel, and Sheree Speakman, "Charter School Funding: Inequity's Last Frontier," paper, Thomas B. Fordham Foundation, Washington, DC, 2005.

2. The external management of schools that is tightly aligned with market-based principals and for-profit objectives is associated with educational management organizations (EMOs). The term *charter management organization* (CMO) originally stems from an effort by the New Schools Venture Fund, a venture philanthropy spun off from the venture capital firm Kleiner, Perkins, Caufield, and Byers, to distinguish nonprofit CMOs from their for-profit EMO counterparts (Steven F. Wilson, "Realizing the Promise of Brand-Name Schools," in *Brookings Papers on Education Policy*, ed. D. Ravitch [Washington, DC: Brookings Institution, 2005], 89–135).

3. Luis A. Huerta and Chad d'Entremont, "Charter School Funding in New York State: Seeking Institutional Legitimacy in a Marketplace of Resources," paper presented at the annual meeting of the American Educational Research Association, New York, March 24–28, 2008; Luis A. Huerta and Andrew Zuckerman, "An Institutional Theory Analysis of Charter Schools: Addressing Challenges to Scale," *Peabody Journal of Education* 84, no. 3 (2009): 414–431. Charter school governance varies by state, according to specific legislation that authorizes and regulates the schools' functioning. Thus, different state contexts may produce different responses to increased autonomy and funding shortfalls. However, all states share a general conceptualization of charter school reform framed around a decentralized theory of action. Charter schools are expected to compete for students in a deregulated quasi-marketplace, advance innovations that challenge traditional schooling norms, and, finally, conform to centralized standards and accountability measures. This contradiction between innovative schooling practices and standardized or traditional regulatory practices is at the root of our analysis.

4. David F. Labaree, "Public Goods, Private Goods: The American Struggle over Educational Goals," *American Educational Research Journal* 34, no. 1 (1997): 39–81.

5. William S. Koski and Jesse Hahnel, "The Past, Present, and Possible Futures of Educational Finance Reform Litigation," in *Handbook of Research in Education Finance and Policy*, ed. Helen F. Ladd and Edward B. Fiske (New York: Routledge, 2008), 42–60.

6. Gary Miron and Christopher Nelson, *What's Public About Charter Schools? Lessons Learned About Choice and Accountability* (Thousand Oaks, CA: Corwin Press, 2002).

7. William S. Koski and Jesse Hahnel, "The Past, Present, and Possible Futures of Educational Finance Reform Litigation," in *Handbook of Research in Education Finance and Policy*, ed. Helen F. Ladd and Edward B. Fiske (New York: Routledge, 2008), 42–60.

8. Brian P. Gill et al., *Rhetoric Versus Reality: What We Know and What We Need to Know About Vouchers and Charter Schools* (Santa Monica, CA: RAND, 2001).

9. Miron and Nelson, *What's Public About Charter Schools?*

10. Finn, Hassel, and Speakman, "Inequity's Next Frontier."

11. Ibid.
12. Nelson, Muir, and Drown, "Paying for the Vision." There are substantial differences in the distribution and use of charter schools and traditional public schools. For example, charter schools are more likely to be elementary schools, which are less expensive to operate than secondary schools, but also are more likely to be located in urban areas, where spending on education tends to be higher. Thus, comparisons between per-pupil expenditures ultimately depend on the revenue sources included in funding formula calculations. Finn, Hassel, and Speakman, "Inequity's Next Frontier," reported that charter schools in Washington, D.C., received 20 percent less funding than did traditional public schools, whereas Nelson, Muir, and Drown, *Venturesome Capital*, found that D.C. charters received more funding. These contradictory findings emphasize that different funding calculations combined with political considerations can lead to very different conclusions about charter school finance. However, we feel confident that the consensus in the current literature is that charter schools receive less funding per student than do traditional public schools (for further reading, see Edward Bodine et al., "Disparities in Charter School Resources: The Influence of State Policy and Community Conditions," *Journal of Education Policy* 23, no. 1 [2008]: 1–33; Carol Ascher et al., "The Finance Gap: Charter Schools and Their Facilities," paper, Institute for Education and Social Policy, New York University, New York, 2004; Fuller et al., "Localized Ideas of Fairness," 93–120; Henig et al., "Growing Pains"; Robin Jacobowitz and Jonathon S. Gyurko, "Charter School Funding in New York: Perspectives of Parity with Traditional Public Schools," Institute for Education and Social Policy, New York University, New York, 2004, http://steinhardt.nyu.edu/iesp/publications/pubs/charter/CharterFinance.pdf; Osberg, "Charter School Funding," 45–69; Nelson, Muir and Drown, *Venturesome Capital*; Hank Prince, "Expenditure Patterns of Michigan's Charter Schools: An Exploratory Story," paper presented at the annual meeting of the American Education Finance Association, Savannah, 1999; U.S. Government Accountability Office, "Charter Schools: New Charter Schools Across the Country and in the District of Columbia Face Similar Start-Up Challenges," GAO Report to Congressional Requesters, U.S. Government Accountability Office, Washington, DC, 2003.
13. Finn, Hassel, and Speakman, "Inequity's Next Frontier."
14. Jacobowitz and Gyurko, "Charter School Funding in New York"; Osberg, "Charter School Funding," 45–69.
15. Nelson, Muir and Drown, *Venturesome Capital*.
16. Ascher et al., "The Finance Gap"; Public Sector Consultants, Inc. and MAXIMUS, Inc., "Michigan's Charter School Initiative: From Theory to Practice," Michigan Department of Education, 1999, www.mde.state.mi.us/reports/psaeval9901/pscfullreport.pdf.
17. Carolyn Sullings and Gary Miron, "Challenges of Starting and Operating Charter Schools: A Multicase Study," Evaluation Center, Western Michigan University, Kalamazoo, 2005, www.wmich.edu/evalctr/charter/cs_challenges_report.pdf; Stephen D. Sugarman, "Charter School Funding Issues,"

Education Policy Analysis Archives 10, no. 34 (2002), http://epaa.asu.edu/epaa/v10n34.html.

18. Ascher et al., "The Finance Gap," studied 2,091 charter school facilities in fourteen states and the District of Columbia and found that charter schools devote 20 to 25 percent of their instructional budgets to repaying debts acquired, in part, to purchase and maintain school buildings. This same study reports that financiers believe that charter schools should not spend more than 12 to 15 percent of per-pupil revenue on debt service.

19. Prince, "Expenditure Patterns of Michigan's Charter Schools."

20. Miron and Nelson, *What's Public About Charter Schools?*

21. Ibid.

22. Finn, Hassel, and Speakman, "Inequity's Next Frontier"; Theodore Kolderie, "Beyond Choice to New Public Schools: Withdrawing the Exclusive Franchise in Public Education," paper, Progressive Policy Institute, Washington, DC, 1990; Joe Nathan, *Charter Schools: Creating Hope and Opportunity for American Education* (San Francisco: Jossey-Bass, 1996).

23. Sally Bomotti, Rick Ginsberg, and Brian Cobb, "Teachers in Charter Schools and Traditional Schools: A Comparative Study," *Education Policy Analysis Archives* 7, no. 22 (1999); M. Burian-Fitzgerald, "Average Teacher Salaries and Returns to Experience in Charter Schools," Occasional Paper Series, National Center for the Study of Privatization in Education, New York, 2005, http://ncspe.org/list-papers.php; Courtney L. Malloy and Priscilla Wohlstetter, "Working Conditions in Charter Schools: What's the Appeal for Teachers?" *Education and Urban Society* 35, no. 2 (2003): 219–241.

24. Miron and Nelson, *What's Public About Charter Schools?*

25. Ibid.; Bodine et al., "Disparities in Charter School Resources." In addition, research examining public school choice programs has reported on how market forces unleashed in the expansion of choice schools resurrect "vertical hierarchies of prestige" that reinforce traditional norms of tracking and nondiverse schools and classrooms (Christopher Lubienski, "Charter School Innovations in Theory and Practice," paper presented at the Educational Issues in Charter Schools Conference, Washington, DC, 2001). What may result is choice schools actively pursuing "more desirable" students from a self-selected population drawn to attributes promoted by each school's mission.

26. RPP International, *State of Charter Schools: Fourth-Year Report* (Washington, DC: U.S. Department of Education, 2000).

27. Osberg, "Charter School Funding," 45–69.

28. Carol Ascher et al., "Going Charter: New Models of Support," Institute for Education and Social Policy, New York University, New York, 2001, http://steinhardt.nyu.edu/iesp/publications/pubs/charter/GoingCharter.pdf.

29. U.S. Government Accountability Office, "Charter Schools: New Charter Schools across the Country."

30. Ascher et al., "The Finance Gap"; Amy Stuart Wells, "Beyond the Rhetoric of Charter School Reform: A Study of Ten California School Districts," paper, University of California, Los Angeles, 1998.

31. Marc D. Millot and Robin J. Lake, "Supplying a System of Charter Schools:

Observations on Early Implementation of the Massachusetts Statute," paper, Institute for Public Policy and Management, University of Washington, Seattle, 1997. Charter schools struggle to secure low-interest loans or issue bonds because they are often viewed as a risky investments in light of their small size, limited cash reserves, and short history (Ascher et al., "The Finance Gap").

32. Ascher et al., "Going Charter: New Models of Support"; Katrina E. Bulkley, "Balancing Act: Education Management Organizations and Charter School Autonomy," in *Taking Account of Charter Schools: What's Happened and What's Next*, ed. Katrina E. Bulkley and Priscilla Wohlstetter (New York: Teachers College Press, 2004), 121–141.

33. Heinz-Dieter Meyer and Brian Rowan, in *The New Institutionalism in Education*, ed. H. D. Meyer and B. Rowan (Albany: State University of New York Press, 2006); John W. Meyer and Brian Rowan, "Institutionalized Organizations: Formal Structure As Myth and Ceremony," *American Journal of Sociology* 83, no. 2 (1977): 340–363; John W. Meyer and Brian Rowan, "The Structure of Educational Organizations," in *Environments and Organizations*, ed. M. W. Meyer et al. (San Francisco: Jossey-Bass, 1978), 78–109; Richard Scott, *Institutions and Organizations* (Thousand Oaks, CA: Sage Publications, 1998); Walter J. Powell and Paul J. DiMaggio, "The Iron Cage Revisited: Institutional Isomorphism and Collective Rationality in Organizational Fields," in *The New Institutionalism in Organizational Analysis*, ed. Walter J. Powell, and Paul J. DiMaggio (Chicago: University of Chicago Press, 1991), 63– 82.

34. Karl L. Weick, "Educational Organizations As Loosely Coupled Systems," *Administrative Science Quarterly* 21, no. 1 (1976): 1–19.

35. Meyer and Rowan, "Institutionalized Organizations"; Meyer and Rowan, "Structure of Educational Organizations," 78–109; John W. Meyer et al., "Institutional and Technical Sources of Organizational Structure: Explaining the Structure of Educational Organizations," *Organizational Environments: Ritual and Rationality*, ed. John W. Meyer and W. R. Scott (Beverly Hills, CA: Sage Publications, 1983), 45–67.

36. Meyer et al., "Institutional and Technical Sources of Organizational Structure," 45–67.

37. Meyer and Rowan, "Structure of Educational Organizations," 80, explain that "ritual classifications are the basic components of the theory (or ideology) of education used by modern societies, and schools gain enormous resources by conforming to them, incorporating them, and controlling them." Ritual classifications are used to control and define who does what within an organization. Thus, educational structures are actually very tightly coupled around the identification or labels given to the activities and actors within an organization—from curriculum to teacher certification. However, the title or role of activities or actors may not adequately identify the actual work that is produced, but rather may provide a classification for upholding the rational organizational structure. In time, these classifications become institutionalized and accepted as norms or rituals within the institutional field of education. Conformity to these norms becomes necessary for organizations to earn legitimacy, both from the

outside and from within the institutional environment (Meyer and Rowan, "Institutionalized Organizations").

38. Powell and DiMaggio, "The Iron Cage Revisited," 63– 82; Bodine et al., "Disparities in Charter School Resources."

39. Luis A. Huerta, "Institutional vs. Technical Environments: Reconciling the Goals of Decentralization in an Evolving Charter School Organization," *Peabody Journal of Education* 84, no. 2 (2009): 244–261; Huerta and Zuckerman, "Institutional Theory Analysis of Charter Schools"; Meyer and Rowan, in *New Institutionalism in Education*.

40. Jeffrey Henig et al., "Privatization, Politics, and Urban Services: The Political Behavior of Charter Schools," *Journal of Urban Affairs* 25, no. 1 (2003): 37–54.

41. For further reading, see ibid.; Katrina E. Bulkley and Priscilla Wohlstetter, eds., *Taking Account of Charter Schools: What's Happened and What's Next* (New York: Teachers College Press, 2004); Gary Miron and Christopher Nelson, "Student Achievement in Charter Schools: What We Know and Why We Know So Little," in *Taking Account of Charter Schools: What's Happened and What's Next*, ed. Katrina E. Bulkley and Priscilla Wohlstetter (New York: Teachers College Press, 2004), 161–175; Priscilla Wohlstetter et al., eds., *Charter School Partnerships: 8 Key Lessons for Success* (Los Angeles: Center on Educational Governance, 2005); Jeffrey Henig et al., "The Influence of Founder Type on Charter School Structures and Operations," *American Journal of Education* 111, no. 4 (2005): 487–522.

42. David Osborne and Ted Gaebler, *Reinventing Government: How the Entrepreneurial Spirit Is Transforming the Public Sector* (Reading, MA: Addison Wesley, 1992).

43. Bodine et al., "Disparities in Charter School Resources."

44. Bruce Fuller et al., "Localized Ideas of Fairness," 93–120. The 1999–2000 SASS is a nationally representative survey, administered by the National Center for Education Statistics (NCES), containing interviews from principals and teachers in 1,010 charter schools, or approximately 86 percent of the charter schools operating during the 1998–1999 and 1999–2000 school years.

45. Cathy Krop and Ron Zimmer, "Charter School Type Matters When Examining Funding and Facilities: Evidence from California," *Education Policy Analysis Archives* 13, no. 50 (2005).

46. Wohlstetter et al., *Charter School Partnerships: 8 Key Lessons.*

47. Henig et al., "Influence of Founder Type"; Krop and Zimmer "Charter School Type Matters."

48. Katrina E. Bulkley, "Balancing Act: Education Management Organizations and Charter School Autonomy," in *Taking Account of Charter Schools: What's Happened and What's Next*, ed. Katrina E. Bulkley and Priscilla Wohlstetter (New York: Teachers College Press, 2004), 121–141.

49. Bodine et al., "Disparities in Charter School Resources."

50. The New York Charter Schools Act of 1998 set an initial cap of one hundred charter schools. In April 2007, the New York State Legislature voted to raise the cap to two hundred schools as part of the state budget process.

51. Jacobowitz and Gyurko, "Charter School Funding in New York."

52. Ibid.
53. Ibid.
54. Finn, Hassel, and Speakman " Inequity's Last Frontier."
55. All the anonymous quotations in this chapter are from interviews with personnel in these three schools conducted from January 18, 2005 to October 13, 2006. We visited each school at least four times over an eighteen-month period (some schools required additional visits). At each school, semistructured interviews were conducted with school-level actors (administrators, teachers, parents, and board members). Interviews followed structured protocols driven by an initial set of indicators identified in the quantitative study that analyzed data from the SASS data set (Bodine et al., "Disparities in Charter School Resources"), including how resources were identified, acquired, and used, as well as controlled by internal and external authorities. We conducted twenty-four interviews, all of which were recorded, transcribed, and then coded. During school visits, the research team also observed classrooms, board meetings, and other school functions.
56. Albert Shanker, "Restructuring Our Schools," *Peabody Journal of Education* 65, no. 3 (1988): 88–100; Bruce Fuller, ed., *Inside Charter Schools* (Cambridge, MA: Harvard University Press, 2000); Amy Stuart Wells, *Where Charter School Policy Fails: The Problems of Accountability and Equity* (New York: Teachers College Press, 2002).
57. Powell and DiMaggio, "The Iron Cage Revisited"; Meyer and Rowan, "Institutionalized Organizations."
58. Russel Berman, "Council Split on Rise in Charter Schools," *New York Sun*, January 8, 2007, A3.
59. Meyer and Rowan, in *The New Institutionalism in Education*; Meyer and Rowan, "Institutionalized Organizations"; Meyer and Rowan, "The Structure of Educational Organizations." The important point here is that when ritual classifications become institutionalized and accepted as proxies for effective schooling, then educational organizations are inclined to adopt such classifications into their formal structure to derive resources and legitimacy from the wider institutional environment.
60. Walter J. Powell and Paul J. DiMaggio, eds., *The New Institutionalism in Organizational Analysis* (Chicago: University of Chicago Press, 1991), 41.
61. Meyer and Rowan, "Institutionalized Organizations," 349.

Chapter 7

1. Todd Ziebarth et al., "The Charter Schools Landscape in 2005," in *Hopes, Fears, & Reality,* ed. Robin J. Lake and Paul T. Hill (Seattle: Center on Reinventing Public Education, 2005).
2. Louann A. Bierlein, "The Charter School Movement," in *New Schools for a New Century*, ed. D. Ravitch and J. P. Viteritti (New Haven, CT: Yale University Press, 1997).
3. Tammi Troy, "The Role of Partnering Organizations in New York City Charter Schools," paper presented at American Educational Research Association annual meeting, New Orleans, April 4, 2002.
4. Janelle Scott and Jennifer Jellison Holme, "Public Schools,

Private Resources: The Role of Social Networks in California Charter School Reform," in *Where Charter School Policy Fails: The Problems of Accountability and Equity*, ed. Amy Stuart Wells (New York: Teachers College Press, 2002), 126.

5. Joanna Smith and Priscilla Wohlstetter, "Understanding the Different Faces of Partnering: A Typology of Public-Private Partnerships," *School Leadership & Management* 26, no. 3 (2006): 249.

6. Chester E. Finn, Bruno V. Manno, and Gregg Vanourek, *Charter Schools in Action* (Princeton, NJ: Princeton University Press, 2000).

7. See, for example, Joe Nathan, *Charter Schools: Creating Hope and Opportunity for American Education* (San Francisco: Jossey-Bass, 1996); Carol Ascher et al., "Governance and Administrative Infrastructure in New York City Charter Schools," paper, Institute for Education and Social Policy, New York University, New York, 2003; Troy, "Partnering Organizations in New York City Charter Schools"; Frank Martinelli, "Charter Schools: How Community-Based Organizations Can Start Charter Schools," paper, Charter Friends National Network, St. Paul, MN, 2001; Paul T. Hill, Robin J. Lake, and Mary Beth Celio, *Charter Schools and Accountability in Public Education* (Washington, DC: Brookings Institution, 2002); Gary Miron and Jerry Horn, "Evaluation of Connecticut Charter Schools and the Charter School Initiative: Final Report," Evaluation Center of Western Michigan University, Kalamazoo, 2002; Smith and Wohlstetter, "Different Faces of Partnering," 249.

8. Priscilla Wohlstetter et al., "Improving Service Delivery in Education: The Role of Cross-Sectoral Alliances," *Social Science Quarterly* 85, no. 5 (2004): 1078–1096.

9. Lloyd Billingsley and Pamela Riley, *Two Steps Forward, One Step Back: The Battle for California's Charter Schools* (San Francisco: Pacific Research Institute for Public Policy, 1999); Legislative Office of Education Oversight, "Community Schools in Ohio: Implementation Issues and Impact on Ohio's Education System," paper, Legislative Office of Education Oversight, Columbus, OH, 2003; Amy Stuart Wells, "Why Public Policy Fails to Live Up to the Potential of Charter School Reform: An Introduction," in *Where Charter School Policy Fails: The Problems of Accountability and Equity*, ed. Amy Stuart Wells (New York: Teachers College Press, 2002); David P. Smole, "Funding for Public Charter School Facilities: Current Federal Policy and H.R.1," in *Charter Schools*, ed. T. Murphy (Huntington, NY: Nova Science Publishers, 2002); Jeffrey R. Henig et al., "Making a Choice, Making a Difference? An Evaluation of Charter Schools in the District of Columbia," paper, Center for Washington Area Studies, George Washington University, Washington, DC, 1999; Troy, "Partnering Organizations in New York City Charter Schools."

10. Smith and Wohlstetter, "Different Faces of Partnering."

11. Ted Kolderie, *The Other Half of the Strategy* (St. Paul, MN: Education|Evolving, 2008), 9.

12. David Osborne and Ted Gaebler, *Reinventing Government: How the Entrepreneurial Spirit Is Transforming the Public Sector* (Reading, MI: William Patrick, 1992), 9.

13. Ibid., 46.
14. Ibid.
15. Ibid.
16. Pauline Vaillancourt Rosenau, "The Strengths and Weaknesses of Public-Private Policy Partnerships," in *Public-Private Policy Partnerships*, ed. P. V. Rosenau (Cambridge, MA: MIT Press, 2000).
17. A.C.A. § 6-23-202.
18. For the District of Columbia law, see D.C. Code § 38-1802.02(14). For the Pennsylvania law, see 24 P.S. § 17-1717-A(2)(i).
19. Va. Code Ann. § 22.1-212.6(B).
20. D.C. Code § 38-1802.05.
21. S.C. Code Ann. § 59-40-60 (F)(7).
22. All the anonymous interview quotations in this chapter are from telephone interviews conducted by June Ahn, Rebecca Cohen, Ally Kuzin, Michelle Nayfack, Jennifer Polhemus, Nina Salomon, Joanna Smith, Nichole Stewart, and Priscilla Wohlstetter that took place from January through July 2007.
23. Della Lamb Community Services, "Della Lamb Elementary Charter School Organization and History," www.dellalamb.org/dlecs_overview.html. Accessed online November 18, 2008.
24. N.M. Stat. Ann. § 22-8B-6.
25. Burns Ind. Code Ann. § 20-20-8-3.
26. NY CLS Educ § 2851.
27. Tex. Educ. Code § 12.101.
28. 24 P.S. § 17-1714-A.
29. Wyo. Stat. Tit. 21, Ch. 3, Art. 3§ 21-3-304.
30. La. R.S. § 17:3997.
31. Idaho Code § 33-5203 (4).
32. C.R.S. § 22-30.5-302(1).
33. NY CLS Educ § 2851.
34. La. R.S. § 17:3983.
35. Alex Molnar, Gary Miron and J. Urschel, "Profiles of For-Profit Educational Management Organizations: Tenth Annual Report," Education Policy Research Unit, Arizona State University, Tempe, 2008, http://epicpolicy.org/files/EMO0708.pdf.
36. Sarah Mead, "Maintenance Required: Charter Schooling in Michigan," Education Sector Report, 2006, www.educationsector.org.
37. Gary Miron and Christopher Nelson, *What's Public About Charter Schools? Lessons Learned About Accountability and Choice* (Thousand Oaks, CA: Corwin Press, 2002).
38. Liane Brouillette, *Charter Schools: Lessons in School Reform* (Mahwah, NJ: Lawrence Erlbaum Associates, 2002).
39. National Resource Center on Charter School Finance and Governance, "Creating Education Partnerships to Meet the Needs of Businesses and Their Employees: JFK Medical Center Charter School, Palm Beach County, Florida," www.charterresource.org/files/Creating_Edu_Partnership--JFK_Medical_Center.pdf.
40. Idaho Code § 33-5203(4); Idaho Code § 33-5206(1).

41. N.J. Stat. § 18A:36A-4.

42. Md. Education Code Ann. § 9-104.

43. Arlo Wagner, "7 Catholic Schools Become Charter," *Washington Times,* November 6, 2007; D.C. Code § 38-1702.05.

44. La. R.S. § 17:3991.

45. ALM GL ch. 71, § 89(j)(5).

46. N.C. Gen. Stat. § 115C-238.29F(b).

47. N.C. Gen. Stat. § 115C-238.29E(e).

48. 14 Del. C. § 504A(6).

49. Minn. Stat. § 124D.10(17).

50. 24 P.S. § 17-1723-A.

Chapter 8

1. Janelle Scott, "The Politics of Venture Philanthropy in Charter School Policy and Advocacy," *Educational Policy* 23, no. 1 (2009): 106–136.

2. For the sake of consistency, we will use the term *MO* to refer to the school management sector in general and use the terms *EMO* or *CMO* when discussing specific organizations.

3. M. K. Sandler, *The Emerging Educational Industry: The First Decade* (Washington, DC: Education Industry Leadership Board, 2002).

4. Alex Andrus, "Venture Capitalism Meets Charter Schools," March 1, 2006, *Philanthropy Roundtable,* www.philanthropyroundtable.org/printarticle. asp?article=837; Education Sector, "Growing Pains: Scaling Up the Nation's Best Charter Schools," paper, Education Sector, Washington, DC, 2009.

5. Alex Molnar et al., "Profiles of For-Profit Management Organizations: Ninth Annual Report, 2006–2007," paper, Commercialism in Education Research Unit, Education Policy Studies Laboratory, Arizona State University, Tempe, 2007; W. Isaacson, "The Greatest Education Lab," *New York Times,* September 6, 2007, http://time.com.time/printout/0,8816,1659767,00.html.

6. John E. Chubb and Terry M. Moe, *Politics, Markets, and America's Schools* (Washington, DC: Brookings Institution, 1990), 227.

7. Stacy Smith, *The Democratic Potential of Charter Schools* (New York: Peter Lang, 2001).

8. Michael Engel, *The Struggle for Control of Public Education: Market Ideology vs. Democratic Values* (Philadelphia: Temple University Press, 2000), 69.

9. Amy Stuart Wells, J. Slayton, and J. Scott, "Defining Democracy in the Neoliberal Age: Charter School Reform and Educational Consumption," *American Educational Research Journal* 39, no. 2 (2002): 307–336.

10. Janelle Scott and Catherine C. DiMartino, "Public Education Under New Management: A Typology of Educational Privatization Applied to New York City's Restructuring," *Peabody Journal of Education* 84, no 3 (2009), 432–452.

11. Alex Molnar, Gary Miron, and J. Urschel, "Profiles of For-Profit Educational Management Organizations: Tenth Annual Report," Education Policy Research Unit, Arizona State University, Tempe, 2008, http://epicpolicy.org/files/EMO0708.pdf.

12. R. Budde, "Education by Charter: Restructuring School Districts," The Regional Laboratory for Educational Improvement of the Northeast & Is-

lands, Andover, MA, 1988; A. Shanker, "Restructuring Our Schools," *Peabody Journal of Education* 65, no. 3 (1988): 88–99.

13. Shanker, "Restructuring Our Schools," 98.
14. Budde, "Education by Charter," 34.
15. See these reports by RPP International for the Office of Educational Research and Improvement, U.S. Department of Education, Washington, DC: "A National Study of Charter Schools: Second-Year Report," 1998; "The State of Charter Schools: Third-Year Report," 1999; "The State of Charter Schools: Fourth-Year Report," 2000. See also RPP International and University of Minnesota, "A Study of Charter Schools: First-Year Report," Department of Education, Washington, DC, 1997.
16. A. S. Wells et al, "Charter Schools As Postmodern Paradox: Rethinking Social Stratification in an Age of Deregulated School Choice," *Harvard Educational review* 69, no. 2(1999): 172–204; Amy Stuart Wells et al., "Underlying Policy Assumptions of Charter School Reform: The Multiple Meanings of a Movement," *Teachers College Record* 100 (1999): 513–535; Bruce Fuller, ed., *Inside Charter Schools* (Cambridge, MA: Harvard University Press, 2000).
17. Robin J. Lake, "Identifying and Replicating the 'DNA' of Successful Charter Schools," paper, Center on Reinventing Public Education, National Charter School Research Project, University of Washington, Seattle, 2007; Education Sector, "Growing Pains."
18. K. Conn, "When School Management Companies Fail: Righting Educational Wrongs," *Journal of Law and Education* 31, no. 3 (2002): 245–269; K. J. Saltman, *The Edison Schools: Corporate Schooling and the Assault on Public Education* (New York: Routledge, 2005).
19. M. Minow, *Partners, Not Rivals: Privatization and the Public Good* (Boston: Beacon Press, 2002); M. Minow, "Public and Private Partnerships: Accounting for the New Religion," *Harvard Law Review* 116, no. 5 (2003): 1229–1270; J. Murphy, *The Privatization of Schooling: Problems and Possibilities* (Thousand Oaks, CA: Corwin Press, 1996).
20. In this chapter, we focus primarily on contracting out for instructional or academic services. School districts have long outsourced ancillary services such as food, transportation, and maintenance, sometimes realizing significant cost savings. These activities have tended to be less controversial than instructional and management outsourcing.
21. Carol Ascher, N. Fruchter and R. Berne, *Hard Lessons: Public Schools and Privatization* (New York: Twentieth Century Fund Press, 1996); P. Carpenter and G. Hall, *Case Studies in Educational Performance Contracting* (Santa Monica, CA: RAND, 1971); E. M. Gramlich and P. P. Koshel, *Educational Performance Contracting: An Evaluation of an Experiment* (Washington, DC: Brookings Institution, 1975); J. A. Mecklenburger, *Performance Contracting* (Worthington, OH: Charles A. Jones, 1972).
22. New American Schools merged with the American Institutes for Research in 2004.
23. M. Berends, S. Bodilly and S. Nataraj, *Facing the Challenges of Whole-School Reform: New American Schools After a Decade* (Santa Monica, CA: RAND, 2002).

24. J. Donahue, *The Privatization Decision: Public Ends, Private Means* (New York: Basic Books, 1989); E. Sclar, *The Privatization of Public Service: Lessons from Case Studies* (Washington, DC: Economic Policy Institute, 1997).

25. J. Hannaway, "Contracting As a Mechanism for Managing Education Services," paper no. RB-28, Consortium for Policy Research in Education, Philadelphia, 1999; Paul T. Hill, L. C. Pierce, and J. W. Guthrie, *Reinventing Public Education: How Contracting Can Transform America's Schools* (Chicago: University of Chicago Press, 1997).

26. M. W. Apple, "How the Conservative Restoration Is Justified: Leadership and Subordination in Educational Policy," *International Journal of Leadership in Education* 1, no. 1 (1998): 3–17; T. C. Pedroni, *Market Movements: African American Involvement in School Voucher Reform* (New York: Routledge, 2007); J. Scott, Christopher Lubienski, and E. DeBray-Pelot, "The Ideological and Political Landscape of School Choice Interest Groups in the Post-*Zelman* Era," in *Handbook of Education Politics and Policy,* ed. B. Cooper, J. Cibulka, and L. Fusarelli (Mahwah, NJ: Lawrence Erlbaum and Associates, 2008): 541–577.

27. National Charter School Research Project, "Quantity Counts: The Growth of Charter School Management Organizations," paper, Center on Reinventing Public Education, University of Washington, Seattle, 2007.

28. Ibid.

29. Ibid.

30. Brian P. Gill et al., *Inspiration, Perspiration, and Time: Operations and Achievement in Edison Schools* (Santa Monica, CA: RAND, 2005).

31. National Charter School Research Project, "Quantity Counts," 16.

32. Ibid.

33. NewSchools Venture Fund (n.d.) "About us" Available at www.newschools .org/about/history. Retrieved May 14, 2010.

34. Gill et al., *Inspiration, Perspiration, and Time.*

35. Molnar et al., "For-Profit Management Organizations: Ninth Annual Report, 2006–2007," 5.

36. Alex Molnar, Gary Miron, and J. Urschel, "Profiles for For-Profit Educational Management Companies: Eleventh Annual Report," Education and the Public Interest Center, Arizona State University, Tempe, 2009, http:// epicpolicy.org/files/08-09%20profiles%20report.pdf; Gary Miron and J. Urschel, "Profiles for Nonprofit Educational Management Companies: 2008–2009," Education and the Public Interest Center, Arizona State University, Tempe, 2009, http://epicpolicy.org/publication/ profiles-nonprofit-emos-2008-09.

37. Julie Bennett, "Brand-Name Charters: The Franchise Model Applied to Schools," *Education Next* 8, no. 3 (2008): 28–34.

38. Ibid., 29.

39. Ibid.

40. Ibid.

41. Education Sector, "Growing Pains."

42. Ibid.

43. Christine Cambell and Brock J. Grubb, "Closing the Skill Gap: New Options for Charter School Leadership Development," paper, Center on Rein-

venting Public Education, University of Washington, Seattle, 2008.
44. Jay Matthews, "Inside the KIPP School Summit," *Washington Post*, August 7, 2007, www.washingtonpost.com/.
45. Susan Colby, Kim Smith and Jim Shelton, "Expanding the Supply of High-Quality Public Schools," September 12, 2005, Bridgespan Group, www.bridgespan.org.
46. Robin Lake (2007). *Identifying and replicating the "DNA" of successful charter schools.* Seattle: University of Washington, National Charter School Research Project, Center on Reinventing Public Education.; Alex Molnar, David R. Garcia, Gary Miron & Shannon Berry (2007). *Profiles of for-profit management organizations: Ninth annual report 2006-2007.* Tempe: Commercialism in Education Research Unit, Education Policy Studies Laboratory, Arizona State University.
47. Robert Maranto, "A Tale of Two Cities: School Privatization in Philadelphia and Chester," *American Journal of Education* 111, no. 2 (2005): 151–185; S. Saunders, "Parents Say 'No' to Edison's Charter School Bid," www.nysut/newyorkteacher/2000-2001/010411edison.html.
48. Associated Press, "L.A. School Board Snubs Charter School Operators," *Education Week*, February 24, 2010, www.edweek.org/tm/articles/2010/02/24/333624clschools_ap.html?qs=LA+school+board.
49. Scott, "Politics of Venture Philanthropy"; R. L. Colvin, "A New Generation of Philanthropists and Their Great Ambitions," in *With the Best of Intentions: How Philanthropy Is Reshaping K–12 Education*, ed. Frederick M. Hess (Cambridge, MA: Harvard Education Press, 2005), 21–48; Frederick M. Hess, ed., *With the Best of Intentions: How Philanthropy Is Reshaping K-12 Education* (Cambridge, MA: Harvard Education Press, 2005).
50. B. Anderson, *A Donor's Guide to School Choice* (Washington, DC: Philanthropy Roundtable, 2004), www.philanthropyroundtable.org/files/choice.pdf; Public Impact, "Jump-Starting the Charter School Movement: A Guide for Donors Washington," Philanthropy Roundtable, Washington, DC, 2004, http://www.philanthropyroundtable.org/files/Jump-starting%20the%20Charter%20School%20Movement.pdf.
51. R. Cohen, "Strategic Grantmaking: Foundations and the School Privatization Movement," paper, National Committee for Responsive Philanthropy, Washington, DC, 2007.
52. Education Sector, "Growing Pains," 14.
53. U.S. Department of Education, Office of Innovation and Improvement, 2009 "Investing in innovation." Retrieved March 7, 2010 from: http://www2ed.gov/programs/innovations/factsheet.html
54. U.S. Department of Education, "Investing in Innovation," U. S. Department of Education, Washington, DC, 2009, www2.ed.gov/programs/innovation/factsheet.html.
55. Education Sector, "Growing Pains."
56. U.S. Department of Education, "Applications Now Available for $3.5 Billion in Title I School Improvement Grants to Turn Around Nation's Lowest Achieving Public Schools," press release, U. S. Department of Education, Washington, DC, 2009, www2.ed.gov/newspressreleases/2009/12/12032009a.html.

57. Carol Ascher et al., "Going Charter: New Models of Support," paper, Institute for Education and Social Policy, New York University, New York, 2001.
58. Ibid., 20.
59. Ibid.
60. Katrina E. Bulkley, "Losing Voice? Educational Management Organizations and Charter Schools' Educational Programs," *Education and Urban Society* 37, no. 2 (2005): 204–234; J. Scott, "Charter School Reform, Privatization, and the Search for Educational Empowerment," unpublished dissertation, University of California, Los Angeles, 2002.
61. C. DiMartino, "Building a Marketplace: Privatization and the New Small Schools Movement," paper presented at the annual meeting of the University Council of Education Administration, 2007.
62. D. Tyack, "School Governance in the United States: Historical Puzzles and Anomalies," in *Decentralization and School Improvement: Can We Fulfill the Promise?* ed. J. Hannaway and Martin Carnoy (San Francisco: Jossey-Bass, 1993), 1–32.
63. National Charter School Research Project, "Quantity Counts."
64. Christopher Lubienski and Sarah Theule Lubienski, "Charter, Private, Public Schools and Academic Achievement: New Evidence from NAEP Mathematics Data," National Center for the Study of Privatization in Education, www.ncspe.org.
65. F. H. Nelson, B. Rosenberg, and N. Van Meter, "Charter School Achievement on the 2003 National Assessment of Educational Progress," paper, American Federation of Teachers, Washington, DC, 2004.
66. U.S. Department of Education, "America's Charter Schools: Results from the NAEP Pilot Study," paper no. NCES 2005-456, Institute of Education Sciences, Washington, DC, 2004.
67. Martin Carnoy et al., *The Charter School Dust-Up: Examining the Evidence on Enrollment and Achievement* (New York: Teachers College Press, 2005); Natalie Lacireno-Paquet et al., "Creaming Versus Cropping: Charter School Enrollment Practices in Response to Market Incentives," *Educational Evaluation and Policy Analysis* 24, no. 2 (2002): 145–158.
68. Carnoy et al., *Charter School Dust-Up*; K. R. Woodworth et al., "San Francisco Bay Area KIPP Schools: A Study of Early Implementation and Achievement, Final Report," paper, SRI International, Menlo Park, CA, 2008.
69. J. David et al., "Bay Area KIPP Schools: A Study of Early Implementation, First Year Report 2004–2005," paper, SRI International, Menlo Park, CA, 2006; Educational Policy Institute, "Focus on Results: An Academic Impact Analysis of the Knowledge Is Power Program (KIPP)," paper, Educational Policy Institute, Washington, DC, 2005; Green Dot, "Green Dot: Key Performance Indicators (KPI) Dashboard," paper, Green Dot, Los Angeles, 2007; A. Thernstrom and S. Thernstrom, *No Excuses: Closing the Racial Achievement Gap in Learning* (New York: Simon and Schuster, 2003).
70. New York City Department of Education, 2008. Duffy, M., Listhaus, A., Meakem, N., Raza, A. & Carson, B. (2009). *Accountability framework for NYC schools: Charter, monitoring, and progress to renewal.* New York City: Department of Education.

71. David R. Garcia, Rebecca T. Barber, and Alex Molnar, "Profiting from Public Education: Education Management Organizations (EMOs) and Student Achievement," *Teachers College Record* 111, no. 5 (2009): 1352–1379.
72. Gary Miron and B. Applegate, "An Evaluation of Student Achievement in Edison Schools Opened in 1995 and 1996," paper, Evaluation Center, Western Michigan University, Kalamazoo, 2000.
73. V. Byrnes, "Getting a Feel for the Market: The Use of Privatized School Management in Philadelphia," *American Journal of Education* 115 (2009): 437–455.
74. Brian P. Gill et al., *State Takeover, School Restructuring, Private Management, and Student Achievement in Philadelphia* (Pittsburgh: RAND, 2007).
75. P. E. Peterson, "School Reform in Philadelphia: A Comparison of Student Achievement at Privately-Managed Schools with Student Achievement in Other District Schools," paper, Program on Educational Policy and Governance, Harvard University, Cambridge, MA, 2007.
76. K. A. Graham, "Philadelphia Taking Back 6 Privatized Schools," *Philadelphia Inquirer* June 19, 2008, www.phily.com/inquirer/education/20080619_Phila__taking_back_6_privatized_schools.html.
77. Peterson, "School Reform in Philadelphia."
78. Natalie Lacireno-Paquet, "Do EMO-Operated Charter Schools Serve Disadvantaged Students? The Influence of State Policies," *Education Policy Analysis Archives* 12, no. 26 (2004).
79. Bruce Fuller et al., "Charter Schools and Inequality: National Disparities in Funding, Teacher Quality, and Student Support," Working Paper Series no. 03-2, Policy Analysis for California Education, Berkeley, 2003; David R. Garcia, "Academic and Racial Segregation in Charter Schools: Do Parents Sort Students into Specialized Charter Schools?" *Education and Urban Society* 40, no. 5 (2008): 590–612; David R. Garcia, "The Impact of School Choice on Racial Segregation in Charter Schools," *Educational Policy* 22 (2008): 805–829; Lacireno-Paquet et al., "Creaming Versus Cropping."
80. Scott and DiMartino, "Public Education Under New Management."
81. Scott, "Politics of Venture Philanthropy."
82. P. C. Bauman, *Governing Education: Public Sector Reform or Privatization* (Boston: Allyn & Bacon, 1996), 166.
83. David F. Labaree, "Public Goods, Private Goods: The American Struggle over Educational Goals," *American Education Research Journal* 34, no. 1 (1997): 39–81.

Chapter 9

1. George Miller, *Building on What Works at Charter Schools*, Education and Labor Committee, June 4, 2009.
2. George Miller, "Building on What Works at Charter Schools," closing remarks to U.S. Congress, Education and Labor Committee, June 4, 2009, videoclip, YouTube, http://www.youtube.com/watch?v=yIj01cfWJAY, transcript by authors.
3. Margaret E. Raymond and Center for Research on Education Outcomes, "Multiple Choice: Charter School Performance in 16 States," paper, Stanford University, Stanford, CA, 2009.

4. Joe Nathan, *Charter Schools: Creating Hope and Opportunity for American Education* (San Francisco: Jossey-Bass, 1996), 207–208.

5. American Legislative Exchange Council, "Model Charter Schools Act," in *American Legislative Exchange Council Policy and Model Legislation* (Washington, DC: American Legislative Exchange Council, 1998).

6. Christopher Lubienski, "Innovation in Education Markets: Theory and Evidence on the Impact of Competition and Choice in Charter Schools," *American Educational Research Journal* 40, no. 2 (2003): 395–443; Mark Schneider and Jack Buckley, "Charter Schools: Hype or Hope?" *Education Finance and Policy* 1, no. 1 (2006):123–138.

7. Clayton Foundation, "The Colorado Charter Schools Evaluation, 1996," paper, Colorado Department of Education, Denver, 1997; Nick Khouri et al., *Michigan's Charter School Initiative: From Theory to Practice* (Lansing: Public Sector Consultants & MAXIMUS, 1999); Gary Miron and Jerry Horn, "Evaluation of Connecticut Charter Schools and the Charter School Initiative," paper, Evaluation Center, Western Michigan University, Kalamazoo, 2002; Gary Miron and Christopher Nelson, "Autonomy in Exchange for Accountability: An Initial Study of Pennsylvania Charter Schools," paper, Evaluation Center, Western Michigan University, Kalamazoo, 2000.

8. Gary Miron and Christopher Nelson, *What's Public About Charter Schools? Lessons Learned About Choice and Accountability* (Thousand Oaks, CA: Corwin Press, 2002).

9. As it turns out, charter schools have also attracted many families from the private school sector, not simply because of more effective academic programs, but by offering a comparable experience without tuition—at no direct cost to the families.

10. Nathan, *Charter Schools*, xviii.

11. Little Hoover Commission, "The Charter Movement: Education Reform School by School," paper, State of California, Sacramento, 1996.

12. Roger W. Bowen, "Charter Schools, Then What?" *New York Times*, January 13, 1999, www.nytimes.com/yr/mo/day/oped/13bowe.html.

13. See, for example, Jeanne Allen and Chester E. Finn, "How Republicans Helped Clinton and Hurt Schools," *Weekly Standard*, December 8, 1997, www.edexcellence.net/library/hijackd.html; Paul T. Hill, "Doing School Choice Right," *American Journal of Education* 111, no. 2 (2005): 141–150.

14. Scott Cowen and Bring New Orleans Back Commission Education Committee, "Rebuilding and Transforming: A Plan for Improving Public Education in New Orleans," paper, Tulane University, New Orleans, 2006; Mark Schneider and Jack Buckley, "Charter Schools: Hype or Hope?" *Education Finance and Policy* 1, no. 1 (2006):123–138.

15. Hill, "Doing School Choice Right," 144.

16. Herbert J. Walberg and Joseph L. Bast, *Education and Capitalism: How Overcoming Our Fear of Markets and Economics Can Improve America's Schools* (Stanford, CA: Hoover Institution Press, 2003).

17. Nathan, *Charter Schools*; Barack Obama, "Remarks by the President to the Hispanic Chamber of Commerce on a Complete and Competitive Ameri-

can Education," paper read at Hispanic Chamber of Commerce, Washington, DC, March 10, 2009.

18. Caroline M. Hoxby, "School Choice and School Productivity (or Could School Choice Be a Tide That Lifts All Boats?" paper, National Bureau of Economic Research, Cambridge, MA, 2002; Mark Schneider et al., "Shopping for Schools: In the Land of the Blind, the One-Eyed Parent May Be Enough," *American Journal of Political Science* 42, no. 3 (1998): 769–794.

19. Ray Budde, "Education by Charter: Restructuring School Districts; Key to Long-Term Continuing Improvement in American Education," paper, Regional Laboratory for Educational Improvement of the Northeast & Islands, Andover, MA, 1988; Albert Shanker, "Restructuring Our Schools," *Peabody Journal of Education* 65, no. 3 (1988): 88–100.

20. Bruno V. Manno et al., "How Charter Schools Are Different: Lessons and Implications for a National Study," *Phi Delta Kappan* 79, no. 7 (1998): 490.

21. Jeanne Allen, "Commentary: Charter Laws and Flawed Research: Expediency for Expediency's Sake," *Education Week*, September 8, 2009.

22. As of this writing, Education Secretary Arne Duncan has affirmed that distinction in his speeches, but implemented policies in Race to the Top funding that endorses charter schools in general.

23. As examples of advocacy pieces, see Two Million Minutes: A 21st Century Solution. 2009 film produced by Robert Compton, directed by Dan Treharne: http://www.2mminutes.com/

24. See, for example, Atila Abdulkadiroglu et al., "Informing the Debate: Comparing Boston's Charter, Pilot and Traditional Schools," paper, Boston Foundation, Boston, 2009; Chester E. Finn, "Beating Up on Charter Schools," *New York Times*, August 24, 1996, http://edreform.com/forum/082496cf.htm; Michigan Association of Public School Academies, "Cap Reached; New Charter Schools Put On Hold," press release, Michigan Association of Public School Academies, Lansing, 1999; Gary Wolfram, "Report of Hillsdale Policy Group on Michigan Charter Schools," paper, Hillsdale Policy Group, Hillsdale, MI, 1999.

25. William J. Bushaw and John A. McNee, "The 41st Annual Phi Delta Kappa/Gallup Poll of the Public's Attitudes Towards the Public Schools," *Phi Delta Kappan* 91, no. 1 (2009); 8–23; Steve Farkas, Jean Johnson, and Tony Foleno, "On Thin Ice: How Advocates and Opponents Could Misread the Public's Views on Vouchers and Charter Schools," paper, Public Agenda, New York, 1999.

26. See, for example, Jonah Goldberg, "Do Away with Public Schools," *Los Angeles Times*, June 12, 2007.

27. John McCain, "John McCain on Education," selected quotes by John McCain, various dates, On the Issues Web page, www.ontheissues.org/2008/John_McCain_Education.htm.

28. See, for example, Commission on Charter Schools, "Charter Schools in Michigan: The Report of the Commission on Charter Schools to the Michigan Legislature," paper, Commission on Charter Schools, East Lansing,

2002; Arne Duncan, "Keynote Address by U.S. Secretary of Education Arne Duncan," paper read at National Charter Schools Conference: Leading Change in Public Education, Washington, DC, June 22, 2009.

29. Joseph L. Bast and Herbert J. Walberg, "Can Parents Choose the Best Schools for Their Children?" *Economics of Education Review* 23, no. 4 (2004): 431–440; John C. Goodman and Fritz F. Steiger, eds., *An Education Agenda: Let Parents Choose Their Children's School* (Dallas: National Center for Policy Analysis, 2001).

30. Roderick Paige, "Remarks of Secretary Paige at the Office of English Language Acquisition Summit," U.S. Department of Education, 2003, www.ed.gov.

31. Bast and Walberg, "Can Parents Choose?" See also Christopher Lubienski, "School Diversification in Second-Best Education Markets: International Evidence and Conflicting Theories of Change," *Educational Policy* 20, no. 2 (2006): 323–344.

32. See, for example, Paul T. Hill, "Doing School Choice Right," *American Journal of Education* 111, no. 2 (2005); Mark Schneider and Jack Buckley, "Charter Schools: Hype or Hope?" *Education Finance and Policy* 1, no. 1 (2006): 130.

33. Justine S. Hastings and Jeffrey M. Weinstein, "Information, School Choice, and Academic Achievement: Evidence from Two Experiments," *Quarterly Journal of Economics* 123, no. 4 (2008): 1373–1414.

34. David J. Armour and Brett M. Peiser, "Interdistrict Choice in Massachusetts," in *Learning from School Choice*, ed. P. E. Peterson and Bryan C. Hassel (Washington, DC: Brookings Institution, 1998); Ellen Goldring and Claire Smrekar, "Community or Anonymity? Patterns of Parent Involvement and Family-School Interactions in Magnet Schools," paper presented at annual conference of the American Educational Research Association, Chicago, 1997); Paul Teske, Jody Fitzpatrick, and Gabriel Kaplan, "Opening Doors: How Low-Income Parents Search for the Right School," paper, Center on Reinventing Public Education, Seattle, 2007; Mark Schneider and Jack Buckley, "What Do Parents Want From Schools? Evidence from the Internet," *Educational Evaluation and Policy Analysis* 24, no. 2 (2002): 133–144; Paul Teske and Mark Schneider, "What Research Can Tell Policymakers About School Choice," *Journal of Policy Analysis and Management* 20 (2001):609–631; John F. Witte, *The Market Approach to Education: An Analysis of America's First Voucher Program* (Princeton, NJ: Princeton University Press, 2000).

35. Teske, Fitzpatrick, and Kaplan, "Opening Doors."

36. Eric A. Hanushek et al., "Charter School Quality and Parental Decision Making With School Choice," paper, National Bureau of Economic Research, Cambridge, MA, 2005.

37. Teske, Fitzpatrick, and Kaplan, "Opening Doors."

38. S. DeJarnatt, "School Choice and the (Ir)rational Parent," *Georgetown Journal on Poverty Law and Policy* 15 (2008), http://papers.ssrn.com/sol3/papers.cfm?abstract_id=1014047.

39. Jeffrey R. Henig, "Choice in Public Schools: An Analysis of Transfer Requests Among Magnet Schools," *Social Science Quarterly* 71 (1990): 69–82;

Salvatore Saporito and Annette Lareau, "School Selection As a Process: The Multiple Dimensions of Race in Framing Educational Choice," *Social Problems* 46, no. 3 (1999): 418–439; Schneider and Buckley, "What Do Parents Want from Schools?"; Hastings and M. Weinstein, "Information, School Choice, and Academic Achievement"; Kimberly A. Goyette, Joshua Freely, and Danielle Farrie, "'This School's Gone Downhill': School Integration and Perceived School Quality," paper read at Population Association of America Annual Meeting, Los Angeles, March 30 to April 1, 2006.

40. Schneider and Buckley, "What Do Parents Want from Schools?"

41. Goyette, Freely, and Farrie, "'This School's Gone Downhill.'"

42. Justine S. Hastings, Thomas J. Kane, and Douglas O. Staiger, "Parental Preferences and School Competition: Evidence from a Public School Choice Program," paper, National Bureau of Economic Research, Cambridge, MA, 2005; Jeffrey R. Henig, "Race and Choice in Montgomery County, Maryland, Magnet Schools," *Teachers College Record* 96 (1995): 729–734.

43. David R. Garcia, "Academic and Racial Segregation in Charter Schools: Do Parents Sort Students into Specialized Charter Schools?" *Education and Urban Society* 40, no. 5 (2008): 590–612; Robert Bifulco and Helen F. Ladd, "The Impacts of Charter Schools on Student Achievement: Evidence from North Carolina," *Education Finance and Policy* 1, no. 1 (2006): 50–90; Robert Bifulco and Helen F. Ladd, "School Choice, Racial Segregation, and Test-Score Gaps: Evidence from North Carolina's Charter School Program," *Journal of Policy Analysis and Management* 26, no. 1 (2006): 31–56.

44. Courtney A. Bell, "All Choices Created Equal? The Role of Choice Sets in the Selection of Schools," *Peabody Journal of Education* 84, no. 2 (2009): 191–208; Goyette, Freely, and Farrie, "'This School's Gone Downhill'"; Teske, Fitzpatrick, and Kaplan, "Opening Doors."

45. Teske, Fitzpatrick, and Kaplan, "Opening Doors."

46. Bell, "All Choices Created Equal?"; Teske, Fitzpatrick, and Kaplan, "Opening Doors"; Hastings, Kane, and Staiger, "Parental Preferences and School Competition."

47. Hastings, Kane, and Staiger, "Parental Preferences and School Competition."

48. Schneider and Buckley, "What Do Parents Want from Schools?"

49. Hastings, Kane, and Staiger, "Parental Preferences and School Competition."

50. Hastings and Weinstein, "Information, School Choice, and Academic Achievement."

51. C. Barone, "Are We There Yet? What Policymakers Can Learn from Tennessee's Growth Model," paper, Education Sector, Washington, DC, 2009.

52. Elissa Gootman, "In Brooklyn, Low Grade for a School of Successes," *New York Times*, September 12, 2008, B1; J. Hernandez, "A School's Grade Plummets, and the Parents Are Confused," *New York Times*, September 22, 2008, B1; Jennifer Medina, "Letter Grades Look Simple, But Realities Are Complex," *New York Times*, November 16, 2008, A39; Jennifer Medina and R. Gebeloff, "Schools Get More A's and Fewer F's," *New York Times*, September 17, 2008, B1.

53. Medina and Gebeloff, "Schools Get More A's and Fewer F's"; S. Freedman,

"How a Middle School Can Be 'Dangerous' and Still Get an A," *New York Times*, December 17, 2007, B7.

54. See, for example, Huw T. O. Davies and Sandra M. Nultey, *Learning More About How Research-Based Knowledge Gets Used: Guidance in the Development of New Empirical Research* (New York: William T. Grant Foundation, 2008); John W. Kingdon, *Agendas, Alternatives, and Public Policies* (New York: HarperCollins, 1984).

55. Christopher Lubienski, "Charter School Innovations in Theory and Practice: Autonomy, R&D, and Curricular Conformity," in *Taking Account of Charter Schools: What's Happened and What's Next?* ed. Katrina E. Bulkley and Priscilla Wohlstetter (New York: Teachers College Press, 2004).

56. Nathan, *Charter Schools*.

57. The original purposes are still largely echoed by umbrella advocacy organizations such as US Charter Schools (see UScharterschools.org).

58. Center for Education Reform, "What the Research Reveals About Charter Schools," paper, Center for Education Reform, Washington, DC, 2001; Bryan C. Hassel et al., "Charter School Achievement: What We Know," paper, National Alliance for Public Charter Schools, Washington, DC, 2007.

59. Clayton Foundation, "1998 Colorado Charter Schools Evaluation Study: The Characteristics, Status and Student Achievement Data of Colorado Charter Schools," paper, Colorado Department of Education, Denver, 1999.

60. See, for example, RPP International and U.S. Department of Education, "The State of Charter Schools: Third-Year Report," Office of Educational Research and Improvement, U.S. Department of Education, Washington, DC, 1999.

61. See, for example, Darcia Harris Bowman, "Mich. Charter Schools Scoring Lower," *Education Week*, November 15, 2000, 8; Public Policy Associates, National Alliance of Business, and Michigan Future, "Redefining Public Education: The Promise of Employer-Linked Charter Schools," paper, Public Policy Associates, Lansing, MI, 1999; Kelly McCutchen, "World Class School Shows Potential of Georgia Charter School Law," paper, Georgia Public Policy Foundation, Atlanta, 1999; Chester E. Finn, "Getting Serious About the Schools," *Weekly Standard*, January 25, 1999; National Governors' Association, "Charter Schools: Challenging Traditions and Changing Attitudes," paper, National Governors' Association, Washington, DC, 1998.

62. Eric P. Bettinger, "The Effect of Charter Schools on Charter Students and Public Schools," *Economics of Education Review* 24, no. 2 (2005): 133–147; Bifulco and Ladd, "School Choice, Racial Segregation, and Test-Score Gaps"; Sarah Theule Lubienski and Christopher Lubienski, "School Sector and Academic Achievement: A Multi-Level Analysis of NAEP Mathematics Data," *American Educational Research Journal* 43, no. 4 (2006): 651–698. See also Henry Braun, Frank Jenkins, and Wendy Grigg, *A Closer Look at Charter Schools Using Hierarchical Linear Modeling*, NCES 2006-460 (Washington, DC: U.S. Department of Education, 2006); Raymond and Center for Research on Education Outcomes, "Multiple Choice."

63. Obama, "Complete and Competitive American Education."

64. Casey D. Cobb and Gene V. Glass, "Ethnic Segregation in Arizona Charter Schools," *Education Policy Analysis Archives* 7, no. 1 (1999); George F. Garcia

and Mary Garcia, "Charter Schools: Another Top-Down Innovation," *Educational Researcher* 25, no. 8 (1996): 34–36; Richard Rothstein et al., "Charter Conundrum," *American Prospect* 9, no. 39 (1998): 46–61; Erica Frankenberg and Chungmei Lee, "Charter Schools and Race: A Lost Opportunity for Integrated Education," *Educational Policy Analysis Archives* 11, no. 32 (2003), http://epaa.asu.edu/epaa/v11n32/.

65. See, for example, Clayton Foundation, "The Colorado Charter Schools Evaluation, 1996," paper, Colorado Department of Education, Denver, 1997; Miron and Horn, "Connecticut Charter Schools"; Gary Miron and Christopher Nelson, "Pennsylvania Charter Schools"; Khouri et al., *Michigan's Charter School Initiative.*

66. Sam Dillon, "Ohio Goes After Charter Schools That Are Failing," *New York Times*, November 8, 2007, www.nytimes.com/2007/11/08/us/08charter.html?th&emc=th.

67. Bryan C. Hassel and Kathleen Kennedy Manzo, "Charter School Achievement: What We Know," *Education Week*, August 15, 2007.

68. John W. Meyer, "Innovation and Knowledge Use in American Public Education," in *Organizational Environments: Ritual and Rationality*, ed. J. W. Meyer and W. R. Scott (Beverly Hills, CA: Sage Publications, 1992).

69. See, for example, Commission on Charter Schools, "Charter Schools in Michigan"; Richard C. Leonardi, "Charter Schools in Ohio: The Rush to Mend Them Should Not End Them," paper, Buckeye Institute for Public Policy Solutions, Dayton, 1998.

Figure 9-1

Texas Center for Educational Research, *Texas Open-Enrollment Charter Schools: Second Year Evaluation, 1997–98*, (December 2008), http://www.tcer.org; Commonwealth of Massachusetts Department of Education *The Massachusetts Charter School Initiative: Expanding the Possibilities of Public Education*, http://www.doe.mass.edu/charter/reports/1998/; Legislative Audit Bureau, *An evaluation: Charter school program*, LAB Report 98-15, (Madison, WI: 1998); Izu, J. A., L. Carlos, K. Yamashiro, L. Picus, N. Tushnet, and P. Wohlstetter, *The Findings and Implications of Increased Flexibility and Accountability: An Evaluation of Charter Schools in Los Angeles Unified School District*, Los Alamitos, CA: WestEd, 1998; Fitzgerald, J., P. Harris, P. Huidekiper, and M. Mani, *1997 Colorado Charter Schools Evaluation Study: The Characteristics, Status, and Student Achievement Data of Colorado Charter Schools*, (Denver: The Clayton Foundation, 1998); Massachusetts Charter School Resource Center, *Massachusetts Charter School Profiles, 1998–99 School Year*, (Boston: 1999); L. A. Mulholland, *Arizona Charter School Progress Evaluation*. (Tempe, AZ: Morrison Institute for Public Policy, Arizona State University, 1999); N. Khouri, R. Kleine, R. White, and L. Cummings *Michigan's Charter School Initiative: From Theory to Practice*, (Lansing, MI: Public Sector Consultants and MAXIMUS, 1999); Clayton Foundation, *1998 Colorado Charter Schools Evaluation Study: The Characteristics, Status and Student Achievement Data of Colorado Charter Schools*, (Denver: Colorado Department of Education, 1999); Gary Miron and Christopher Nelson, "Autonomy in Exchange for

Accountability: An Initial Study of Pennsylvania Charter Schools," paper, (Kalamazoo, MI: Western Michigan University, 2000); Jerry Horn and Gary Miron, *An Evaluation of the Michigan Public School Academy Initiative.* (Kalamazoo, MI: The Evaluation Center, Western Michigan University, 2000); Jessica Whitt, *Broken Promises: Charter Schools in Texas* (Austin: Texas Freedom Network Education Fund, 2000); Colorado Department of Education, *1998–1999 Colorado Charter Schools Evaluation Study: The Characteristics, Status and Performance Record of Colorado Charter Schools,* 2000; Timothy J. Gronberg and Dennis W. Jansen, *Navigating Newly Chartered Waters: An Analysis of Texas Charter School Performance,* (Austin: Texas Public Policy Foundation, 2001); George W. Noblit and Corbett Dickson, *North Carolina Charter School Evaluation Report,* (Raleigh: North Carolina State Board of Education, 2001); Jeffrey R Henig, Thomas T. Holyoke, Natalie Lacireno-Paquet, and Michele Moser, *Growing Pains: an Evaluation of Charter Schools in the District Of Columbia: 1999–2000,* (Washington, DC: George Washington University, Center for Washington Area Studies, 2001); Eric A. Hanushek, John F. Kain, and Steven G. Rivkin, "The Impact of Charter Schools on Academic Achievement," unpublished manuscript, University of Texas at Dallas, 2002; Gary Miron and Jerry Horn, "Evaluation of Connecticut Charter Schools and the Charter School Initiative," paper, (Kalamazoo, MI: Evaluation Center, Western Michigan University, 2002); Gary Miron and Christopher Nelson, *What's Public About Charter Schools? Lessons Learned About Choice and Accountability,* (Thousand Oaks, CA: Corwin, 2002); Gary Miron, Christopher Nelson, and John Risley, with Carolyn Sullins, "Strengthening Pennsylvania's Charter School Reform: Findings from the Statewide Evaluation and Discussion of Relevant Policy Issues," paper, (Kalamazoo, MI: Evaluation Center, Western Michigan University, 2002); W. Randall and Kevin M. Hollenbeck, "Impact of Charter School Attendance on Student Achievement in Michigan," working paper no. 02-080, (Kalamazoo, MI: W.E. Upjohn Institute for Employment Research, 2002); Christopher Nelson and Gary Miron, *The Evaluation of the Illinois Charter School Reform: Final Report,* (Springfield, IL: Illinois State Board of Education, 2002); Jay P. Greene, Greg Forster, and Marcus A. Winters, "Apples to Apples: An Evaluation Of Charter Schools Serving General Student Populations," Education Working Paper no. 1, (New York City: Manhattan Institute, Center for Civic Innovation, 2003); Tom Loveless, *The 2003 Brown Center Report on American Education: Charter Schools: Achievement, Accountability, and the Role of Expertise,* (Washington, DC: The Brookings Institution, 2003); New York Board of Regents, *Report to the Governor, the Temporary President of the Senate, and the Speaker of the Assembly on the Educational Effectiveness of the Charter School Approach in New York State,* 2003, http://www.emsc.nysed.gov/psc/5yearreport/fiveyearreport.htm; Margaret E. Raymond, *The Performance of California Charter Schools,* (Stanford, CA: Center For Research On Education Outcomes, Hoover Institution at Stanford University, 2003); David Rogosa, "Student Progress in California Charter Schools, 1999–2002," unpublished manuscript, (Stanford University, 2003); Simeon P. Slovacek, Antony J.

Kunnan, and Hae-Jin Kim, *California Charter Schools Serving Low-SES Students: An Analysis of the Academic Performance Index,* (Los Angeles: California State University, Los Angeles, 2002); Ron Zimmer, et al, *Charter School Operations and Performance: Evidence from California,* (Santa Monica, CA: RAND, 2003); Colorado Department of Education, *2001–2002 Colorado Charter Schools Evaluation Study: The Characteristics, Status and Performance Record of Colorado Charter Schools,* (Denver: 2003); Legislative Office of Education Oversight, *Community Schools in Ohio: Final Report on Student Performance, Parent Satisfaction, and Accountability,* (Columbus, OH: 2003).

Conclusion

1. David F. Labaree, "Public Goods, Private Goods: The American Struggle over Educational Goals," *American Educational Research Journal* 34, no. 1 (1997): 39–81.
2. Diane Ravitch, *The Death and Life of the Great American School System: How Testing and Choice Are Undermining Education* (New York: Basic Books, 2009).
3. Larry Cuban, "Why Some Reforms Last: The Case of the Kindergarten," *American Journal of Education* 100, no. 1 (1992): 166–194.
4. Richard Arnot and J. Rowse, "Peer Group Effects and Educational Attainment," *Journal of Public Economics* 32, no. 3 (1987): 287–305; Eric A. Hanushek et al., "Does Peer Ability Affect Student Achievement?" *Journal of Applied Econometrics* 18, no. 5 (2003): 527–544.
5. Paul Teske, Mark Schneider, and E. Cassese, "Local School Boards As Authorizers of Charter Schools," in *Besieged: School Boards and the Future of Education Politics,* ed. W. G. Howell (Washington, DC: Brookings Institution, 2006), 130.
6. Sandra Vergari, "The Politics of Charter Schools," *Educational Policy* 21, no. 1 (2007): 15–39; Lee Anderson et al., "A Decade of Public Charter Schools: Evaluation of the Public Charter Schools Program; 2000–2001 Evaluation Report," paper, Department of Education, Washington, DC, 2002; Louann A. Bierlein-Palmer and Rebecca Gau, "Charter School Authorizing: Policy Implications from a National Study," *Phi Delta Kappan* 86, no. 5 (2005): 352–357.
7. Bruce Fuller, "The Public Square, Big or Small? Charter Schools in Political Context," in *Inside Charter Schools: The Paradox of Radical Decentralization,* ed. Bruce Fuller (Cambridge, MA: Harvard University Press, 2000).
8. Ibid.; Jay P. Greene, Greg Forster, and Marcus A. Winters, "Apples to Apples: An Evaluation of Charter Schools Serving General Student Populations," paper, Center for Civic Innovation, Manhattan Institute, New York, 2003.
9. Teske, Schneider, and Cassese, "Local School Boards As Authorizers."
10. Heath Brown, Thomas T. Holyoke, and Jeffrey R. Henig, "Shopping in the Political Arena: Strategic Venue Selection by Private Organized Interests," paper, National Center for the Study of Privatization in Education, New York, 2008; Jeffrey R. Henig et al., "Privatization, Politics, and Urban Services: The Political Behavior of Charter Schools," *Journal of Urban Affairs* 25, no. 1 (2003): 37–54; Thomas T. Holyoke et al., "Institution Advocacy and the Political Behavior of Charter Schools," *Political Research Quarterly* 60, no. 2 (2007): 202–214.

11. Diane Ravitch, *The Death and Life of the Great American School System: How Testing and Choice Are Undermining Education* (New York: Basic Books, 2009).

12. David Arsen, David N. Plank, and Gary Sykes, "School Choice Policies in Michigan: The Rules Matter," paper, Michigan State University, East Lansing, 1999.

13. Christopher Lubienski, Charisse Gulosino, and Peter Weitzel, "School Choice and Competitive Incentives: Mapping the Distribution of Educational Opportunities Across Local Education Markets," *American Journal of Education* 115, no. 4 (2009): 601–647.

About the Editors

Christopher A. Lubienski is an associate professor of education policy and a fellow at The Forum on the Future of Public Education at the University of Illinois. He is also a fellow with the Education Policy Research Unit at Arizona State University and the Education and the Public Interest Center at the University of Colorado at Boulder. His research focuses on education policy, reform, and the political economy of education, with a particular concern for issues of equity and access. His recent work examines organizational responses to competitive conditions in local education markets, including geo-spatial analyses of charter schools in post-Katrina New Orleans and a report on innovation in education markets for the Organisation for Economic Co-operation and Development. After earning a PhD in education policy and social analysis at Michigan State University, Lubienski held post-doctoral fellowships with the National Academy of Education and the Advanced Studies Fellowship Program at Brown University, and he was recently named a Fulbright Senior Scholar for New Zealand. He has authored both theoretical and empirical journal articles on questions of innovation and achievement in school choice systems, and he is the coeditor of *School Choice Policies and Outcomes: Empirical and Philosophical Perspectives* (coedited with Walter Feinberg, SUNY Press, 2008).

Peter C. Weitzel is an advanced doctoral student in educational organization and leadership at the University of Illinois at Urbana-Champaign, where he studies issues of school choice and urban educational governance. He has been working on issues of school choice for five years, and his research has appeared in *Educational Policy, American Journal of Education,* and other professional journals. As a graduate student, he has worked with the Institute of Government and Public Affairs, the Dean's Office in the College of Education at the University of Illinois, and The Forum on the Future of Public Education. His recent school choice research includes a geo-spatial analysis of the post-Katrina New Orleans educational market and a large scale sociological analysis of choosers and nonchoosers. Peter's studies and research have been recognized with numerous awards and scholarships from the College of Education, including the highest award given to doctoral students. Prior to graduate studies, he was the director of an AmeriCorps program that provided tutoring, character education, service learning, and a range of other services to students in high-needs communities in South Carolina. Peter received a BA in secondary education and English from Washington University in St. Louis in 2001 and an EdM from the University of Illinois at Urbana-Champaign in 2008.

About the Contributors

David Arsen is a professor of education policy and administration at Michigan State University. He received his PhD in economics from the University of California at Berkeley. His current research focuses on school choice, school capital facilities, Michigan school finance, and the privatization of educational services.

Chad d'Entremont is currently the research and policy director at Strategies for Children, Inc., a public policy organization focused on early childhood education. His scholarly research focuses on how ideology shapes education policy, with specific attention paid to school choice and the privatization of educational services. He has published papers on cyber and homeschool charter schools, educational vouchers, and tuition tax credits. Chad is currently a doctoral candidate in the politics and education program at Teachers College, Columbia University.

Catherine C. DiMartino is an assistant professor in the Department of Foundations, Leadership and Policy Studies at Hofstra University. Prior to her position at Hofstra, she taught middle and high school social studies, had a fellowship at the Educational Testing Service and, most recently, worked for the RAND Corporation. Her research focuses on the politics of public-private partnerships, the implications of marketization and privatization for school leaders and the impact of mayoral control on urban school communities. She earned a PhD in educational leadership from New York University, an MA in social studies education from Teachers College, Columbia University, and a BA in anthropology from Haverford College.

Suzanne E. Eckes is an associate professor in the Educational Leadership and Policy Studies Department at Indiana University. Suzanne has published over sixty articles related to school legal issues. She is an editor of *The Principal's Legal Handbook* and a member of the board of directors for the Education Law Association. She is the recipient of the Jack A. Culbertson Award for outstanding achievements in education from the University Council of Educational Administration. Prior to joining the faculty at Indiana University, Suzanne was a public high school French teacher and an attorney. She earned her master's in education from Harvard University and her law degree and PhD from the University of Wisconsin–Madison.

David R. Garcia is an associate professor in the Mary Lou Fulton Teachers College at Arizona State University. Garcia's professional experience includes extensive work in state education policy development and implementation. Prior to his appointment at ASU, he served as the associate superintendent of public instruction for the state of Arizona and worked for the Arizona state legislature. His research interests include school choice, accountability, and the study of factors that facilitate or distort policy implementation in public education. He received his doctorate from the University of Chicago in education policy, research, and institutional studies.

Jeffrey R. Henig is a professor of political science and education at Teachers College and professor of political science at Columbia University. He earned his PhD in political science at Northwestern University in 1978. Among his books on education politics are *Rethinking School Choice: Limits of the Market Metaphor* (Princeton University Press, 1994); *The Color of School Reform: Race, Politics and the Challenge of Urban Education* (Princeton University Press, 1999), named by the Urban Politics Section of the American Political Science Association (APSA) as the "best book written on urban politics" in 1999; and *Building Civic Capacity: The Politics of Reforming Urban Schools* (Kansas, 2001), named by the Urban Politics Section of the APSA as the "best book written on urban politics" in 2001, and *Mayors in the Middle: Politics, Race, and Mayoral Control of Urban Schools* (Princeton University Press, 2004). His most recent book, *Spin Cycle: How Research Is Used in Policy Debates: The Case of Charter Schools*, was published by the Russell Sage Foundation/Century Foundation in 2008. Professor Henig's scholarly work on urban politics, racial politics, privatization, and school reform has appeared in such varied journals as *American Journal of Education, Educational Evaluation and Policy Analysis, Journal of Urban Affairs, Policy Sciences, Policy Studies Review, Political Research Quarterly, Political Science Quarterly, Social Science Quarterly,* and *Urban* Affairs Review.

Luis A. Huerta is an associate professor of education and public policy at Teachers College, Columbia University. He earned his PhD in education policy from the University of California, Berkeley in 2002. He teaches courses in policy analysis and implementation, school finance and organizational sociology. His research and scholarship focus on school choice reforms and school finance policy. His research on school choice reforms examines policies that advance both decentralized and market models of schooling—including charter schools, homeschooling, tuition tax credits and vouchers. His research also examines school finance policy and research, with a specific focus on how legal and legislative battles over finance equity in schools and the research which has analyzed the effects of resources on student achievement, have consistently overlooked how resources are used within schools. His recent scholarship on school choice and school finance is published in *Educational Policy, Journal of Education Finance, Teachers College Record, Peabody Journal of Education, Journal of Education Policy,* and *Phi Delta Kappan.*

Gary Miron is a professor of education at Western Michigan University. He has extensive experience evaluating school reforms and education policies. Over the past two decades he has conducted several studies of school choice programs in Europe and the United States, including nine state evaluations of charter school reforms. In recent years, his research has increasingly focused on education management organizations (EMOs) and efforts to create systemic change in urban schools in Michigan and rural schools in Louisiana. Before coming to Western Michigan University, Miron worked for ten years at Stockholm University in Sweden.

Yongmei Ni is assistant professor in the Department of Educational Leadership and Policy at the University of Utah. Her research interests focus on school choice and charter schools, school finance, and school effectiveness. Her recent research has examined the effects of school choice policies on racial/ethnic segregation and social stratification, as well as their competitive impact on the effectiveness of traditional public schools. Her ongoing work involves investigation of how school choice influences teachers' working conditions and resource allocations. Professor Ni was an associate editor of *Educational Administration Quarterly* and currently serves on the editorial board of the journal. She holds a PhD in education policy and a master's degree in economics from Michigan State University.

Janelle T. Scott is an assistant professor at the University of California at Berkeley in the Graduate School of Education and the African American Studies Department. She is also a fellow with the Education Policy Research Unit at Arizona State University and the Education and the Public Interest Center at the University of Colorado at Boulder. She earned a PhD in education policy from the University of California at Los Angeles' Graduate School of Education and Information Studies and a BA in political science from the University of California at Berkeley, and was a 2008 National Academy of Education/Spencer Foundation Postdoctoral Fellow. Prior to earning her doctorate, she taught elementary school in Oakland, California. Her research explores the relationship between education, policy, and equality of opportunity, and centers on three related policy strands: the racial politics of public education; the politics of school choice, marketization, and privatization; and the politics of advocacy in public education. Her work has appeared in several edited books and journals, including *Peabody Journal of Education, Educational Policy, American Educational Research Journal,* and *Harvard Educational Review.* She is the editor of *School Choice and Diversity: What the Evidence Says* (Teachers College Press, 2005).

Joanna Smith is a research professor at the University of Southern California's Rossier School of Education and assistant director of USC's Center on Educational Governance (CEG). Smith's research utilizes qualitative approaches to exploring education policy, innovation, and reform. Currently, she is leading CEG's systematic review of charter school research (2000–2010) as part of a U.S. Department of Education–funded study. Her work has been published in journals including *Education Finance and Policy, School Leadership and Management, Policy Studies Journal,* and *Educational Administration Quarterly.* Smith received her PhD in urban educational policy from USC in 2004. Prior to her tenure at USC, Smith taught high school English at an Islamic school in Melbourne, Australia. She earned her bachelor's degree in English from Haverford College.

Priscilla Wohlstetter is the Diane and MacDonald Becket Professor in Educational Policy at the University of Southern California's Rossier

School of Education, where she also directs USC's Center on Educational Governance. Her research explores K–12 urban education policy and the relationship between school governance and improved school performance. Wohlstetter has served as principal investigator for numerous national and international studies focusing on urban reform. She currently serves as co-principal investigator on a project funded by the U.S. Department of Education to evaluate charter schools and the federal charter schools program. Her publications include articles on federal and state education policies, local governance, public-private partnerships, educational innovations, and the use of data-driven decision making to improve school performance. Recent books include *Taking Account of Charter Schools: What's Happened and What's Next, Federalism Reconsidered: The Case of the No Child Left Behind Act,* and *School-Based Management: Organizing for High Performance.* She received her master's in education and social policy from Harvard Graduate School of Education and her PhD in public policy from Northwestern University.

Index

Date Due
